Chris Townsend is possibly the world's most experienced long distance walker who also writes. He is the author of many books including *Grizzly Bears and Razor Clams*, his account of the Pacific Northwest Trail, and *Rattlesnakes and Bald Eagles*, his account of the Pacific Crest Trail, both published by Sandstone Press. He is gear correspondent for The Great Outdoors Magazine and has a website as Chris Townsend Outdoors where his popular blog receives many thousands of visitors.

Also published by Sandstone Press

Grizzly Bears and Razor Clams: walking America's
Pacific Northwest Trail

Rattlesnakes and Bald Eagles: hiking the Pacific Crest
Trail

OUT THERE

A VOICE FROM THE WILD

Chris Townsend

Foreword by
Cameron McNeish

SANDSTONEPRESS
HIGHLAND | SCOTLAND

First published in Great Britain
and the United States of America
Sandstone Press Ltd
Dochcarty Road
Dingwall
Ross-shire
IV15 9UG
Scotland.

www.sandstonepress.com

Editor: Robert Davidson

The publisher acknowledges support from
Creative Scotland towards publication of this volume.

ISBN: 978-1-910124-72-7
ISBNe: 978-1-910124-73-4

Cover design by Raspberry Creative Type, Edinburgh
Typeset by Iolaire Typesetting, Newtonmore.
Printed and bound by CPI Group (UK) Ltd, Croydon CR0 4YY.

To Denise

CONTENTS

ACKNOWLEDGMENTS

Far too many people have shared, assisted and supported my journeys over the years for me to mention them all here. Indeed, some of their names I can no longer recollect. My thanks to them all.

Many of the pieces here first appeared in various magazines over the years, especially The Great Outdoors aka TGO. I have edited them to make a more unified book so they're not exactly as they first appeared.

My thanks to these editors for publishing my writing – Emily Rodway, Daniel Neilson and Cameron McNeish at The Great Outdoors, Alun Davies at AT Adventure Travel, Geoff Birtles at High Mountain Sports, Tom Prentice at Climber, and Mike Merchant at the John Muir Trust Journal. Also thanks to Roger Smith and Sandy Allan for their assistance.

Robert Davidson of Sandstone Press for his help and encouragement. Temperature units have been left as in the original publication.

My partner Denise Thorn who, as always, listened patiently to me talking about the book time and time again and who read through the text making many corrections and useful suggestions.

FOREWORD

Man's relationship with the wild places of the world has been well documented in recent years and one of the fascinating issues that presents itself time and time again is our increasing yearning for simplicity.

I don't think many folk would dispute the notion that we are living in increasingly complex times. We have more riches than our parents and grandparents could ever have dreamed of - books by the zillion, great music from various digital appliances, fabulous films and television programmes and the opportunity to move around the world virtually as we please.

But for increasing numbers of us that richness can occasionally appear tarnished and lose its appeal, and we begin to ache for an element of simplicity in our lives. The Welsh/American outdoor writer Colin Fletcher defined it well: an opportunity to take respite from our eternal wrestling with the abstract, and instead, grapple with the tangible.

On a personal level I periodically leap off the twenty-first century treadmill and embrace what I've realised is another world; a parallel ecosphere that exists alongside the busy, frenetic, technological world that most of us inhabit, a world where there is a natural order of things that allows us to slow down and become an integral part of something older, wiser and infinitely more beautiful, a world where wildness reigns supreme.

The Harvard socio-biologist EO Wilson once wrote; 'Wilderness settles peace on the soul because it needs no help. It is beyond human contrivance.'

Beyond human contrivance! I find that a comforting thought.

Walking through a pristine and unspoiled landscape – a wild landscape - offers us an opportunity to find space. No interference to our thoughts. Nothing to distract us in an environment that is essentially peaceful. We can find renewal in the stillness of a forest, or on a wind scoured mountain top - the drift of cloud against the sky, the movement of sun and shadow, the warbling, liquid call of a curlew. In our chaotic, fast-paced and continuously changing world these things speak to us of *eternal* values, things that have always been, as ancient as the duration of days. All of them are completely and utterly unplanned, and most important of all, none of them have been arranged or rehearsed or manufactured by man.

That, I believe, is the real issue. And that is predominantly the issue that Chris Townsend explores in this book. Some may call it mountaineering. Others may call it hillwalking or long distance hiking or backpacking, but the real issue goes deeper than that. The issue in question is more fundamental than an outdoor activity, or a sport or a recreation, and Chris Townsend is one of a very tiny band of outdoor writers who has grasped that notion and has explored it in detail so that others may understand.

Part of that modern world I referred to has produced a crop of personality/television adventurers who treat the great outdoors as a racetrack, a place to prove themselves to others, or even more tragic, as a natural arena to be 'conquered'. In their strive for limelight, for sponsorship deals and for personal glory they completely fail to understand the natural world for what it is – the major part of the web of creation of which we, mankind, are also part and parcel.

Because we are part of that web of creation we are reliant on it. We endlessly discuss ideas about 'protecting the natural world' but in essence it is the natural world that protects us! If we choose to wage war on it then we will ultimately be the loser. This spinning globe we call Earth has the ability to simply slough us off and heal itself – it doesn't need us, but we need it! Boy, do we need the natural world. If you don't understand this concept of reliance then try and hold your breath for a minute or two...

Many more years ago than I care to remember - I think it might be in the region of almost four decades - as I first wrestled with these notions, I met another young man who was similarly absorbed by the complexities of the natural world and our relationship with it.

Over the years our friendship has grown and I have come to hugely respect Chris Townsend's sane and logical thinking processes, his respectful and passionate pleas for conservation of our planet and his bold and ambitious expeditions across the continents. A handful of Americans may have walked longer or further but they have not endured the tough walking conditions that we have here in Scotland, where sign posts are mostly non-existent, where the weather ranges from Alpine to Arctic inside moments, and where the voracious highland midge can make life so difficult that suicide appears as a welcome option!

Chris' walking achievements are legendary. He is widely

OUT THERE

acknowledged as the UK's outdoor gear guru. He has performed various roles with conservation and outdoor NGO's but above all Chris Townsend is an evangelist, spreading the good news about the natural world, and an advocate for the importance of that other world. It's in these roles that his wisdom truly shines through.

Throughout this book, whether Chris is writing about camping, hiking, skiing, the changing seasons or those heroes who have inspired him, a vital element becomes brightly apparent – his passion for wild places and his joy in communicating that passion to others. I commend that passion to you.

Cameron McNeish
Newtonmore
October 2015

xiv

INTRODUCTION

When I was growing up I wanted to be a writer and an explorer. Somehow, to my surprise, I have achieved both, after a fashion. As a boy my passions were reading and exploring the countryside around my home on the Lancashire coast. I climbed trees, fell in ditches, got lost in thickets, built dens, and imagined myself as the children in the books I read, especially those in the Arthur Ransome *Swallows and Amazons* stories and the Richmal Crompton *Just William* stories.

I also read true stories of exploration and discovery from classics like John Hunt's *The Ascent of Everest* to the Zoo Quest tales of a young David Attenborough. Imagining myself on Everest or in the jungles of South America was beyond me at ten years old but I could imagine being in Ransome's Lake District while the imaginary countryside of William Brown was very similar to the real one all around me.

I never lost my dreams, though in my teens and early twenties they were pushed aside a little by the pressing concerns of adolescence, and I never stopped wandering in the countryside or scribbling in notebooks. I never thought either of them could be a way of making a living though and no-one ever suggested they could. My life as

1

a long distance walker and outdoor writer came about gradually, unplanned and with many fortuitous twists and turns.

I wrote a few articles about long walks I'd done in the late 1970s and discovered that magazine editors quite liked them so I wrote some more and then expanded them to cover my thoughts and feelings about the outdoors and outdoor activities. I'm still writing many decades later and a selection of these essays make up this book, revised and with some changes to bring them up to date.

My previous books have been stories of long walks such as *Rattlesnakes and Bald Eagles*, 'how-to' books like *The Backpacker's Handbook* and guidebooks such as *World Mountain Ranges: Scotland*. The essays in this book cover a greater range of topics and many of the ideas that appear in my earlier books are expanded and considered in more depth.

My interests are in wild land and the outdoors in all its aspects so you'll find my thoughts on rewilding, forests, mountains, wilderness writers, outdoor gear and more, plus accounts of ski tours in places like Spitsbergen and Greenland, and trekking in the Himalayas as well as walks long and short.

My passion for wild places and for communicating my joy in them hasn't dimmed over the years. If anything it has grown. Along with it has come a growing desire to help defend these places and work for their conservation and restoration. *Out There* tells the story of my outdoor life and shows the importance of wild places to me. My hope is that it will enhance your own experience of 'out there' or, if you haven't been yet, inspire you to think and feel about it with something of my own affection, enthusiasm and concern.

1

IDEAS & INSPIRATION

Thinking of the mistakes I made as a novice backpacker makes me shudder. Did I really suffer that much? With no instruction or mentors I learnt initially by trial and error, mostly the latter. Sleeping out in the rain in a feather and down sleeping bag in a plastic survival bag showed me the joys of condensation and a wet bag; trying to sleep on frozen ground with no insulating mat taught me why these pieces of expensive foam are needed; buying a piece of open cell foam from a market because it was cheaper than a real camping mat taught me just how much water it absorbed when sleeping in a single-skin tent with no vents to let condensation escape. Result: another sodden sleeping bag. Then there was humping an external frame pack round the English Lake District with no hipbelt (these were 'optional extras' in Britain in the early 1970s). A shocked American hiker had me try on his pack with hipbelt, and I've been in loved with hipbelts ever since.

I also learned that one of those compass things might be a good idea after getting lost on the featureless moorland of Kinder Scout in a November storm and descending in the dark, cold and wet. A torch would have been useful too, as I stumbled into bogs and fell over rocks. Just a week later I realised that carrying spare batteries was also a good idea when my new torch failed. It had accidentally switched on in the pack and again I found myself slipping and sliding downwards in the darkness. When my cheap thin nylon cagoule leaked through the seams I went to the other extreme with a bulky, heavy neoprene coated cagoule with taped seams. The condensation was horrendous (this was long before any fabrics that let moisture out) but it never let in a drop of rain.

Those episodes and more taught me a great deal, as they would anyone who survived them. I don't recommend following my example though. Far better to learn from those with more experience, whether in the wilds or from books, blogs and articles. Back in my early days the Internet didn't exist so I couldn't just pull up advice and gear reviews in an instant. Instead, when I realised that I would like to be safer and more comfortable, I read backpacking manuals and joined The Backpacker's Club, a new organisation in Britain at the time. Those books – Peter Lumley's *Teach Yourself Backpacking* and Derrick Booth's *The Backpacker's Handbook* (whose title I pinched for my own how-to book a few decades later) – were invaluable. I still have them and when I glance through them now, although the gear seems old-fashioned the advice is sound. I also went on Backpacker's Club meets and learnt much by talking to experienced backpackers as well as hiking with them and observing their techniques.

Along with instructional books I read books about long-distance hikes and soon aspired to undertake similar walks. My first really long walk was inspired by John Hillaby's *Journey Through Britain*, the story of a backpacking trip from the farthest apart points on the British mainland, Land's End and John O'Groats. Hiking 1250 miles (2000km) that spring was a revelation. Two weeks and 270 miles (430km) was my previous longest walk. This one was long enough to become 'what I did', my way of life for the 3 months it took. This, I realised, was really living, this was what I wanted to do. I also discovered my love for real wildness as I crossed the Scottish Highlands and revelled in the remoteness and vastness compared with the English countryside. I still didn't know what real wilderness was though. And I didn't know I didn't know either.

After Hillaby came Hamish Brown and his wonderful *Hamish's Mountain Walk*, the story of the first ever walk over all the Munros (mountains over 3,000 feet/914m high) in Scotland in a single trip, and still one of the best long distance hiking books I've ever read. Inspired by Hamish I set out to climb all the Munros on backpacking trips. It took me four years, during which I undertook two 500 mile (800km) hikes and several shorter ones, and I learnt much in the stormy Highlands where camps are often exposed and subject to high winds and heavy rain. I think that if you learn backpacking skills there, you can easily adapt them to anywhere else. (Many years later I spent four and a half months on a continuous walk over all the Munros plus the subsidiary Tops during a wet summer that really tested my skills and my perseverance).

Whilst bagging the Munros I was lent a book an acquaintance had picked up in the USA, a book that would change my life even more than Hillaby's and Brown's had done. It was *The Thousand-Mile Summer* by Colin Fletcher. Reading Fletcher's wonderful prose about backpacking in big wilderness in California inspired me to think about hiking overseas. A little research (again, without the Internet, I can't imagine how I did it!) turned up the Pacific Crest Trail. I knew the moment I read about it that I wanted to hike it, and the year after completing the Munros I took my first very nervous steps north from the Mexican border.

Although still early April it was hot. The desert landscape was completely alien to me and I had much to learn. My first lesson was that a half litre water bottle is nowhere near adequate in dry places. In Scotland I barely ever carried water – there were always plenty of streams and pools. Once I'd added some soda bottles to my load all was well though and I began to enjoy and appreciate the strange landscape.

The next challenge came as I approached the High Sierra. Late snow meant it was completely snowbound. I bought snowshoes and crampons and teamed up with three other hikers and, together, we made it through, taking three weeks on the longest section. My pack was so heavy at the start that I couldn't actually lift it. I had to sit down, put it on, and gingerly stand up. Every hour or so I had to rest as my shoulders and hips were going numb. At least that's what my journal says. I can't now remember the weight or the pain but I can remember the joy of spending so many days without leaving the wilderness. The weight was ridiculous and I've never carried such a stupid load since but the rewards made the effort worthwhile.

For much of the PCT the beauty and wildness of the landscape had me floating on a high. I was astounded and overjoyed to discover such wilderness. The whole trail was an inspiration. It remains the one walk that stands out in my memory; the one where I discovered real wilderness and the great pleasure of hiking and living in it. Since the PCT I've done many other long walks, most recently the

6

Pacific Northwest Trail and the Scottish Watershed, and all have been great experiences. None has quite the magic or power of the PCT though. That was my first wilderness walk and as such remains special.

Going solo

The best way to experience wild places is to go alone. The full intensity of being in nature, of feeling part of it and blending in only comes with solitude, when you can open up to the world around you. By myself in the hills or the woods I often achieve a feeling of heightened awareness, of being in touch, never reached when I am with others. The reasons for this are deep, varied, complex and not completely clear, at least to me, but I shall try and identify them. Firstly of course, being alone means no distractions. When I walk with companions their company is a key part of the trip so involvement with nature is no longer central. Just removing the distractions of others is superficial though, it's what emerges without those distractions that matters. Time alone in the wilds is time to connect and the longer the time the deeper the connection, which is why backpacking is much more intense than day walking. This connection is a mix of understanding and feeling.

Being alone also helps ensure a connection with the wild, allowing free interaction with

weather, landscape, internal feelings and external stimuli. On one overnight trip I wandered into a corrie in the Cairngorms and came upon a granite seat facing a curve of ragged cliffs and snow-choked gullies. I accepted the invitation and sat for a while watching rocks, clouds and a trickling spring, absorbing the atmosphere. When it seemed the right time I shouldered my pack and left the corrie, which now seemed familiar and known. Being alone it was completely my decision when to stop and when to move on.

This freedom applies to a host of decisions from the moment of waking. Do I spring up, pack and stride off or do I roll over and sleep a little more? Do I linger over an extended breakfast? Choosing the route, choosing the frequency, length and whereabouts of rest stops, deciding how far to walk each day, picking a campsite early because it looks too wonderful to pass, or walking into the evening and camping in the dark because I'm enjoying the dusk. Doing whatever I feel like when I feel like it allows me to relax and follow what feels a natural rhythm unbroken by the desires, needs or abilities of others. Sometimes I go into an almost trance like state where I am not really conscious of my body and walk for several hours, completely absorbed in where I am not who I am.

Sometimes I come out of these reveries astonished at how far I've walked and for how long. Yet at the same time, because I am walking at a speed and with a rhythm that suits me, I can deal almost automatically with changes in terrain, barely conscious of the need to cross boulders with care or slow down and shorten my steps when climbing steep slopes. Without conscious thought I'm engrossed in the landscape, observing every detail.

Falling into a natural rhythm is most obvious when walking but it is also present when you rest, camp, eat and sleep. I have my own camp routine, honed in Britain's wet and cold weather but applied even in warm dry places. I sort out my shelter first (which may mean pitching a tent or just laying out a groundsheet and mat), then unpack gear into its place and finally start the stove. This procedure allows me to relax and feel organised and protected.

As I become more awake as the day goes on I tend to walk, camp and sleep late. This does not suit everyone and when I walk with others I usually adapt to doing things earlier. Following my own rhythms and habits means I am at ease and able to relate more easily to where I am. It is a way of putting the necessary routines of backpacking into the background so they do not intrude on my real reasons for being there.

Two frequently put objections to solo backpacking are loneliness and safety. I've often been asked how I cope with being on my own. I find this an extremely difficult question to answer because I don't find being alone a problem. In the wilds there is always so much to see and do, from the practicalities of campcraft, route finding and dealing with the weather, to watching everything from the landscape as a whole to a devil's coach horse beetle struggling up a loose gravel slope. Solitude and loneliness are very different. I have never been lonely in the wilds.

Safety is a consideration, of course, but I find that being alone, and always taking that into account, adds to the intensity of the experience. There is no one to ask for advice, no one to share decision making with, no one to tell you your judgement is faulty or your choice unwise. Only you can decide what route to take, where to camp, whether to ford a river or make other choices. Your thinking becomes deeper (or at least it should do) because you and only you have to live with the results. With others safety is an issue and care is needed but it is shared. On your own every action must be weighed carefully and the risk assessed without consultation.

This becomes still more significant on backpacking trips, especially multi-week ones in remote places. On my thousand-mile hike through the Yukon Territory I went ten days without seeing another person (and I met very few in the whole trip). I was hiking cross country in terrain ranging from dense forest to open meadows and rocky ridges, and route finding was a matter of going with the nature of the land.

Following braided wide shallow rivers, wading between gravel banks, was easier than bushwhacking through the dense undergrowth on either side. At other times I escaped the tangled forest by climbing up to long bare terraces running high on the hillside. Constantly having to assess the terrain and choose a route kept me profoundly involved with the landscape. With a companion or in a group I would not have been so absorbed. I knew that I was far from help, that no one expected to hear from me for a few weeks and that the route I'd left with contacts was very approximate. At any time I could be several miles from it. This gave me every incentive to be careful and to concentrate all the time which, in turn, made the experience very powerful.

Thoughts on peak bagging

Looking out of my window, I can see a small heather-clad hill a few miles away. It goes under the prosaic if appropriate name of Tom Mor - Big Knoll. It's not, as far as I know, in any tables of hills. At just 484 metres high and a mere 70 metres above the saddle linking it to the nearest higher hill, it doesn't fit the criteria for even the most obscure and esoteric list. Over the years though, I've climbed up Tom Mor many times, sometimes in deep winter snow when it looks as though it could be part of the Arctic, sometimes on warm summer evenings when the sun glows red on the bright thread of the river twisting through the valley below and the distant Cairngorms fade into black.

There are mountain hares on Tom Mor, along with red grouse, meadow pipits and the occasional raven. Two big well-built cairns decorate the summit, plus a less attractive modern communications mast. I've never seen anyone else up there or even any footprints. I go because the route is interesting, the view pleasant and, when the light is right, spectacular. The distance is just right for a half-day or evening walk and, of course, it's close to home.

Even though I've been there many times before, I always go to the summit of Tom Mor. To bypass it would make the walk seem incomplete. It's a destination, a goal, an objective that gives a purpose, a meaning, to the walk. Afterwards it defines what I did. I went up Tom Mor. Although the real enjoyment is in the going up and the coming down and in what I *see* and experience along the way, not in reaching the top, having a summit to climb to gives a shape to the walk, a picture I can see in my mind.

Of course, if I just climbed that one little hill over and over, I would have a very clear image of a very small area. Some people do that and are content. I once knew somebody who went to Edale in the Peak District in England and climbed Kinder Scout every weekend. He liked Kinder and also liked the familiarity, the friendliness, of the known.

While I enjoy my strolls up Tom Mor, I also like to seek out the unknown and the different, the potentially challenging and the uncertain. But oh, how difficult this can sometimes be! How much easier to stick to the same paths and the same summits. Often a stimulus is needed to get me to venture into new territory. Curiosity is the usual spur. No hill is identical to any other, so every hill has something different to see and enjoy. Each way up is different, too, offering a new perspective on a perhaps familiar summit. This alone, the desire for the new and the unfamiliar, is enough to justify peak bagging.

There's more, though. Working through a list of hills means building up a picture of an area until you can see it as a totality. Climb all the Lakeland Fells (I have to say I hate the neologism 'Wainwrights' - the man himself never compiled a list or gave his name to one) and you will have a clear overview of the area, of how the different hills and dales link together to form the whole. Work your way through the Munros and the Corbetts (and maybe the Grahams as well) and your knowledge of the Scottish hills should be fairly comprehensive. Go out in all types of weather, as peak baggers tend to do, and you'll know what the hills are like in storms as well as sunshine, again giving a depth of knowledge unknown to those who only venture out when it's fine.

In Britain, there is a particular reason for peak bagging too, and that is that most of our truly wild country lies high up, on and around the summits. To experience that wildness, we need to climb. In other places where there is real wildness in the valleys as well as on the heights, I don't feel such a desire to reach the summits.

In wild places abroad, I've walked for weeks and months at a time and hardly climbed any peaks as I was in wilderness anyway. I did, however, bag a few in the White Mountains of New Hampshire, specifically for the views as the mountains are mostly densely forested and only the highest summits and ridges rise above the trees. To see anything, you have to climb. There are 48 summits over 4000ft (1220m) in New Hampshire and, on a ten day backpacking trip I climbed 22. Maybe I'll go back and climb the rest one day.

While essentially a pointless pursuit, in that reaching summits has no extrinsic value, peak bagging is healthy and harmless (apart from some erosion on popular routes) and should cause no offence. Yet there are those who feel so threatened by peak baggers that they attack it as 'list ticking', 'stamp collecting' and even as 'sacrilegious'. These critics seem to think that peak baggers have no appreciation of the mountains they climb, no desire to understand the nature of the land and no feeling for the beauty of wild country.

There probably are peak baggers for whom reaching a summit and ticking off a list are all that matters (philosophically, this may be the existentialist approach, as with Mallory's 'because it's there'), but I venture to guess that they soon give up, as the effort and time required would be too much if there is little enjoyment. In my experience, most peak baggers have as much awareness and understanding of the hills as their critics, and often more due to their greater experience.

Those who decry peak bagging as mere list ticking fail to understand the commitment, challenge and pleasure involved. They also seem unaware of the rewards of exploring new country, of learning how the topography of a region works, of experiencing a range of hills in all weathers at all times of year. Collecting summits means collecting experiences.

Why some walkers should feel smug and superior (which is how they often appear) because they don't bag peaks leaves me baffled and not a little irritated. It seems such an intolerant and elitist attitude, a way of saying that their way of doing things is right and anyone else's is wrong. You never read of peak baggers criticising other walkers for not doing all the Munros or all the Lakeland

Peaks. Why should they? Yet somehow those who set out to climb these peaks disturb those who don't so much that they feel they must denigrate them.

Those of us who love the hills should be tolerant of different ways of doing things, as long as they don't damage the wilds. There is nothing better about admiring the hills from below than there is about climbing them. Repeated ascents of the same peak are no less or more valuable or valid than climbing a different hill every day. How we enjoy the hills is a personal matter and not one that should engender criticism or censure.

Planning and spontaneity

Long distance walks are usually planned carefully. Information is put together on the nature of the terrain, possible camp sites, resupply points, water sources and more so that a detailed plan can be assembled. Once this is done you can, if you wish, know where you'll spend each night, how far you'll walk each day, where there is water and whether there are any hazards such as stream fords. Such plans are good for safety and peace of mind. They also ensure that you can complete your walk in the time available. I make plans similar to this for my long walks, but not in so much detail. Certainly not down to where I'll camp or how far I'll walk each day. Rather I need to know how far it is between resupply points so I know how many days to allow for each section. Any more than that takes out some of the adventure and excitement.

I like not knowing what to expect and the freedom of decision making. Raining at dawn? Let's have a second breakfast and read some more of my book. A late start might mean a shorter distance but so what? Discover a beautiful camp site mid-afternoon? Then stop early and enjoy it. On other days, feeling strong and with a beautiful dusk unfolding, I might walk until after dark, making camp by headlamp. This approach sometimes means I have to walk further than perhaps intended. On the Pacific Northwest Trail I lingered on the summit of 2,225 metre Abercrombie Mountain as the setting sun turned the sky dark red and a half moon rose followed by a single bright star. I had intended to camp at the first water I could find back down in the forest. I did camp at the first water too – but 1,200 metres down and four hours later.

This less structured approach reaches its epitome on trips with no plans at all. I often do this over one and two nights where I can let desire, terrain and weather determine how far I go and where I camp.

A friend from Derbyshire found himself with a few days free and made a flying visit for a trip onto the Cairngorm Plateau. The forecast was good so we wandered across the plateau to the summit of Ben Macdui where a brisk wind sent us down to the headwaters of the Garbh Uisge Mor and a spectacular camp looking across the plateau to Cairn Gorm. The evening was lovely with soft light, drifting pale pink clouds and a slowly darkening sky. Morning came with low mist and drizzle. Cairn Gorm had vanished. With no set plans we decided to cross Ben Macdui again and descend into the Lairig Ghru and follow this out of the mountains. It was a good choice as the clouds lingered on the summits all day while down below we had views of the burns, pools and rocks of this dramatic pass. With no schedule to adhere to we could adapt to the weather.

On another trip I headed up alone onto the huge Moine Mhor (Great Moss) above Glen Feshie, a wonderful place for aimless wandering as there are a myriad possible camp

15

sites and the terrain is good for walking. The weather forecast was promising and I was hoping for a couple of fine camp sites. My first was in the heart of the plateau with extensive views of streams, pools, rolling tundra and hills all around – totally wild, totally beautiful. Feeling energetic the next morning, probably inspired by the clear sky and warm sunshine, I decided on the superb high level walk along the rim of An Garbh Choire from Braeriach to Cairn Toul. I could have done this as a day trip from camp but wanted the option of camping elsewhere that night.

The day was magnificent with sharp, clear views and the Moine Mhor shimmered in the sunlight. This really is big country. Coming off Cairn Toul I was entranced by the many springs surrounded by bright green and red moss and, low down on the hillside, found a curious, long, wide, grassy shelf like a road cut across the slope for several hundred metres. Possibly it was the shore of an ancient loch. Mostly smooth and mostly dry it was a fine place for a camp with a view to the gully-riven craggy north face of Beinn Bhrotain. I'd walked 15 kilometres but was only four kilometres from where I'd camped the night before. I could easily have left my camp there, but that would have taken the spontaneity and freedom out of the day.

Trips like these with no destination, no purpose other than to be in wild places and relish the natural world, are in some ways the most perfect ones. No pressure, no schedule, just the freedom of the outdoors.

A sense of space

One warm sunny evening early in the summer I walked into the great bowl of Coire Ardair in the Creag Meagaidh National Nature Reserve, admired the dark snow-streaked cliffs rising above the lochan, and climbed the steep stony slopes to the narrow notch known as The Window. Here the world suddenly opened up. Until now I had been in the corrie, surrounded by its steep walls rising to long rippling ridges. The corrie was wide and there was no sense of being closed in but I could not see beyond its confines. From The Window I could look out to wave after wave of shadowy mountains vanishing into the distance. The sudden sense of space was liberating. I revelled in the vastness as I climbed the last slopes to the big plateau of Creag Meagaidh, that broad bulky mountain set in the heart of the Highlands. Up here there was just sky and mountain and wildness and this seemingly untouched landscape stretched to the horizon all around with only a few signs of human interference, not enough to do more than slightly detract from the scene.

I camped just fifty metres below the summit, my tiny tent dwarfed by the immensity of the mountain. The western horizon turned pink, the sun sank behind distant clouds, the first stars emerged. The ranges of hills became silhouettes, the corries below pools of blackness. The feeling of a huge world remained.

Morning came with a hazy sunrise. Far off hills were pale and vague, hovering in the cool air. Slowly as the sun rose and strengthened they hardened and sharpened. I gazed at the spreading view from Creag Meagaidh's summit cairn then set off on the long high level walk over a series of tops to Carn Liath. I was above the world, striding over the hills free from the concerns of the locked-in land far below. From Carn Liath I began a slow descent and as I came down the land closed in, the world shrank, the mountains rose on either side. I felt restricted. The freedom of the summits had gone.

17

This sense of space and freedom is for me one of the great joys of the hills. I can find it on any summit but most especially on big plateaux or long ridges, places where I can stay high for hour after hour. I've also felt it on wide beaches, particularly remote ones such as Sandwood Bay, and there's a hint of it in wide meadows in forests. In deserts it sometimes seems all there is. In such places nature is dominant and nature is large. Size is a key component of this feeling of space. It has to be seen spreading out all around. This is why in Britain mountain tops and ridges are the places to find it. High passes can provide it too but we don't have many of those, unlike the High Sierra in California or the Himalaya, both places where I've enjoyed the vastness of the landscape without climbing summits.

As well as size I find naturalness important. The curving, flowing lines of the landscape, unbroken by human straight lines, have a beauty that speaks of space. In Britain it's rare to have a completely unsullied view. Even from Creag Meagaidh, surrounded by hills, I could see blemishes – a distant wind farm, the white blades catching the eye; the pale slashes of bulldozed roads; the stark War of the Worlds marching metal towers of electricity pylons; blocks of conifer plantations – but these were tiny in the great scale of the landscape. Every new turbine, pylon or road has an effect though, gradually diminishing the beauty and sense of space.

This sense of space, of a world unconstrained and free, matters. We need to know such places still exist, that there is still somewhere to go that is beautiful and wild and in which we can lose ourselves. Of course glens, forests, corries can all be magnificent and wonderful but they don't, can't, have the same feeling of space. I love them for the details of nature, for the protection they offer from storms, for the views up to the summits, but to really see them I think you need to climb high above them and look down. The regenerating woodlands of Coire Ardair are lovely and inspiring and walking through them is a pleasure but to see how extensive they are you need to be on the hills above. From the heights you can see the shape of the land too, the shape of the corries and glens, the shape of the lochs and rivers. I love watching the landscape and seeing how it is constructed, how the parts fit together.

Backpacking is the ideal way to see the world like this, as long as the world itself is big enough to embrace multi-day journeys. Carve the wild up into little pieces and that will be lost. We need space for freedom and beauty.

2

NIGHTS IN THE WILD

The finest roof when camping is the open sky. Falling asleep watching the stars and the ragged silhouette of mountains, and waking as the first pale light glows in the east is the most thrilling way to spend a night in the wilds.

In dry areas such nights can be the norm. During both my two month long Arizona Trail walk and a five week hike in the High Sierra I spent more nights under the stars than in shelters. Sleeping out like this means keeping in touch with nature, in touch with the world. Breezes ripple the sleeping bag and brush your face; the sounds of animals scurrying nearby are loud and clear. If you stir in the night you half-awake to stars, trees, rocks, grass and the whole spreading natural world, and when you properly wake at dawn you are already outdoors with no need to unzip the tent to see what's happening.

There are nights when the wind blows too hard or the rain starts to fall or biting insects launch an attack, and then you need a shelter. Even those scurrying animals can force you under cover. One night in the Grand Canyon mice running over my sleeping bag kept disturbing my sleep until, in the early hours of the morning, I pitched my tent and sealed myself inside.

After the open sky the next best shelter is a roomy tarp

pitched so you can see all around. Next again, a tent with doors that open wide, again providing a good view and some contact with the outside world. Only when high winds blow and heavy rain or snow falls or insects are biting do I close up a tent. I don't go outside to be inside. It's just that I'm not out there to suffer. If it's more comfortable sealed into my tent then that's where I'll be.

Lying in a warm sleeping bag, listening to the rain rattling on the flysheet and the wind roaring in great gusts can be strangely relaxing. Feeling snug and secure inside a tiny shelter is satisfying, but few such camps are really unforgettable. The lack of contact with the outside reduces them to the simple function of survival in a storm, with nothing distinctive to remember them by.

Sometimes, though, stormy nights can be surprisingly memorable as well as pleasurable. On my walk over the Munros and Tops I descended from a cloud-wrapped summit on a day of torrential rain and strong winds into a glen that was waterlogged with pools of water on every flattish spot and cascades pouring down the valley sides. I stumbled through the wetness, cursing the rain as I searched for a site. I wanted warmth and shelter, food and rest. Eventually I found a flattish knoll that wasn't too wet and had just enough room for my little tent. I pitched, tightening the guylines against the wind, stripped off my wet waterproofs, boots and socks and crawled in. Suddenly I had shelter. I donned a dry fleece sweater and slid into my dry sleeping bag. Now I had warmth. Lighting the stove I made a hot drink. Outside lay a saturated world, the rain still hammering down, but now it looked wild and exciting and I was glad to be there.

More usually wild camps are remembered because of a beautiful or spectacular situation and weather that doesn't force you into a closed tent. Camps where the tarp or tent function only as a bedroom are ideal. After that I like it when I can look out from my shelter, protected from wind and rain but not cut off from the outside. Whilst sleeping under the stars is not possible that often in Britain (and by sleeping under the stars I mean just in a sleeping bag with the hood open, not sealed in a bivi bag, which I find more confining than a tent), camps where you can sit outside or look out from your shelter occur surprisingly frequently, especially outside of summer. This might seem surprising but the one horror that can force me inside a tent with the doors shut tight are the ravenous hordes of midges that roam the hills searching for campers in the summer months.

Midges are usually associated with the Highlands but I have memories of midge-ridden nights in the Lake District too. Outside of midge season wild camping in the British hills can be a delight. The number of possible sites is legion. I discover more every year and the list of those I've passed by, but intend returning to, would last several lifetimes.

Taking pleasure in camping means that I rarely walk from dawn until dusk as this allows no time to enjoy a camp site. For me contemplation and slowly absorbing my surroundings are important, and remaining in one place gives the opportunity to notice the sort of subtleties that are easily missed while walking. Wildlife is more likely to be observed from a camp too, another reason not to be closed away from the outside. Tents and tarps make good hides.

On one TGO Challenge I camped on the edge of a small pinewood and woke at dawn to the strange bubbling calls of black grouse. Lying in the tent I watched these magnificent birds strutting and preening and fanning their wide tails as they competed for mates, a wonderful start to my day. On other walks in other places I have been woken by deer grazing in a meadow just feet from the tent and porcupines shuffling through the grass.

Having time in camp means being able to watch how the passage of the sun and the fading and strengthening of the light changes the landscape, altering how it looks and feels. In the evening the shadows grow and colours fade, hills turn dark and lose detail, sunset turns clouds pink and orange before the sky blackens and the first stars appear. The world becomes mysterious and hidden until, at dawn, the darkness fades as the sun lightens the sky and the flat, black, featureless hills gradually reveal themselves as ridges, cliffs and gullies appear. The first sharp rays of the sun touch a hill top, turning it red and gold. Slowly the sunshine creeps down the mountainside and across the land, approaching camp and bringing the promise of warmth and life.

Just a few days before I wrote this I lay in my sleeping bag on a frosty morning in the Highlands watching the sun turning the white, shivering land a warm, sumptuous golden brown. Gradually, oh so gradually, the sunshine slipped towards my frosted tent. I relished the anticipation of its warmth then revelled in the sudden heat and light. I never tire of those moments, the return of light and life to the world, which make wild camping an incomparable joy.

Stealth Camping

As the name suggests, stealth camping is camping where you are unlikely to be seen. I've practised it since I began backpacking, long before I heard the term itself. I like it though; it suggests quietness and a lack of disturbance. It comes to mind particularly on routes that pass through more developed areas and where wild sites are hard to find - as was the case one spring when I hiked the Southern Upland and the Annandale Ways.

Scotland's enlightened access legislation, which gives a right to camp wild, meant I didn't have to hide my camps but, nonetheless, as both paths run through farmland and lowland woods in places, there were times when I preferred to be out of sight. South of the border, in England, stealth camping is rather more of a necessity as wild camping isn't a legal right. High in the hills it's usually accepted but in many lowland areas it's wise to be invisible.

I learnt much on a Land's End to John o'Groats walk, including making camp late and leaving early. At the same time I also found that passing by a prospective site because I wanted to walk a few more miles could mean difficulties in actually finding somewhere, so sometimes I stopped early but didn't pitch until it grew dark.

A stealth camp is one where you are unlikely to be seen by others because you are out of sight not only of roads, buildings and footpaths but also bothies, huts and popular wild sites. If there are signs that people camp there regularly then it's not a stealth camp site.

Along most long distance paths and in popular walking areas there are wild sites that are used almost every night in the summer. Yet by only venturing a short distance it's usually possible to camp in solitude. Finding a stealth site means a combination of studying the map and studying the terrain. In lowland areas, woods are excellent, just wander away from the path and find a flat area. This doesn't necessarily mean being surrounded by trees with no views either.

Towards the end of one of my TGO Challenge cross-Scotland routes there is a spot beside a fine rushing river with a lovely view back up the glen that is hidden from the nearby road by a steep wooded bank. I've camped there four times and have never seen another person. (And no, I'm not going to tell you where it is!). In open hill country stealth camping can be more difficult. I look for wrinkles and dips in the terrain, and have found that sometimes such spots can lie surprisingly close to footpaths.

In my view the main reason for stealth camping isn't to hide from other people (I'm not that anti-social!) but to be in closer contact with nature. I'm out in the wilds to experience the landscape, the wild life, the trees, the flowers and the whole magnificent natural world and I want that to be part of the camping as well as the walking.

I don't want the wildlife to be disturbed by people walking by, as can happen when camping near a footpath, or by other people talking, as can happen at popular wild sites. I don't want to look at other tents either or hear vehicles on a road or tractors in a field, so if I see another tent I give it a wide berth, assuming those campers are also seeking solitude. Not everyone does this. Once in a big corrie I deliberately went well away from the path and the used camp sites and camped out of sight behind some boulders. The next morning I went for a stroll up a nearby hill and, when I returned, there was another tent only fifty feet or so away from mine. In all that vast area, which could have held a dozen or more tents all hidden from each other, they had chosen to camp next to the only other tent there. I packed up and left, as intended, hoping that the other campers didn't think I'd taken offence and moved because of them. Mind you, if I'd been staying a second night I might have moved for that very reason!

Stealth sites are usually undisturbed and pristine. They don't look like camp sites and ideally there is nothing human left visible. They certainly don't have rings of stones, flattened vegetation, bare patches of earth, stone windbreak walls or camp fire scars. Sites with these are the opposite of stealth ones, showing overuse. I pass them by or, if I do use one, restore it a little by breaking up the stone rings and demolishing structures. When leaving a stealth site it should look as though no-one has ever camped there. Perhaps there's some flattened grass, but this will quickly recover if it was used for one night only. The idea is that if someone else does camp in that area they probably won't choose exactly the same spot so a new visible site doesn't appear.

For these reasons stealth camps should be for one night only and new paths shouldn't be trampled from the nearest footpath or to the nearest water (something more likely with groups). Indeed, stealth camps may not be near water at all. I've often carried enough water for camp for the last hour or two to a fine but waterless site. I carried water for camps twice on the Annandale Way and each time found a lovely, quiet and relaxing woodland site.

No special equipment is required for stealth camping but a dull green or brown-coloured shelter is useful, especially when camping in open country. There's nothing like vivid red or orange nylon for attracting the eye. That said, I used a quite bright gold-coloured tent on the Pacific Northwest Trail and made several stealth camps by simply heading off into dense forest and thick undergrowth. Despite the colour of the tent anyone would have had to be fairly close to spot it.

I think stealth camping is in fact the natural form of backpacking camping. It's what wild camping should be.

Summit Camps

Ideally a wild camp should be in a spectacular location and the weather should be fine so you don't have to be cooped up inside. The most dramatic and stunning locations for wild camps are mountain tops and it is on these that I have had some of my most memorable nights. They also have the wildest weather and are not places it's easy to escape from in the dark. That in itself makes summit camps special and gives them an edge and sense of uncertainty that is rarely felt in low level camps.

Sometimes mountain top camps are unwise or impossible and lower sites have to be sought. On many occasions I've turned away from planned summit camps to look for somewhere sheltered. At other times I've not intended to camp on summits but fortuitous circumstances have led me to do so. Such was the case on one TGO Challenge when I camped on the summit of Ben Nevis. This had not been planned and only grew as an idea as I approached the snow-capped mountain from the west. When snow free the big summit plateau is a vast rock field with nowhere for a comfortable camp and no water, but snow makes a comfortable bed and can be melted.

The forecast was for a calm clear night so I left Fort William on a sunny evening and climbed to the summit, passing many walkers descending, most of whom looked puzzled at seeing someone heading up that late in the day. Many warned me of the time and the snow on the summit. (Heading up late for a high camp does disturb some people – many years ago I was stopped by a walker

27

in the Lake District who was furious that I was going up in the evening despite my big pack, informing me that I was both inexperienced and irresponsible). On Ben Nevis I think the fact that I was wearing sandals shocked some people too.

By the time I reached the summit plateau I was alone. I pitched the tent on deep snow near the trig point and wandered round, watching the hills slowly sinking into night. Across Glen Nevis the long rippling ridge of the Mamores turned a rich red and gold. Beyond the dark cliffs of the Ben's North Face Loch Eil glowed gold beneath the last pink of thin clouds far to the west. A raven wheeled overhead and a snow bunting hopped about, hoping for crumbs. A half-moon rose and the first stars glittered. All was calm and silent and I felt both excited and peaceful in such perfect conditions. The snow made for the softest and least bumpy pitch of the whole walk and I slept well. Dawn came with wet mist and a gusty wind but the sun soon burned the dampness away for me to look down on cloud-filled glens with peaks rising out of them, sharp and clear.

After fourteen hours alone on the summit, which is usually crowded during the day, I departed, still marvelling at my wondrous night. After crossing the Carn Mor Dearg arête I looked back at the vast magnificent North Face of Ben Nevis, amazed that I'd camped on the summit. It was the high point of the walk, both literally and emotionally.

Sleeping on a mountain can mean waking to a storm, perhaps in the middle of the night. On Coinnich Mhor, one of the subsidiary summits of Beinn Eighe in Torridon (and whose name means 'big moss', a hint that it might make a good camp site) I was woken at 4.30 a.m. by heavy rain lashing the tent. Everything was damp with condensation running down the walls (a situation made worse by the fact that I was testing a small not very well-ventilated single skin tent – gear testing isn't always fun!). I unzipped the door and looked out only for my head lamp beam to bounce back at me from the thick mist surrounding the tent. I felt disappointed, as I'd climbed Coinnich Mhor on a fine evening with a forecast for a clear night and sunny weather. There'd been a red sky at dusk too, with lovely colours over the hills of Fisherfield and Ruadh-stac Mor, the highest peak on Beinn Eighe. The rain didn't ease despite the forecast and the next day was one of low cloud and downpours. The evening light had made the high camp worthwhile though (and I now knew a great deal about that tent!).

However there's no need to climb the highest peaks for wonderful summit camps. Lower peaks can offer just as splendid views and just as remote and wild a feel. North-west of Ben Nevis, across the Great Glen, lies a long flat-topped hill called Druim Fada (which means long ridge). The high point of only 744 metres, called Stob a'Grianain, is at the east end and here I camped, a few yards from the summit cairn, one early autumn evening after a long day. The weather was sunny but there was a cold west wind that kept the air sharp and clear. Below I could see Corpach and Fort William with Ben Nevis and the Mamores rising above them.

In daylight the towns looked rather mundane. Looking away from them to the west all I could see was hills and glens. The feeling was of being situated on the edge of the wild, between civilisation and nature. As the sun set and the light dimmed, the landscape became more mysterious and atmospheric. Ben Nevis glowed in the low late rays of the sun and a full moon, huge and orange, rose over the misty pale landscape of the Great Glen. The towns became daubs of bright lights, decorations rather than real places even though I could hear traffic whenever the wind paused. By dawn the towns were in grey shadow and Ben Nevis was cloud-capped, but out west the sky was red and golden and pale mist filled the glens below the purple shaded hills. The day was hazy and dull but again it was the night and dusk and dawn that had worked magic.

Winter is a more serious time for high camps as nights are long and cold and storms severe. Snow can transform undistinguished hills though, and make camping on them an exciting adventure. One February, when deep snow lay from the glens to the summits, I went from my front door up little Carn na Loine, a heathery bump just 549 metres high in the far north-east corner of the Cairngorms National Park. Snow free, this is a rolling heather moorland hill managed for grouse-shooting; under snow it is more like an arctic wilderness. The sky was overcast as I pitched camp but at dusk the sun sank below the cloud, turning the snow pink and the western sky red and orange. Night brought a clearing sky, a full moon, stars and a temperature of -8°C, and I was glad of my down jacket as I watched the wildness and listened to the silence. Home was just a few miles away but it could have been on another planet. Indeed, it seemed as though it was.

The world of the summits is different. Camping there takes you into a special place where the flatlands can be forgotten and wildness embraced.

Entertainment in Camp

Midwinter nights in the Scottish Highlands are long. With over seventeen hours of darkness the sun sets in the middle of the afternoon. On moonlit and starry nights I like to walk long after dark and spend time outside my tent star gazing, but when the sky is overcast and the weather stormy I'm usually in my shelter soon after sunset. The question then becomes: what to do with all that time? With no views, just blackness outside, you can't watch the night evolve through the open door. Cooking and eating don't take up much time either, though in winter I carry more food that needs cooking than when daylight hours are long.

On long winter nights like this, and nights at any time of year when stormy weather or biting insects make it preferable to be inside my shelter, I occupy myself mainly with reading and writing. Some people like to listen to music or podcasts or even watch videos or films (options that weren't available until quite recently). I don't usually like anything that requires sound though, as I find it cuts me off from the world in a way that reading doesn't. A bird or animal cry, the rattle of rain on the flysheet, a change in the wind - I like to register all these. I do have music on my smartphone and, very occasionally, listen to this, but when it feels out of place I soon turn it off.

Reading used to mean a paperback book and on many long walks I spent rest days scouring shops, for a second-hand book preferably as I'd leave it in the next town or pass it on. In small towns there is usually little choice, and I've read some strange stuff over the years. This has all changed with the e-reader, which I think is one of the greatest inventions for backpackers in recent years. Even paperbacks are quite heavy so I never carried more than a couple at a time. With an e-reader I can carry a whole library for the same weight (and much less bulk) than a small paperback. The size of the books doesn't matter either. The complete works of Dickens and a slim paperback are exactly the same with an e-reader.

On my 55-day Scottish Watershed walk I read thirteen books, all downloaded before the walk, including several that were sizeable hardbacks in physical form such as George Monbiot's *Feral* and Wade Davis's *Into the Silence*. I'd never have carried these except in digital form. With a wide selection available I never became bored either. If I couldn't concentrate on something fairly heavy like *Into the Silence* I had the *Complete Sherlock Holmes* and some Neil Gaiman novels for light relief. With paperback books I had no choice if I wanted a change.

Whilst for reading I've gone with the latest technology, for writing I've stuck with traditional means - pen and paper. I've tried writing on tiny keyboards, both real and virtual, and just find it too difficult in the confines of the tent, where I'm usually lying on my side and often have cold fingers. Many typing mistakes can make writing unintelligible too. I can always read my scrawled writing (though others might have difficulty!). I like notebooks with waterproof covers (Alwych brand) and I use pens with waterproof ink (Nite Ize Inka Pens and Fisher Space Pens) that will also write at any angle and on greasy paper. Of course, I started keeping a journal long before smartphones and tablets and other electronic devices existed. Maybe if I was starting out now I'd find tiny keyboards usable.

Keeping a journal doesn't just occupy time, it also means that you have a record of your trips for future enjoyment and as a spur to memory. When writing my book on the Pacific Crest Trail, *Rattlesnakes and Bald Eagles*, I reread my journals, written over thirty years before and found that, whilst I could recall much of the walk, there were details I'd forgotten and I was fascinated to read about some actual incidents I couldn't actually remember!

If you don't hike solo, finding activities to fill hours in camp isn't so difficult. Even when talking to each other pales you can produce a pack of cards and play endless games. However, in big storms even groups may find it hard to pass the time. I once led a ski tour in Greenland and, at our highest camp, on the ice cap, stormy weather kept us trapped in the tents for four days. A few people had brought paperback books which became highly valuable. The generous owners allowed them to be torn into sections and passed round so everyone had something to read at least some of the time. Those book pages were more valuable than anything else for those few days.

Bothies

On those trips where the rain beats down day after day and the wind thrashes your tent through the nights, lying inside a small and increasingly damp piece of nylon can eventually become unappealing, and that's when bothies enter their own. These simple unlocked shelters have two big advantages over a tent in stormy weather. Firstly, they don't shake noisily in the wind and flick condensation at you. Secondly, they have space in which you can stand and move around without having to don all your clothes and venture into the wind and rain. Bothies only have basic facilities, sometimes being no more than one room with a wooden floor. Many have several rooms though, plus wooden sleeping platforms, old chairs, tables and a fireplace or stove. There often isn't any fallen wood nearby so fuel may need to be carried in if you want a fire.

My first introduction to bothies was during a Pennine

Way walk one April long ago. Coming off Cross Fell in
dense wet mist I found Greg's Hut and spent a warm night
there after drying out damp gear in front of a fire. Since
then I have spent many nights in bothies and grown to love
the individual quirks and designs of the many different
buildings that have been pressed into service.

Bothies are particularly welcome on winter trips, especially when the weather is stormy, as spending long hours
cooped up in a small tent can become wearisome. I was
reminded of this one February when I hiked the Southern
Upland Way, a thirteen day trip on which the weather
was mostly wet and windy. My second day was spent
in wind, rain and low cloud and by the time I reached
the little wooden Beehive bothy amongst dripping trees
in Galloway Forest Park. I was very glad of its shelter
as I had a damp tent from the night before and the wet
mist meant that any camp would be very soggy indeed.
Next day the weather was worse, starting with drizzle and
finishing with several hours of heavy rain, and throughout
I was in thick damp mist. Rather than camp I decided to
press on to the next bothy, White Laggan, which I reached
long after dark, having been out for eleven hours during
which I sloshed through some 42 kilometres. The bothy
had a good store of wood and a stove so I was soon sitting
in the warm, cooking my late supper and feeling amazingly relieved.

Next morning I stuck my head outside as the first light
was creeping over the land. My journal entry tells the
story – 'mist blasting past the bothy in wet waves. Very
windy. No visibility'. I was glad I hadn't spent the night
in my damp tent.

Bothies are also a place to meet other outdoors people
and share experiences. I have had many interesting

conversations with walkers and climbers over a hot brew and a bothy fire. Of course sometimes bothies can be crowded. Many years ago fifteen of us crammed into little Corrour bothy in the Cairngorms, which was really only big enough for half that number, and since then I have always carried a tent or tarp and been prepared to camp out if a bothy is full.

The only exception was when I planned a TGO Challenge Route across the Highlands using bothies plus a few B&Bs the whole way, including one high level rickety wooden hut that was blown down by the wind a few years later. On this trip I found another disadvantage of not carrying a tent – you have to reach the bothy regardless of conditions. Overall it was a difficult crossing, the hardest of the fifteen Challenges I have done. There was still deep snow on the hills and the weather was windy and frosty. An ice axe was essential and our route was changed a few times to deal with the conditions (we were blown back from an attempt on Ben Nevis).

On reaching the Cairngorms we stayed in Ruigh Aiteachain bothy in Glen Feshie before crossing the Moine Mhor to Corrour bothy. The going was hard work due to the deep soft snow and it was late when we arrived on the rim of Coire Odhar high above the bothy. The snow on the steep upper slopes of the corrie was hard and icy and, having no crampons, we had to cut steps with our ice axes, slowly zigzagging back and forth across the slope until we reached easier ground. All the time we could see tents outside the bothy so we had the added worry that it might be full. To our great relief it proved to be empty. If we'd had tents we'd have camped on the tops or found an easier way down.

Another attraction of bothies is the bothy book where

visitors can record their thoughts, feelings and experiences. Here you can learn about suggested routes in the area, weather conditions at different times of year, problems with river crossings and see how many people use the bothy and at what times of year. (There is one bothy in the Eastern Cairngorms – the Shielin' of Mark – that has a sudden spike in visitors in the middle of May when TGO Challengers pass by and hardly any visitors at any other time.)

Bothies require maintenance if they are to remain safe and watertight of course. A wonderful volunteer organisation, the Mountain Bothies Association, does the work and deserves the support of everyone who ever uses a bothy. I joined it after my stay in Greg's Hut and have been a member ever since.

Camp Fires

Flickering brightly as the flames gathered strength, overcoming the hissing of the damp wood, the fire lit up a small circle in the dark rainy forest. Inside the orange light there was warmth and comfort. Outside, the night was black, forbidding, almost sinister.

The day had been frustrating, progress slow up the pathless, densely wooded valley where the going was awkward and finding a rhythm impossible. The sky was overcast, rain fell and the landscape and my mood were gloomy. Cooking away from my tent, as this was the Yukon Territory and grizzly and black bears lived here, I erected a tarp as a kitchen shelter.

Sitting under it in the damp darkness I stared out at the shadowy trees and shivered. Craving warmth and light I scraped around for some dry tinder and 'not too wet' sticks, cleared a patch of soil in the mouth of the tarp and lit a small fire. The transformation was instantaneous. The world changed and with it my mood. Heat and brightness made my little camp a home rather than a functional necessity, friendly and cosy inside the circle of firelight. Outside, in the darkness, the rain fell relentlessly and the forbidding forest hung dark and oppressive, but I was no longer in that world. I was in one that was warm, bright and welcoming.

Camp fires can do that, and have been doing so since humans first learnt to control fire. The desire to see those flames flickering and coals glowing is deeply ingrained in us. When wild camping, far from electric lights and heating, the yearning for a fire grows, especially if the weather is wet or cold. For some it's not really camping if there's no fire. Whilst I camp without a fire far more than with one I well understand the attraction. When I don't have a fire it's because I can't light one without leaving a scar or because there is no suitable fuel. On some walks in remote wilderness areas such as the Yukon and the Canadian Rockies I have lit fires so regularly that it's been worth bringing a light grill as a pot support, the weight justified by the stove fuel I didn't need to carry. In most areas though fires are too damaging and a practical but rather soulless stove replaces them.

Despite my delight in them I'd accepted that camp fires were a rare luxury, especially in the UK, but when little, lightweight, wood burning stoves appeared it became possible to have a miniature camp fire without leaving scars or even needing much wood. Just a handful of twigs produces a roaring blaze that is warming, enthralling and invigorating. I carried one of these stoves on the Pacific Northwest Trail and was delighted with my little camp fires.

Once I'd cooked my meal and boiled water I could remove the pot, add more fuel and stare into the flames. Such a little, contained fire still had the power of a much, bigger open one, still produced the same enchantment and was just as absorbing. Back home I've used such a stove with pine cones in the woods and dead heather twigs in the hills.

Warmth, light, cooking – all practical reasons to have a fire. The deeper reasons are the real ones though, and these are ethereal and internal with no immediately obvious function. Just watching the fire can seem like a pointless activity. It's not though.

The complex, ever-changing patterns of flames and slowly disintegrating twigs have a hypnotic, seductive power. Hours can pass as I stare into the fire, watching the embers glow and the sticks dissolve into pale ash, my face glowing from the heat. 'Dreaming the fire', a lovely phrase I learnt from Colin Fletcher's *The Thousand-Mile Summer*, takes me out of time, into a world where the fire is all that exists. I find it to be amazingly relaxing and soothing, a marvellous way to unwind after a day's walking, a way to empty my mind and allow whatever images the fire brings to enter my psyche.

In the flames strange shapes and ideas are conjured, a magical world where nothing exists for more than a second. Outside the fire the other world still exists and sometimes softly intrudes on my meditations. The pale shapes of trees and rocks assure me I am in a natural place, the call of an owl from somewhere in the woods and the rustle of an animal in the bushes reminds me life goes on, the swish of wind in the branches and the gentle patter of rain remind me that the weather is not still. Glancing up when the sky is clear I marvel at the vast starry expanse, a universe of unimaginable size, and look back down into the tiny yet no less wonderful world of the fire. Often it's only when the last flames die that I shake myself, surprised to discover how much time has passed. It feels as though only seconds have gone by.

3

BACKPACKING TALES

Footpaths, trails and tracks lead the backpacker through the wilds, over the hills and down the dales. A nice clear path makes walking easy and route finding simple. Just follow that narrow ribbon of dirt to your destination. I can walk many miles a day on a good path, and if the trail is smooth and wide I can look round and enjoy the country. Of course, many paths are bumpy and uneven, beset with stones, roots, puddles and holes. They still lead you towards your goal but you do have to pay attention. Then there are those trails that fade away, perhaps to reappear after a few hundred yards, perhaps not, or are thin and indistinct.

I like footpaths and have followed thousands of miles of them over the years, but there is a little problem with that strip of worn ground disappearing into the distance. It holds you away from nature, away from the trees, the rocks, the tussocks, the bogs, the hard reality of the landscape. Compared with the alienation from the wild produced by motorised travel (culminating in the total lack of contact with anywhere in jet planes) this is slight - but it is real, and the more manicured and waymarked the path the more it intrudes. Many, particularly in areas like the Alps, are like those found in urban parks: sanitised, denatured, tame. Wilderness paths should be rough and rugged, even harsh and jagged. They should fit the landscape and not be imposed on it as if dropped from on high, but even these are still made by people, still barriers to the full experience.

Step off the path and the world changes. Suddenly there is no line leading you on. There is just the wild. You are in the landscape and not, merely, on the edge looking in. The direction you go in will now be decided by the nature of the land and by your desires. Now there is freedom but also responsibility. You cannot let the path make the decisions anymore.

Reaching a destination cross-country and reaching it via a path are different experiences. The cross-country journey will probably need to be broken down into short sections – how to get through this band of forest or stretch of marsh, how to get down this ridge or up to this col – and you may have to retreat at times and look for another way past an obstacle. The relation between time and distance changes. Sometimes you may still be able to stride out, or you may find it takes an hour to progress a mile. Off-trail travel is not for those who like to make high mileages and cover big distances every day. It is for those who want close contact with nature and who want to learn about the landscape and how best to make a way through it.

The most direct route is often the slowest and hardest when there is no trail. Finding the easiest way through the terrain becomes important and even then you may end up bruised, muddy, and exhausted only to find that you've made hardly any progress. I remember stumbling and clawing through almost impenetrable willow and alder thickets in the Little Twelve Mile River valley in the Tombstone Mountains in the Yukon Territory, clothes snagging and tearing on branches, soaked in sweat. A mile in an hour was good. I camped on a strip of stones overhung by willows wondering how to avoid doing it again. A thigh-deep river ford and a steep 600 metre climb through the forest to alpine tundra was the answer.

Studying the formation of the hills, the relationship between meadows and forest, cliffs and ridges, rivers and gorges can enable you to plan ahead. I've sat on summits and high passes scanning the land ahead through binoculars to work out a line that doesn't look too difficult. In the Yukon Territory, when I walked hundreds of miles cross-country through dense forests and swamps, I found that where the rivers were wide and braided it was easier to wade between sandbanks rather than bushwhack through the forest. Where the rivers were too deep and fast, climbing above the trees to wide terraces that ran high above the valleys also made walking easier even when cliffs or ravines eventually forced me back down.

Hiking this way I learnt how the land worked, how all the different features fitted together, and that made me feel closer and more a part of it. Putting my hands to rocks and trees, wading rivers and get muddy in bogs means physical contact with nature, feeling as well as seeing the wilds. The landscape becomes more than scenery, more than something to look at. You experience it with every sense.

Leaving the trails behind is to become an explorer, discarding knowledge of what is to come and finding out for yourself.

I have been lucky, privileged in fact, to hike many trails in their infancy, often when they were trails in name only. The Pacific Crest, Continental Divide, Arizona and Pacific Northwest Trails all had long sections of cross-country travel (the last three still have some). These long trails will never be easy, even when there is a path the whole way, as they run through remote and rugged deserts and mountains, but hiking them so early in their existence did add to the pleasure.

I learnt the skills needed for cross-country hills in the British hills, in particular the peat groughs and bogs of the Dark Peak. Bleaklow and Kinder Scout are excellent hills for practising route finding and keeping your temper. In the Scottish Highlands I discovered that there were far more ways up and through the hills than those marked on maps and described in guidebooks. Wandering away from the paths I learnt much more than I would have done otherwise.

Feeling confident about leaving paths brings great rewards and is part of the freedom of the wilds. It can be hard, gruelling even, but being in such direct contact with the land is worth any effort. Paths are good when you need to get somewhere but abandoning them is better when you want to wander and explore. Here are some tales of trips that involved trails ranging from the well-marked to the almost invisible as well as cross-country sections. What they have in common is that they all took me into wild country for many days at a time so there was a feeling of immersion in nature as well as the need for good route-finding skills.

Backpacking Suilven

Rising abruptly from an undulating land of bog and loch, Suilven is one of the great mountains of the Scottish Highlands, a massive and distinctive wedge of dark Torridonian sandstone standing alone on a plinth of pale striped metamorphic Lewisian gneiss.

Suilven looks ancient, a gnarled and battered giant, and it is. At around 3000 million years old Lewisian gneiss is one of the oldest rocks in the world. At just 1,500 million to 850 million years old the Torridonian sandstone is young by comparison, but still much older than many rocks. From the sides this slice of layered stone is an undulating 2.5km ridge with an off-centre low point, a bulging summit at the west end, the highest point, and a split summit at the east end. Viewed from the east Suilven rises as a finely tapered pyramid, the easternmost top, Meall Bheag, being lower than the next one, Meall Mheadhonach, so they appear as one. From the west, steep terraced cliffs rise to the bulky, rounded summit of Caisteal Liath, the Grey Castle. From everywhere Suilven looks striking and imposing, a grand mountain in a grand setting. The name comes from the Norse for 'pillar' and probably refers to its appearance from the sea and its use as a landmark by the Vikings as they sailed their longboats along the west coast of Scotland. A mighty mountain indeed, yet it is only 731 metres high, not even reaching Corbett status. So much for categorising mountains by height then, for Suilven is finer and more distinctive than many that rise hundreds of metres higher.

As Suilven lies in solitary splendour in the district of Assynt, a huge roadless area between the coast and the road north from Ullapool, all approaches are lengthy. It is usually climbed from the path running west from the scattered village of Elphin to the little fishing port of Lochinver, a good through-route. This path passes below the north face of Suilven where a rougher trail leads to the low point on the ridge, the Bealach Mor, a geological fault line. A more interesting route that explores some of the wonderful country surrounding the hill and crosses

Suilven from south to north can be walked in one long day. I think it's more satisfying though, to take two days and spend a night in this vast landscape, really absorbing and sinking into the atmosphere. Waking in such a place greatly enhances the feel of being part of it, of belonging, and deepens the joy and satisfaction of walking in the wilds.

With this in mind two of us managed to tear ourselves away from the attractions of the Achins tearoom and bookshop at Inverkirkaig Bridge, and set off one late spring afternoon along a path through lovely woodland, a rich mix of alder, rowan and birch with a few pines, beside the River Kirkaig. This path rises to moorland above the ravine and leads to the Falls of Kirkaig, a ferociously powerful cataract that plunges eighteen metres between sheer cliffs into a black rippling pool. Trees frame the cliffs and the situation is one of natural perfection, beautiful and severe at the same time.

As we climbed onto open, boggy, heather moorland rain began to fall with clouds hiding the hills we knew rose splendidly all around. A typical Lewisian gneiss landscape of pools, bogs and low hummocky, rocky knolls, this terrain is known as 'cnoc and lochan'. The ragged twisting path led across wet ground to long Fionn Loch where we found a lovely camp site on the north shore near a burn running down from high Coire Mor. Swirling low clouds and grey sky added to the feeling of wildness and remoteness.

Nothing was visible but cloud and water, bog and rock, heather and grass. A breeze off the loch kept the midges away and I lay in the tent with the doors wide open staring at the wetness. Slowly the world became distinct and I started to notice movement other than that of cloud and water and to hear sounds other than the patter of rain and gentle hiss of wind. On a spit of gravel at the mouth of the burn two little birds ran like clockwork across the shore. I scanned them with my binoculars. Ringed plover, birds of the water's edge. Out on the loch a dark silhouette rode the wind-rippled water. The streamlined shape and long pointed bill showed it was a diver, though whether red or black-throated I could not tell. A cuckoo called from afar and grouse cackled somewhere. Just water and wind, rain and moor, birds and rocks. It was enough. I dozed off content with the world.

Later my sleep was disturbed by the wild shriek of a diver and the drumming of a snipe and, at dawn, the more insistent repetitive call of a cuckoo. More noisy cries had me looking out of the tent to see a line of long-necked ducks flying overhead. The clouds slowly began to dissolve and across the loch strange shapes began to materialise in the mists, the splendid peaks of Cul Mor, Cul Beag and Stac Pollaidh and, to the east, Suilven, steep, dark and foreboding. The world brightened as the sun rose through swirling clouds until by 8.00 am the sky was clear and the temperature was already 17°C.

Not much further along the shores of Fionn Loch we turned towards the mountain, following a rough eroded path across hummocky moorland to the steep southern flanks of Suilven. The path headed straight up these slopes and cut across the face to the Bealach Mor, a stony, steep climb. The views were spacious and exhilarating. Out of the undulating, shining, sparkling, watery landscape rose a series of distinctively shaped and named hills: Cul Mor, Cul Beag and Stac Pollaidh now sharp and clear to the south, Canisp just to the north with Quinag in the distance. Further away other peaks came into view, most clearly the ragged edge of An Teallach to the south and the twisting ridges of Arkle and Foinaven far to the north. Eastwards a long dark line marked Conival and Ben More Assynt.

Turning west we followed the ridge, with some easy scrambling, up to Caisteal Liath, Suilven's highest summit. From this spacious high vantage point there were superb views across the moorland to the blue island-dotted sea, the distant hazy Western Isles and back east to the soaring eastern spire of Suilven, Meall Mheadhonach. Everywhere lochs and lochs and lochs, water filling every dip and hollow, each one ground out by the glaciers that carved this landscape, including Suilven, itself sculpted by ice grinding past as it flowed from east to west.

There is no walkers' way off Caisteal Liath, which is ringed with crags on three sides, except via the Bealach Mor so to this we returned, crossing again the curious, not to say crazy, wall that runs over Suilven just above the low point. Who built it and why? No one seems to know. From the bealach we descended the wide eroded gully of scree, heather and rock (which is rather loose and nasty at the top) that runs north down to Loch na Gainimh. This is the most popular ascent route, as the worn path shows. On the descent the whaleback of Canisp to the east and distant Quinag to the north dominated the view. The summits of these peaks are paler and greyer than the slopes below, with caps of Cambrian Quartzite lying over the dark Torridonian sandstone.

Once out of the gully the walking became easier before we reached the Elphin to Lochinver path. Turning west-wards we headed for the coast, pausing frequently to turn and contemplate the ever-changing, slowly dwindling views of Suilven. The moorland faded too as we passed

Glencanisp Lodge and walked through some pleasant quiet woods to reach a road for the last two kilometres into Lochinver and a celebratory meal of the famous pies at Lochinver Larder.

Wild days on Rum

Stormy nights in a tent are one of the joys of backpacking. So I told myself as I lay in my tiny shelter listening to the wind lashing the tent with rain and shaking the thin nylon walls. I was camped in Coire Dubh on the island of Rum below the mist-shrouded walls of Barkeval and Hallival on the first night of a four day trip during which I hoped to traverse the Rum Cuillin, the finest Hebridean mountains outside the Cuillin of Skye. Like their larger namesake the Rum Cuillin are the jagged remnants of an ancient volcano.

Earlier in the day I'd arrived on the ferry from Mallaig after a pleasant trip spent watching birds and staring at the ominous dark cloud hiding Rum. In the little village of Kinloch, the only one on the island, the midges were biting, ending the temptation to camp there rather than start my walk in such, dull misty weather. Instead I passed by the grand Edwardian pile of Kinloch Castle, a rather incongruous feature on this wild island, and climbed a muddy path into the cloud to camp on a breeze-catching knoll in the mouth of the corrie.

That evening, in the hope of clearing skies and a colourful sunset, I climbed 591 metre Barkeval, a rugged hill built of peridotite, an extremely rough red-brown volcanic rock. I clambered up rock and bog in thick mist and steady drizzle. The summit came and went, barely noticed in the increasingly stormy weather, and

48

a compass bearing led to the Bealach Bairc-mheall from where I dropped back down into Coire Dubh and shelter from the wind. Immediately, clouds of midges swarmed round me and I had to run to escape, producing copious condensation inside my waterproofs. Wet rain jacket, wet windshirt, wet shoes, wet socks, wet trousers, I stripped off and dived into the merely damp confines of the tent and an already clammy sleeping bag. The gusty wind kept the midges at bay, though they sprang up whenever it dropped for more than a few seconds. During the night the strengthening wind woke me several times. By morning the strongest gusts were reaching 30mph. The tent was shrouded in damp mist and the flysheet was soaked inside and out.

Adopting my wet weather strategy – stay in the tent and hope it clears – I put on another brew and settled down to read my book, the story of Scottish plant collector David Douglas, who put up with far more than wet nights in search of seeds in the Rocky Mountains. Eventually I was rewarded for my sloth with a brief clearance and a sudden view down to the woods in Kinloch Glen. I started packing. The clouds soon closed back in but I went anyway, climbing back up through the dark mist to the Bealach Bairc-mheall where standing was difficult and the anemometer recorded a gust of 57.7 mph. It took only seconds to realise that the traverse of the Cuillin would be foolhardy, if not indeed impossible, in such weather and I was soon descending steep, rough slopes into huge Atlantic Corrie, then on east down Glen Harris, a lovely, wild valley with a noisy river crashing down in a series of waterfalls and water slides, culminating in one big white foamed fall straight into the matching white foamed sea.

Here, on the south-west coast of Rum, I camped on the

beautiful flower-strewn machair above a wild sea, with grey water breaking in ragged white waves, their crests ripped into spinning foam by the wind. A herd of wild goats stared down at me from a ridge, their shaggy coats, curved horns and manic eyes appropriate to this elemental place. Four curlews circled above the camp.

The crossing of the ridge had taken only half a day. Reluctant to spend more hours than necessary in my damp camp I spent the afternoon exploring the coast and visiting the Greek temple-like mausoleum built by the Bullough family, former owners of the island. The ferry to South Uist bounced past and I was glad I wasn't on board. Inland the hills were still cloud-shrouded, dark masses looming in the dull air.

The wind and rain finally eased at dawn, perfectly timed for the midges to come out as I was breakfasting. To the south-west thin lines of blue sky wavered below the steel grey cloud. Gradually the cloud rose, revealing 528 metre Ruinsival with bands of cloud drifting below the summit. By now the sea was gentler and more rhythmic rather than a storm driven staccato crashing, and the world was beginning to look brighter and more colourful.

As the sky continued to lighten I climbed beside lovely white waterslides to Loch Fiachanis, set in a wonderful corrie backed by the great walls of Trallval and Ainshval. More wild goats watched me from a rocky knoll. Steep slopes led up to Ruinsival and a long ridge to Ainshval, second highest summit on Rum at 781 metres and one of the islands two Corbetts. Good views on the approach faded as the clouds descended again. A walker was just leaving the summit, the first person I'd seen in two days.

I took a bad line on the descent to the Bealach an Fhuarain and found myself on some very steep, loose, slippery, broken ground that ended in a stubby crag. As I was trying to traverse to easier terrain the clouds lifted again and I had splendid views down Glen Dibidil and across a blue sea to the isle of Eigg. Across the glen the intimidating steep screes of the south-west face of Askival, the highest Rum peak at 812 metres, rose into the cloud. Skirting the base of a rather too loose boulder field I reached a little stream on a grassy sward high on the mountainside, hanging far above Glen Dibidil. It was a magnificent situation and I knew immediately I wanted to camp there. Seeing the bealach away to the left I realised I had descended too far to the east, fortuitously finding this grassy ledge, from which relatively easy ground led back to the ridge.

Showers and midges between the gusts soon drove me into the tent, where I massaged my toes, now grey and cold after three days in wet shoes and socks. My spare dry merino wool socks felt luxurious and I soon slipped my legs into my sleeping bag to further warm my feet. Outside, the cloud thickened and visibility shrank to barely twenty metres. The sense of space and depth was gone and the world reverted to a patch of wet grass and dense grey mist. The temperature in the tent was 13°C but it felt colder due to the dampness.

Bursts of rain and a hammering wind woke me during the night. Looking out I could see the distant lights of Mallaig on the mainland, shining below the cloud. As the storm eased briefly I heard strange, throaty shrieks and cries, masses and masses of them. These were the calls of Manx shearwaters, sea birds that nest in burrows high on the hillsides, only coming in to land after dark when they are safe from predation by skuas and gulls. Over 70,000 pairs nest on Rum. The Vikings who ruled these islands

51

1000 years ago thought that their weird calls were the voices of trolls in the mountains. They named one of the hills Trollaval – mountain of the trolls.

Most of the hill names on Rum are Norse. 'Val' comes from 'fjall', which became 'fell' in Northern England. Askival is hill of the ash spear, Ainshval hill of the rocky ridge, Ruinsival hill of the heap of rocks, Hallival hill of the ledge and Barkeval hill of the precipice. Prosaic but descriptive names all, letting you know just what these hills are like.

The storm continued at dawn. The Bealach an Fhuarain was very windy and swirling with mist. Having had enough of wet rocky slopes in minimal visibility and with a ferry to catch that afternoon I decided Askival would have to wait for another visit. Turning downhill I descended Glen Dibidil, another lovely valley with a rushing stream and many waterfalls. At its foot a bothy sits in an idyllic situation looking over the sea to Eigg. Fine cliffs surround Dibidil Bay from where I followed a wet and muddy but very scenic path around the coast to Kinloch where the sun shone between showers. From the ferry I looked back at the dark silhouette of Rum, the Cuillin now visible below a clearing sky. I would be back.

Wandering in the Colorado Rockies

Mount Massive Wilderness, read the sign. Beyond it the dark line of the trail snaked into the depths of the silent conifer forest. I had only a vague idea of where I would go, a rough route worked out in snatched moments during a hectic weekend.

Not having a specific trail to walk, a clear destination, worried me at first. Where would I go, and why? The

Colorado Rockies are ideal for aimless venture as they are made up of small pockets of wilderness that can be escaped easily when you need to resupply.

My tentative route involved a couple of cross-country sections that might or might not 'go'. Although I hoped to reach the town of Aspen within a week, I'd brought along food for ten days or so just in case they didn't, which seemed quite likely in the circumstances. My pack then was heavy, maybe as much as 60lbs (27kg), as I set off up the trail. Burdensome though it seemed, the load also gave me the freedom of knowing I could live comfortably without needing to visit civilisation for the whole of my trip.

The forest was quiet and peaceful, allowing me to unwind slowly from the rush of the previous few days. It was good to be alone. I didn't go far that first afternoon, camping in a spruce grove above a rushing cool stream called Willow Creek after only a couple of hours. It was enough though. Content to be in the wilderness again, I wanted to walk slowly and quietly through the woods and over the hills, absorbing the wildness all around. Miles travelled were even less relevant than usual.

Wanting to eat into my load a little before continuing, I stayed at the Willow Creek camp for two nights, spending the intervening day on a walk up Mount Massive, at 4,397 metres the second highest peak in the Colorado Rockies. I'd climbed the highest, 4,400 metres Mount Elbert, just two days previously with a large group. Climbing the two peaks fulfilled a long held ambition. In September 1985 I walked past these peaks on my Continental Divide hike from Canada to Mexico. I'd planned on climbing them then but early season snow and thick clouds, along with the pressures of a long walk, meant I had passed them by. I'd always hoped to return though I never believed I ever would. I was a little surprised, therefore, to find myself standing on Mount Massive's small rocky summit surveying the grand sweep of wilderness that stretched all around. I shared the summit with a man from Kentucky and met several other walkers on the mountain. There's plenty of space though as the mountain is aptly named, the summit ridge being three miles long.

The real pleasure though was in the climb, in leaving the dark confines of the forest to wander up a gradually steepening hillside and marvelling at the mountain vista that slowly unfolded on every side. At one point I passed a yellow tent pitched by a tiny pool and envied the campers, wishing I'd lugged my tent out of the trees. But there would be other nights, other sites, and that night as thunder shook the skies and rain lashed down I valued the security of my deep forest camp.

Knowing the first cross country section was coming up gave an edge of tension to the next day even though most of it was spent on a dirt road beside pretty Halfmoon Creek. Far up the creek lay the tottering wooden shell of the long abandoned Champion Mine, a reminder that it was prospecting, mostly for silver, that opened up these hills. Aspen is an old mining town. A locked gate topped by a Private sign blocked the road near the mine but I went on anyway, up a steepening track to a high col. The ground dropped away steeply into a forested valley on the far side. The map showed a trail down Lackawanna Gulch, as the valley was called, but warned that it was 'considered impassable'. Again I went anyway, to find the descent easy though the trail came and went.

Half the problematic part of my route was now over. After a night spent camped in a willow thicket beside North

Fork Lake Creek, I set off to cross the Continental Divide above Blue Lake and make a cross country link between the Mount Massive and Hunter Fryingpan Wilderness Areas. The day began on the trail to Blue Lake, a slippery trail of loose soil and gravel up through the forest. At one point hands were needed as the route went directly up a small crag with precipitous drops to either side. After this the cross country section over a 4,000 metre col and down to the next valley was quite easy, the open grassy hillsides allowing for a myriad of routes.

The Hunter Fryingpan Wilderness now lay before me, its trails leading eventually to Aspen. (The strange name comes from the names of the two creeks that dominate the area.) This is a gentle land of dense forests and rolling alpine tundra, the peaks lower and less rugged than those of surrounding areas. Lost Man Trail, Midway Trail, Hunter Creek Trail merged into one another, a continuous ribbon of easy walking over grassy passes with views of distant rugged peaks and beside slow quiet creeks in sombre, soothing forests.

Away from people and moving softly I began to see the inhabitants of the land; fat black and gold marmots scuttling amongst the rocks on the high passes, brown flickers swooping through the trees, red-tailed hawks soaring high above the forest and elk crashing through the undergrowth, their antlers held high. I heard the elk too, their weird bugling call a sign of the coming of autumn. On one steep trail a tiny mouse emerged from a hole in a log to prospect a way across a trickle of stream. A safe way found, the mouse scurried back to reappear with an even tinier baby mouse held gently in its jaws which it then carried across the water.

I walked on, high above Hunter Creek. Across the valley

of the Roaring Fork River, in which lay Aspen, rose the jagged pyramidal summits of the Maroon Bells, perhaps the most distinctive and well-known peaks in Colorado. They looked attractive and, after watching them for a while, I knew where I would go next.

Aspen was an aberration in the wilderness. The mining days are long gone and it's now a luxury ski resort, favoured by rich celebrities, especially film stars, hence the average property price of millions of dollars. It is smart, clean, expensive and totally unreal, almost Disneyland like in its purity. I stayed a day and a half, overnighting in a half-closed ski lodge, the cheapest accommodation in town, and marvelling at the prices in the shops.

The main trailhead for the Maroon Bells Snowmass Wilderness lies ten miles up the Maroon Creek valley. To prevent traffic congestion and pollution the Forest Service bans private vehicles from its single road between 8.30am and 5.30pm. Instead a shuttle bus runs several times an hour from Aspen to the trailhead.

I took the bus. One nice feature of not being on a through-walk was that I didn't feel obliged to walk every step of the way. Beyond Maroon Lake the twin peaks of the Maroon Bells, named for the dark red colour of the rock, rose into a cloudy sky. These are steep mountains with loose, rocky slopes and narrow exposed ridges. Walkers with a good head for heights can scramble up but they are not for heavily laden backpackers who, perforce, are channelled up the valleys to each side.

With no route to follow I could take any of the trails into the mountains. That to the south, beside West Maroon Creek was the least steep, a good enough reason for going that way. I had six days before I needed to be back at the trailhead. The map showed a network of trails, any number of which could be linked to a circular route. Which I'd take I had no idea.

What decided me was the lakes. Whilst the area is known for its spectacular peaks I remember it best for the beautiful timberline lakes. Geneva, Avalanche, Capitol and Snowmass, all pristine waters that reflect the grandeur of the mountains while lying in calm solitude on the edge of the forest. My route linked them via high mountain passes like West Maroon Pass, a mere notch in a steep castellated red rock ridge; wide green valleys full of dying flower meadows and whitewater creeks tumbling in cascades; and dense forests where I walked in a silence so loud you could almost hear it.

Ideas of climbing any of the peaks, not very strong to begin with as I preferred to see what was over the next pass, were blown away by the weather. Every day at any time between mid-morning and late afternoon clouds would pile up over the summits to burst in savage thunderstorms. I had no desire to tread high mountain ridges under threat of lightning. I could not swoop away in seconds like the eagle I saw hanging black against an approaching storm. Crossing some of the passes was unnerving enough, with distant flashes and rumbles and tendrils of cloud reaching from the black heart of the storm towards me. Twice I fled in the night from camp-sites chosen for views rather than shelter to cower among the trees as lightning flashed all around.

Despite these night-time panics the camp-sites were a joy. At Geneva Lake, a lovely deep green tarn backed by pale screes and cliffs, I woke in the night to a sky alive with stars edged by the deep blackness of the forest and the mountains. The next night at Avalanche Lake the last rays of the fading sun lit up the lake and the reflections of the mountains with a golden glow and at dawn I woke to the first rays catching the tip of the highest peak. The lake shone green and grey, reflecting the rocks and trees in the cool clear water.

Finally though it was time to come down from the mountains. I'd walked over a hundred miles and ascended nearly 30,000 feet. The figures didn't matter though. I'd lived for a time in the wilderness. That was what mattered.

I had one last night out in Minnehaha Gulch under the shadow of North Maroon Peak. A storm raged most of the night and into the morning. As I headed down in heavy rain I could see below the ragged edges of the clouds the white traces of fresh snow high on the mountainsides. Summer was ending.

The Great Outdoors Challenge, an appreciation

Lochailort: May 9th, 1980. I greeted a fellow Challenger called Ron Reynolds then set off for Loch Beoraid and Glen Finnan on a hot, humid, hazy day. The first Challenge, (then called the Ultimate Challenge after the sponsor), a coast-to-coast walk across the Scottish Highlands held in May and organised by The Great Outdoors (TGO) magazine, had begun. Twenty days later on May 28 I walked into the Park Hotel in Montrose, my crossing complete.

Fast forward 27 years to May 24, 2007. Again I walked into the Park Hotel, my eleventh crossing complete (by 2015 I had done fifteen). A Challenger greeted me. It was Ron Reynolds, who I'd first met in Lochailort all those years before on the first day of the first Challenge. He'd just finished his nineteenth.

The reason we were both still there, after all the years,

is that the Challenge is a very special event, one to which many people develop an emotional attachment and to which they are drawn again and again. At the end of the first I wrote some prescient words in my journal: 'A good trek. Already thinking of next year'. How many others have done the same as they walked the last miles to the east coast I wonder? It won't be a small number. The Challenge is unique, a non-competitive backpacking event where participants plan their own routes and start and finish in different places before meeting up for celebrations. There really is nothing else like it.

That it takes place in the finest backpacking country in Britain naturally makes it very attractive, as does the fact that it's a coast to coast walk, which gives it a clear beginning and end. Crossing a country on foot, even a small one like Scotland, is an appealing idea although, of course, you can do this without taking part in the Challenge, and many do. The secret to its success doesn't lie in the hills, the wildness, the beauty of the landscape, wonderful though these are, but in the people. The key words are community and involvement, and right from the start a bond was formed between participants. We felt like pioneers, a small handful of people (there were only 60 the first year) testing out a new idea.

The bond goes right back to the founding of the event when Hamish Brown, the man who first climbed all the Munros in one continuous walk, put his proposal to Roger Smith, then TGO editor, and Bill Wilkins of Ultimate Equipment, now long-gone. (In my imagination this always sounds like one of those deals cooked up in a smoky room by dubious politicians or business men – 'with this plan we can take over the backpacking world'. No offence meant, Hamish, Roger and Bill!). Since then

Hamish has become the father figure of the event, the man who inspired us all, while Roger has became its heart, the motivator, encourager, recorder and, for many years, organiser. However, Bill Wilkins left Ultimate Equipment and vanished from the Challenge story after a few years. Eventually Ultimate Equipment closed and the event was named after TGO, which had promoted and organised it from the beginning.

Over the years the community of Challengers has grown from a purely UK phenomenon to an international one. In the early days information spread slowly via TGO's annual Challenge issue. The Internet didn't exist so there were no websites, blogs, podcasts or forums and often there was little or no contact among Challengers between events, but still the sense of community grew. Gatherings were organised so people could get together and swap experiences. This spread to the event itself with Challengers planning their routes so they could meet others along the way (most notoriously in the Fife Arms in Braemar – there has always been a fair amount of hedonism involved!).

Communities along the way became involved too and the first Challengers became almost like the first cuckoo – a sign that spring was here. On the 1993 Challenge two of us stopped at a B&B in South Laggan in the Great Glen and the owner greeted us with relief and the words 'I was beginning to worry I might not be getting any Challengers this year'. She then offered to drive us to the nearest restaurant as she didn't do evening meals (we accepted gratefully). That hospitality is now found right across Scotland but especially in Tarfside at St Drostan's Hostel and at Lochcallater Lodge.

In a sense the Challenge has become part of the fabric of the Highlands in spring. Many Challengers have become involved in helping the event, vetting routes and working at Control in Montrose, and the Park Hotel itself has become an integral part of the event. I never thought back in 1980 as I walked down John Street that over thirty years later I would be taking the same last steps of the Challenge down the same now very familiar street to the same hotel. Back then I wondered what I would find (just Roger in fact – the first Challenge was three weeks long and I finished well after everyone else, since then it's been two weeks only). Now I take those steps with eager anticipation – who will I meet, what stories will I hear? I've never been that involved with the social scene during the Challenge. I'm pleased if I meet people but don't arrange to do so or plan my route to call in at popular gathering spots. (On the 25th Challenge I met no one else until I was a few yards from the Park Hotel.) However I do look forward to meeting others in Montrose and sharing stories and experiences. This is a major part of the whole Challenge experience.

The Challenge is an adventure, an exciting journey shared with many others. It is always challenging and completing it is an achievement, especially for the first time but also every time. Crossing the Highlands in May is never to be taken for granted. I have strode out on brilliant sunny days with vast views when the walking was easy, but I have also battled against wind and rain on compass bearings across mist-shrouded boggy hills.

Perhaps most exciting and intimidating is snow, which is possible in May. 1983 is the snowiest Challenge I remember. Having scared ourselves on a snowy Sgurr na Ciche – Sgurr nan Coireachan traverse in Knoydart, two of us acquired ice axes in Fort William and were grateful later on when we had to cut steps down into Coire Odhar in the Cairngorms. There was snow on the tops the whole way across.

The Challenge has been part of my life since that first day in 1980 and I am very grateful for the pleasure, inspiration and experiences it has given me. Thank you, Hamish. Thank you, Roger. Thank you Challengers. Long may it long continue.

Exploring the Grand Canyon

I wasn't prepared for the Grand Canyon. I'd read books, gazed at photographs, studied the maps, but I still wasn't ready for its overwhelming presence.

After a long drive through flat, wooded country the bus from Flagstaff dumped me outside a rustic building labelled *Bright Angel Lodge* in Grand Canyon Village. Tourists wandered everywhere and a large car park dominated the place. With darkness less than an hour away my main concern was in finding the campground, but first I thought I'd take a quick glance at the canyon. I ambled towards a low parapet. Suddenly, there it was — beyond the neat wall chaos reigned. The ground fell away into a confusion of multi-coloured rock towers and buttresses , terraces dropped towards dark, hidden depths and rose again towards the far distant rim. To either side the chasm appeared as a contorted slash in the landscape, snaking its way towards a hazy horizon.

I stared down, unable to comprehend the scale. I was overawed and not a little nervous. Was I really to spend two weeks walking in that alien world? I retreated into the forest for the night.

The next day I went back. It was still there, only now, in the bright morning light, it seemed even bigger. For the next two days I prepared for my walk, buying food, checking water sources, arranging for a food drop at the bottom of the canyon. Every so often I went back to the rim and stared into the wild world below. Each time the scale seemed vaster than before.

The Grand Canyon is indeed huge. The statistics are hard to grasp. The length is about 450km while the width varies from 6 to 25km. The South Rim, where I first looked into the Canyon, ranges in height from 1,850 to 2,300 metres, the North Rim from 2,300 to 2,600. The Colorado River lies from 1,050 to 1,830 metres below. Inside this massive gorge there are side canyons that would be major landmarks in their own right anywhere else and mountains that soar 1,200-1,500m above the Colorado yet still aren't as high as the rim. Happily this stupendous wilderness is protected as a national park, though plans for damming the canyon are still regularly submitted.

The overwhelming nature of the canyon, its incredible presence, inspired one visitor in the nineteenth century, a geologist named Clarence Dutton, to name the many towers and buttes after eastern religious deities. Thus I was to walk below the Tower of Set, Isis Temple, Cheops Pyramid, Buddha Temple and, most impressive of all, Zoroaster Temple. Curiously, these names seemed totally appropriate in their monumental setting.

Walking in the canyon is like hill walking in reverse. You start in the cool forests of the rims then descend through the steep tiers of rock to the hot desert below. At the end of the trip, whether it's a day or a month, you climb back up to the flatlands. Deep inside the canyon the topography is just about ideal for long walks as a wide band of gently sloping shale lies about two-thirds of the way down. This forms a terrace known as the Tonto

Platform, which you can walk along for miles. Steep red and yellow cliffs rise above while dark, sombre crags lie below, rimming the narrow Inner Gorge. Stream beds and gullies break up the cliffs and it is mostly down these that ways can be found in and out of the canyon and down to the river. Passable sections are often linked by narrow terraces that run dramatically across the cliffs to the next place where a descent or ascent can be made.

There are many paths in the Grand Canyon but only a few are maintained, the popular Corridor Trails that link the North and South Rims. Most paths are rough and narrow in places with scrambling required at times. Rockslides and dense vegetation may hide the paths in places too. The biggest problem in the canyon is the lack of water. There are only a few streams and some of these are seasonal. There is the Colorado River of course, but this can only be reached in a few places.

I had twelve days to spend wandering in the Canyon. To make the most of them my plan was to descend the unmaintained but fairly popular Hermit Trail, walk for several days along the Tonto Platform, drop down for a night beside the Colorado, then cross the river by one of the only two bridges. I would then head up to the North Rim where I would spend a few days before returning to the South Rim via the North Kaibab and Bright Angel Trails, both Corridor Routes.

After breakfasting on a litre of water and a muffin I set off down the Hermit Trail carrying three litres of liquid and feeling more nervous than normal at the start of a backpacking trip. This was a very strange place which didn't relate in any way to my previous backpacking experience. 'Everything so new I can't judge it,' I wrote in my journal. Steep switchbacks led down to tree dotted but waterless Hermit Basin where the trail levelled off. The Hermit Gorge is inaccessible at this point so I followed the trail on a long traverse high on the side of the canyon through the red Supai cliffs, a breathtaking walk along a series of narrow terraces. Below lay the major barrier of the Redwall, a very steep 150m-plus high limestone cliff stained red by seepage from the rocks above. A series of tight, steep switchbacks known as the Cathedral Stairs eventually cut down a break in the cliffs.

This descent takes you to the Tonto Platform and as soon as you reach it all feelings of claustrophobia vanish. Dotted with pale green desert plants, this gently sloping terrace is wide enough to suggest space, almost like being on a high mountain plateau. Steep cliffs still rise all around, but rather than just two confining walls these form separate mountains and ridges split by deep side valleys. Beyond the farthest, highest tree-topped cliffs lay flat woodland, but such a landscape seemed incomprehensible down here. My emotions responded eagerly to the world before me, a complex, exciting and colourful mountain world, but my body was responding to the temperature. Although it was mid-October it was very, very hot.

I spent four days wandering along the Tonto Platform from Boucher Creek to Lonetree Canyon, following its sinuous course in and out of innumerable side canyons, camping by the few trickling creeks in the shade of spiny catclaw acacia trees and thickets of tamarisk bushes. Far below, the winding green course of the Colorado River could occasionally be seen, walled by the steep cliffs of the Inner Gorge. There are a few breaks in this barrier and I followed one, the canyon of Monument Creek, down to the river where I camped on gravel banks beside the roaring surge of Granite Rapids. Down here, by the raging waters, you begin to understand the eroding powers of the river, carving out this great defile in the face of the earth.

From the Tonto Platform I descended the lower part of the South Kaibab Trail, one of the Corridor Routes and therefore popular with mule trains and overnight hikers, who normally descend one day and climb out the next. The trail leads to one of the only two bridges across the Colorado, both of them close to the confluence with Bright Angel Creek. On the north side of the bridge there's a campground, complete with picnic tables and with a bar and dining room nearby at Phantom Ranch. There's a ranger station too and it was here that I collected my supplies for the second half of my walk.

Two days took me from Phantom Ranch up the long North Kaibab Trail to the North Rim. At first the path winds through a narrow gorge called The Box, but then follows the wide valley of Bright Angel Creek to Roaring Springs Canyon. From here it climbs steadily, curving round the steep cliffs on narrow terraces before switch-backing tightly up to the forested rim. En route a side trip leads to pretty Ribbon Falls where the lime-rich waters of Ribbon Creek have built up a moss-covered cone of soft travertine rock below the cascade.

The North Rim is little visited compared to the south and by late October all the facilities have closed for the season. My four nights here were spent alone. During the day I wandered along the rim watching the canyon below and enjoying the antics of the beautiful kaibab squirrels with their bushy white tails. On one day I descended the unmaintained and little used Old Bright Angel Trail and was surprised at how much bushwhacking was required to get through the dense, thorny bushes. These canyon-lands might be classed as desert but there is a surprising amount of plant life. My last two days were spent crossing the canyon from rim to rim in dull, rainy weather, a sign of the winter to come. Although by now I felt comfortable in the canyon the feeling of wonder hadn't dimmed. Even now, many years later, I still feel in awe of it. The Grand Canyon remains the most incredible place I have ever been.

The White Mountains of New Hampshire

'STOP. THE AREA AHEAD HAS THE WORST WEATHER IN AMERICA. Many have died there from exposure. Turn back now if the weather is bad'.

Bold black lettering leapt out at me from a battered yellow sign that loomed out of the grey, snow-filled sky. The warning was a little late. I had already crossed the area of worst weather and was descending.

The sign referred to Mount Washington, at 1,917m (6,288 ft) the highest peak in New England and notorious for stormy weather. Way back in 1934 the wind reached an unimaginable 231mph; still the highest speed ever recorded anywhere. Wind speeds of 100mph+ occur every month, snow can fall all year round and the summit is cloud-capped 75 percent of the time. Rain is common in the summer too. This isn't a place for calm, clear weather or easy hiking.

Mount Washington is the heart of the Presidential Range in New Hampshire, itself part of the larger Appalachian Mountain chain. The timberline lies at around 1500 metres and only a few areas rise above the trees that blanket most of the area. Washington is over 150 metres higher than the next highest summit, and like many peaks that tower over their neighbours catches the full force of the weather. Long ridges run north and south over four peaks of 5,000-plus feet and another two topping 4,000. This is the largest area above timberline in the White Mountains and there is a glorious traverse over all the summits which was my first aim on a two-week trip in the area.

I set off from the Appalachian Mountain Club's lodge at Pinkham Notch on a warm sunny day. Stripped to T-shirt and shorts I ambled through dense forest, past tumbling brooks and delicate waterfalls. Two moose crossed my path, odd, ungainly looking creatures that paused to stare at this undoubtedly equally odd looking humpbacked human.

A trail sign — the White Mountains are full of trail signs — pointed steeply upwards to something called Lowe's Bald Spot 0.2 miles away. A short, steep, rocky path led to a series of rock ledges rising above the forest and my first view of the mountains, the summits of Mounts Madison and Adams rising above vast waves of green and yellow trees that filled the Great Gulf, the deep valley lying between these peaks and the big rather hazy hump of Mount Washington itself.

That night I encountered my first tent platforms at the Osgood Tentsite. These raised blocks of planks have their good points, providing flat sites on steep slopes and minimising the impact of campers, but pitching tents on them is difficult, especially with a single hoop model that requires pegging down just to stand up. Without the 15 metres of cord I'd bought at the last minute (on the advice of a friend in Boston) erecting the tent would have been impossible.

Snowflakes started to fall in the strengthening wind and grey clouds swirled round the head of the Great Gulf as I reached the summit of Mount Madison the next day.

Rocky slopes led down to the closed Madison Hut. Two walkers, the first I'd seen, were heading up. 'Interesting weather', said one.

The mountains were jumbled piles of loose greasy rocks and scree dotted with patches of krumholz (wind-battered dwarf conifers), the trails just lines of cairns leading into the mist. Mount Adams, the second highest in the range, was a struggle in the increasingly wild storm. Going on over Washington and all the other peaks seemed less and less attractive or even possible.

At Pinkham Notch a ranger had told me there was a campsite called The Perch down in the forest below Adams, 'there's nowhere else to camp without descending a long way, it's too steep'. I dropped down into the wet forest and into rain rather than snow to find a set of small tent platforms and a dry wooden lean-to. I had just settled into the empty shelter when a school party of eleven arrived - the lean-to held ten - who looked tired and damp. I moved out and set up the tent, to be rewarded with a share of their dinner of rice and spicy beans as the rain turned to wet, heavy snow.

Stuffing a frozen tent into the mesh pocket of my pack the next day was awkward but not as painful as stuffing my feet into frozen trail shoes. The steep climb back up soon warmed my feet. Mount Jefferson, the next peak, was in cloud but it was breaking and I soon had a view of the great bulk of snow-streaked Mount Washington.

A puff of black smoke rose from the flanks, a sign of the cog railway that has been in operation since 1869. There's more than a railway on Mount Washington. There's a road and a scattering of buildings, the main one holding a meteorological observatory, a visitor centre, a post office, gift shop, museum, café and more. In the past there have been hotels, a military research centre and even a daily summit paper. The first vehicle was driven up the road in 1899 and cows once grazed on the scanty pasture.

Soot on the snow showed I was nearing the summit, then the railway line appeared and soon afterwards a surreal tangle of masts and buildings fading in and out of the drifting cloud and the intermittent snow showers. The temperature was —4C and the wind was gusting to 39 mph. I went inside, into warmth, bright artificial light and a cluster of car and train borne visitors, a bubble of urban life transported to an alien, hostile, mountain summit

Within minutes of leaving this bizarre aberration the unreal vision evaporated and I was alone in the grey half-light of the mist and the soft pale snow. Briefly the clouds parted to give a dizzying view down to a small lake. I felt as though I could fall through the hole in the swirling whiteness but it soon closed again as the winds strengthened and the snow fell more thickly while I staggered over Mounts Monroe, Franklin and Eisenhower.

Visibility in the blizzard was no more than ten yards and it was hard to tell if I was actually making progress. The first krumholz appeared and soon afterwards small trees as I crossed the last summit, Mount Pierce. Darkness came suddenly and the day ended with a slippery-slithery descent down a steep narrow trail of wet greasy rock slabs. Tired, storm battered, damp and hungry I arrived at the Mizpah Spring Hut and decided to stay, blundering into the dazzling light and warmth. 'There's two big school parties in, we could find a space on the floor'. I blundered out and pitched the still frozen tent on a platform in the nearby woods. Heavy snow continued to fall.

By dawn all my wet gear had frozen. I set off down the Crawford Path, built in 1819 and the oldest continuously maintained trail in North America, into warm sunshine at Crawford Notch, where a highway and railway cross the mountains and the AMC has an environmentally friendly lodge called the Highland Centre where I was able to dry everything out.

West of Crawford Notch is a large roadless area, the heart of which is preserved in the Pemigewasset Wilderness. Most of the area is covered by dense forest with just a few areas protruding above the trees, most notably Franconia Ridge. A network of trails links the summits and the main valleys. The hills are steep and rocky and the trails are often no more than strips of boulders and bare rock rising steeply. In some places easy scrambling is required, in others wooden steps and ladders are provided.

My plan was to circle through this area over as many summits as possible (during the walk I climbed 22 of the 48 summits over 4,000 feet (1,220m) in New Hampshire).

From Crawford Notch I took the Avalon and A-Z Trails (the last named because it links the Avalon and Zealand Trails) up into the mountain forest and a camp, a real camp on real ground, near Mount Field Brook. At 900 metres I was below the lying snow. The forest glowed wet with raindrops.

The patter of leaves and pine needles hitting the tent woke me in the morning. High above the wind rushed through the trees. Rather than lightening, the sky was darkening as the next storm roared in. The temperatures were warmer and the clouds brought rain rather than snow, torrents of rain crashing down out of the blackness. The forest dripped and shook water in the wind like a wet dog. Swollen brooks rushed and tumbled over mossy rocks.

I went above timberline on Mount Guyot into mist and

71

a wind that had me staggering. By early afternoon I was camped on another plank platform on steep slopes, and in the heart of the Pemigewasset Wilderness. The rain poured on and winds shook the tent. During the afternoon other sodden walkers arrived. Each year thousands of people use these tent sites. It's a busy wilderness.

The storm blew out during the night, the temperature dropped and by dawn the tent was frozen inside and out. Squirrels chattered loudly, birds sang and patches of blue sky showed through racing white clouds. Leaving the tent and camping gear to air and, hopefully, start to dry I set off for West Bond, Mount Bond and Bondcliff, three of the remotest summits in the White Mountains. The most interesting summit was Bondcliff, a thin rocky ridge with ravens hanging in the wind above it.

Collecting the tent I then followed steep rocky trails past the wonderfully situated Galehead Hut to camp on yet another tent platform 150 metres below the summit of Mount Garfield. The sun shone in between short, sharp hail and snow showers. By dawn the clouds had closed in again and were brushing the tops of the trees above camp.

Beyond Mount Garfield the trail rose slowly to timber-line. Once out of the trees there were large patches of snow and the rocks were covered with ice. The wind was strong and cold, the mist thick. Slipping on steep slopes I wondered whether it was wise to continue when the summit of 1600 metre Mount Lafayette, the highest on the ridge, loomed up in front of me, its cluster of signs covered with rime ice. A day walker appeared. 'Nothing to see', he said glumly and was gone into the cloud. A chipmunk popped out of a hole in the rocks and ran round on the snow, searching for any food scraps dropped by walkers.

Franconia Ridge ran for five miles to the south, undulating over four more summits, three of which were cloud free. On the south ridge of Mount Lincoln the shattered cliffs and pinnacles were white with rime ice. To the west the ridge dropped precipitately to Franconia Notch, to the east the line of the Bond range rose above the deep forested Lincoln Brook valley. From the last summit, Mount Flume, a series of wooden ladders led down steep slopes to flat ground where I camped.

Forest trails led me north as I completed my circular walk. Placid ponds dotted the flat marshy woods and there were many moose tracks. I climbed three final peaks, camping near the summit of the last one, Mount Torn, from where I watched as the sun set to leave a delicate pink wash over the sky. As the last sunlight faded the full moon rose and I made my way back to camp by its cool eerie light, the shadows black and impenetrable.

At dawn a pale pink glow appeared above Mount Jackson, just across Crawford Notch, and deepened to a richer red. A thin curve of fiery orange appeared above the mountain followed by the first edge of the sun and I headed down the trail, my journey in the White Mountains over.

Through the Uinta Mountains in Utah

Ragged black clouds crashed, swirled and rolled around the cliffs and ridges. Thunder rumbled and roared. Lightning lashed across the sky, briefly illuminating the trees and the mountains with ghastly yellow light. Torrential rain hammered down, bouncing off the ground, at times turning to hail and whitening the landscape.

Our high camp, above 3,350 metres on the edge of the last cluster of trees, felt very exposed. Huddling in the protection of a dense thicket we watched the storm circle the wide basin, waiting for it to fade and move away. 'Maybe someone should stand further away so they can resuscitate the rest of us if lightning strikes,' someone joked.

Out in the open our dinner was cooking, steam emerging from a black pan perched on a little stove and every so often someone would pull their hood over their head and dash out to see how the meal was doing. After a long day high in the mountains we wanted that food.

The day had begun many, many hours earlier when we'd set off in the dark for Utah's highest mountain, 4,125m (13,528 ft) King's Peak. The predawn start meant we could be off the summit before any afternoon thunderstorms, common here due to the hot air from the deserts that lie below the mountains rising and meeting the cool air above the peaks. Watching the lightning bounce round the valley and thinking of those we'd met still heading up as we descended I was glad of that dark start to the day though at the time, stumbling round half-asleep in the cold, I'd resented it. There'd been a storm the previous night too, with torrential rain, distant flickers of lightning and very strong winds. None of us had slept undisturbed.

To climb King's Peak was why we were there so sleeping in, while desirable, seemed rather pointless. King's Peak lies in the heart of the Uinta Mountains, a western spur of the Rocky Mountains in north-east Utah, just south of the border with Wyoming. Utah usually conjures up images of desert canyons and red slick rock but the Uinta are alpine mountains, snow-covered for more than half the year and with a myriad lakes and streams. Forests rise to around 11,000 feet (3,350m). Above the trees are vast open grassy bowls dotted with lakes, above which rise long, steep, rocky ridges. Most of the area is protected in the 460,000 acre High Uintas Wilderness, the largest wilderness area in Utah and a wonderful region for back-packing, hill-walking and scrambling.

I had arrived in a ten-strong party with the aim of shrugging off the noise, tension and frenetic activity of a trade show by spending a few peaceful nights in the wilderness, taking in an ascent of King's Peak. But the weather was disturbing the hoped-for tranquillity a little. The walk-in to base camp, through gradually-thinning conifer forest, had been pleasant, a gentle ascent into a magnificent bowl, but by the time we made camp it was raining heavily with thunder and lightning all around.

As grey light slowly crept across the mountains on the morning of the ascent we saw dark clouds capping the mountain ridges; below them a bright white edging of fresh snow. Bundled up against the dawn chill we gulped down a quick breakfast before setting off for a notch known as Gunsight Pass in the ridge above. Beyond the pass huge Painter Basin faded into distant dark forest. King's Peak, at the head of the basin, rose into the grey cloud.

The trail led to yet another pass, Anderson, that lay just 300m below the summit. The last climb up the north ridge of the mountain was the slowest and hardest part of the day; clambering over the steep rocks and boulders was halfway between walking and scrambling. On one side the west face fell away steeply in a rocky tangle of crags, towers and buttresses.

The slowness of the ascent had a benefit though. As we climbed the clouds rose and by the time we reached it the little airy summit was clear, though the sky remained overcast and threatening. The wind was cool too and we didn't linger, soon heading back to camp, reaching it just before the storm broke. It raged through the evening but faded away with the daylight to leave a calm, dry night with a stunningly bright sky, the thickly-packed stars of the Milky Way seeming surprisingly close.

Early the following day, while it was still dark, the others returned to the world of flights, cars and cities while I remained in the wilderness for another nine days, a prospect I relished. In a sense the real journey was only now beginning, the previous two days having been no more than a taster, a brief but enjoyable dash into the wilderness in the company of nine others. Now I could slow down, ease more gently into the wilds and notice the wildlife, the rocks, the plants, the details of the landscape.

The Uinta Mountains are the largest east-west running mountain range in the US outside Alaska. My plan was to head to the eastern end, cross the main ridge and walk to the western end along the Highline Trail, which runs at or above timberline and crosses many high passes.

I began with a two-day wander through deep conifer woods and huge grassy meadows where the last flowers of summer still gave a touch of colour. Once off the well-worn King's Peak path I met no one and the trail was often faint. The only tracks were those of elk and mule deer, the only sounds those of squirrels, birds, creeks and the wind in the trees. At night I camped on the edge of meadows, sheltering under big firs and spruces from the rain showers and the night frosts that whitened the grass. Above, big rounded rolling hills added to the sense of quiet and gentleness.

The walking was peaceful and relaxing and I gradually unwound from the excitement of the storms and King's Peak and being with so many people. On my third day alone I crossed the crest of the mountains at Divide Pass between Island and Fox Lakes. A party on horseback passed me, the first people I'd seen since setting off by myself.

The walk's calm was in danger of becoming soporific as I approached Kidney Lakes, especially as the light remained dull and the sun, if visible at all, was hazy and weak behind the clouds. The hills around me were gentle and soothing too but not overly impressive. I was now so relaxed I needed some stimulation, which was when the wilderness came to life.

Wait long enough and nature will always reveal something. As I walked through the trees some distance from the shore of one of the Kidney Lakes I caught a glimpse of something moving in the water, something very big. A huge bull moose with a massive rack of antlers was standing in the shallows. Dropping the pack I crept to the edge of the water, binoculars and camera in hand. Two moose cows were also out in the lake, one vigorously plunging her head into the water and emerging with a dripping green veil of waterweeds. For an hour and more I lay on the ground watching these ungainly yet magnificent animals, the largest members of the deer family. The bull barely moved during this time but the cows were quite active, one eventually swimming to shore and trotting into the forest.

I camped near the lakes and returned at dusk to watch the moose. The clouds cleared: reeds, forest, hill, clouds and sky glowing in the low sun, their reflections shining in the blue water. Moose were everywhere: in the lake, in the meadows, in the forest. One had watched me make camp from a distance of just 15 metres. Six were in the water together with more on the shore. Other animals were about too: elk running through the trees, more nervous than the moose, coyotes yipping and yapping not far away.

I had my stimulation. I returned to camp in the dark feeling overwhelmed, gratified, exhilarated and excited.

Shrieking gray jays woke me the next morning. The meadows were white with frost and crunched underfoot. My breath was visible in the air and a brightness in the east suggested the sun was near. The treetops shone with that warm golden-green glow that always enlivens and inspires with the warmth and promise of a perfect day in a perfect place. Dawn light on the lakes was beautiful with gently rippling reflections. The moose were still there.

For the next five days the sun shone from a deep blue sky, the light sharp and clear, giving a luminous edge to the landscape. The incipient dullness had gone from my mind and I spent the rest of the trip feeling elated. From Kidney Lakes I walked up vast Painter Basin with its wall of rocky peaks, including King's Peak, shining ahead of me. On Anderson Pass I encountered many people, my first hikers since King's Peak. With this vast wilderness to explore, most were intent only on the highest peak.

The descent from the pass was tremendous, an exciting mile-long narrow traverse across steep stony slopes above a line of cliffs. Above me the west face of King's Peak was banded with red and gold rock, giving a feel of the Southwest, a hint of the desert canyons that lay not far away. Like those canyons the Uinta Mountains are composed of sedimentary rocks: sandstone, shale and quartzite. Below the rocks Yellowstone Basin was another great parkland-like sweep of meadows and tree groves. Camp was in a cluster of tall sub-alpine fir with mountains all around, the long wooded Yellowstone valley breaking the undulating ring of stark stony slopes.

The pattern of the walk was now set. A succession of high steep passes -- Tungsten, Porcupine, Red Knob, Dead Horse, Rocky Sea — led to more huge meadow-filled basins — Garfield, Oweep, Lake Fork, Rocky — with long wooded valleys reaching down to the distant lowlands. I climbed two more summits, 11,884-foot Yellow Peak (3,623m) and 13,080-foot Wilson Peak (3,987m), the first an easy walk, the second a steep scramble up loose rubble that required concentration but rewarded with beautiful and spectacular views from the long flat summit ridge. Below, to the north, lay the dark waters of Red Castle Lakes with the bright shattered rocks of Red Castle rising above.

Care was needed on the steep loose descent of Porcupine Pass. The narrow trail cut across the stony mountainside above a series of small cliffs before switchbacking down into the meadows below. Above me rose the massive five-mile long ridge of a mountain just called Stone, its long tiers of cliffs flaming red in the setting sun.

One of the joys of crossing passes is the anticipation as to what lies on the other side, the growing sense of excitement as the moment of discovery approaches. Sometimes the suddenly-revealed vista is breathtaking and you stop to gaze in wonder. This was the case at Red Knob Pass where I was amazed by the soaring pinnacles of Mount Beulah, its steep south face a mass of buttresses and cliffs, towering above the West Fork Blacks Fork valley.

From Dead Horse Pass, a broad saddle reached by a steep ascent on shattered slopes through a chaos of loose boulders, scree and small crags, I looked down to the brilliant turquoise waters of Dead Horse Lake shimmering on the edge of the long, dark, forested slash of the valley. South of the pass Ledge Lake lay at the foot of crumbling cliffs down which cascades of water crashed and tumbled noisily. A bull moose grazed among the lakeside willows. From a camp in the trees I watched the beast as it browsed through the bushes. Across the water the slopes of Squaw and Explorer Peaks turned gold in the evening sun.

The site was too beautiful to abandon after just one night so I spent a day here, watching the light changing on the mountains and the water, absorbing the depths of the landscape and scrambling up a minor summit above the camp. The ascent was on increasingly steep and loose rock where great care was needed not to slip or roll a stone on to a foot. As the climbing became more intense nothing existed beyond the next foot hold: reach the security of the next rock... balance on wobbling stones... pick out the best route... My only concern was staying alive and uninjured, but every time I looked up there was beauty all around and I forgot the precariousness of my situation.

A slow, awkward descent led to a col. Above me rose Explorer Peak, with a narrow rocky arête leading to its summit. Clouds were building rapidly beyond it and this was no place to be in a thunderstorm, so I cautiously retreated into the Fall Creek valley, picking a way through broken bands of crags and slithering down loose scree gullies. A blast of strong wind and a touch of hail swept over me and then the storm passed and faded into the distance.

Crossing the head of Rock Creek the next day, a superb walk past a number of beautiful timberline lakes, clouds again built up to the south. This time they failed to dissipate and by the time I reached the last pass of the walk, Rocky Sea, the sky was already darkening. I attempted one of the peaks above the pass but was still far from the top when a crash of thunder shook the air and I found myself running, slipping and skittering over the rocks back to the pass.

Grabbing my pack I sped towards the shelter of the forest where two hikers were sheltering under the first large tree, waiting for the storm to clear before crossing the pass. They had a long wait. Soon after I entered the trees the rain started and my last camp was deep in the forest, sheltering from the thunder and lightning that rang and flashed all around. It was still raining at dawn and the thunder continued as I walked out to Minor Lake and the highway. I didn't mind.

Traversing Corsica on the GR20

Seven hours after a cool early morning start in Scotland I was sweating uphill with my companion Cameron McNeish in ridiculous temperatures above the burnt orange roofs of Calenzana. We'd already hiked through the maws, a mix of fine scented spiky shrubs and flowers that tore at our legs and arms leaving thin trickles of blood to congeal in the sun. Now we'd ascended into the high rocky mountains and pine forests where our trail would remain until the final day and descent into Conca, far to the south.

We were just starting out on the Grand Randonneé 20, a long-distance path that runs north-south along the length of the mountainous spine of Corsica, a volcanic island rising steeply over the deep blue of the Mediterranean Sea.

Threading a way through the mountains and staying as close to the watershed as possible the GR20 is an exciting, adventurous, complex, route with much closer contact to steep rock and exposed situations than walkers usually find on waymarked footpaths. Initially the idea of following the red and white painted stripes that mark GR routes may seem a little tame and easy. It's not on the GR20, especially when you come face to face with some of the terrain where those paint splashes go.

This route is unrelentingly steep and exacting, a real challenge to the mountain walker. From the first day you'll find yourself grappling with rock and learning with gratitude just how adhesive rough granite is, and also how easily it strips away skin if you get too close. You can identify GR20 walkers by the scars and abrasions on their arms and legs.

The upside of this strenuous, difficult and sometimes scary trail is immersion in a complex, rocky wilderness of high peaks, vertical cliffs, spires, pinnacles, slabs and every other form of rock architecture imaginable. The route twists and turns, constantly rises and falls as it contours the way of least resistance through the terrain. I was impressed by the imagination of the creator, the alpinist Michel Fabrikant, and the skill of those who helped plot the route. This is not a trail for those who like to stride out and cover great distances. There are few places where any sort of rhythm is possible for more than a few hundred metres. The descents cannot be rushed; they drop steeply down scree, boulders and slabs and twist around cliffs and gullies. There are sections through gentle valleys and forests that are easier, but these are few.

Starting in the north means most of the really difficult terrain comes in the first four days, including the exposed Spasimata slabs and the notorious Cirque de la Solitude. But don't think the southern half is easy or gentle, as is often implied. It's still harder than most trails, just not as extreme as the terrain to the north.

Most of the route lies between 1200 and 2000 metres

in altitude. The highest point is the Breche de Capitellu at 2225 metres, the lowest (forgetting the start and finish), is at Vizzavona, the half way point that ducks just under 920 metres. For those who care about such things, the loftiest summit in Corsica is Monte Cinto (2706m), which you can climb as a side trip.

The few easier sections in the forests are enjoyable, a quiet, shady respite from the scrambling and the sun. Many of the tall Laricio pines have their tops blasted by lightning. There are some oversized spruce trees here too, one of which was the biggest tree in Europe until lightning lopped off the top few metres. Above the forest, low juniper, alder and yellow flowered broom spread over what ground they can, adding softness and colour to the hard, harsh terrain.

The forests and mountains are full of flowers, many of them familiar, some more exotic including the alpine columbine and the orange lily. There is wildlife; lizards dart everywhere and yellow-billed choughs circle over passes waiting to scavenge the scraps left by hikers. Most spectacular are the huge lammergeier, great vultures with a wingspan of almost three metres.

The crux of the GR 20 — and the rock climbing term is apt — is the crossing of the Cirque de la Solitude on the fourth day. The walls of the cirque plunge steeply down from the Bocca Tumasginesca (a *bocca* is a col or pass) and then rise equally steeply to the Bocca Minute. The first sight of the cirque filled me with awe and horror, more so when I saw trekkers inching down extremely steep rock over sheer drops. I'd never ventured into such terrain without being roped up.

Technically, the climbing and scrambling was easy and there are chains bolted in place on the steepest sections. It is sustained though and psychologically I was at my limit, especially on the terrifying descent, and welcomed the patient encouragement and assistance of Cameron, a much more experienced rock climber who relished the scrambling.

The cirque is magnificently wild, savage and exciting, with tremendous views of huge pinnacles and specatcular cliffs, and it was wonderful to be there, amongst such grandeur, despite the fear and the exposure. That said, I felt great relief on reaching the Bocca Minute with the cirque over and done with. Crossing it is as tough and as challenging a mountaineering adventure as most hikers will ever encounter.

Appropriately the day ended with a thunderstorm raging in the mountains to the south. A dramatic end to a dramatic day with just the edge of the storm buffeting our camp with a light shower and a gust of wind. The storm brought relief in the form of cooler temperatures and improved views with sharper, clearer light that lasted to the end of the trail.

The day following the Cirque is one of the easiest on the route with only one steep rocky ascent. Much of the day is spent in cool forest or descending the picturesque Golo valley beside refreshing cascades and deep pools. The end to the day isn't so scenic - the Castel du Verghio ski resort is a collection of blockhouse style buildings, rusting ski lifts and bare eroded pistes.

'Wild pigs ate my sandal!' begins my journal entry for the morning at Castel du Verghio. Feral pigs roam the resort and will eat anything they can get so campers are corralled in a dusty, shade-less field surrounded by a high mesh fence. A warm breeze rattled across the site, rustling the tents, and it was that wind, I thought, that woke me in the night.

I sat up to see my food stuffsack being dragged under the flysheet by something small and dark. Hearing me move the creature fled. The stuffsack was slimy with saliva but unharmed. I shone my headlamp around and checked my gear. A sandal was missing. Surely not, I thought. Maybe I'd left it outside. I shone my headlamp round. No sandal. I searched the whole site and the area round it the next morning. Still no sandal. I assume a piglet small enough to creep under the fence had stolen and probably eaten it. Luckily I had a pair of trail shoes. I slept with them for the rest of the hike.

The landscape south of Castel du Verghio is more open and spacious than that to the north, less hemmed in by rock walls and mountains, especially at the Lac de Nino near the Refuge de Manganu. This large high level lake (1743 metres) lies in an area of expansive wet meadows cut by small streams and dotted with pools (called *pozzi* in Corsican). The bright green grass and blue water make for an idyllic pastoral interlude in the island of harsh rock and stone that makes up most of the GR20.

Manganu marks a return to the scrambling. Above this refuge lies a steep cirque rimmed with peaks up which the GR20 climbs to the highest point on the route, the Breche de Capitellu, a narrow notch below a twisted, towering pinnacle, from where you look down into a vast cirque with the jagged crest of Monte Rotondo, Corsica's second highest mountain, rising beyond it.

Two beautiful lakes decorate the cirque, the Lac de Capitellu and the Lac de Melu, the waters deep bright blue add a splash of colour in a rich brown granite landscape. By an optical quirk the two lakes appear to be almost on the same level. In fact Lac de Melu is over 200 metres lower than Lac de Capitellu, as is evidenced later in the walk.

From the Breche de Capitellu the GR20 stays high, winding across the slopes of Punta Alle Porta over steep scree and boulder fields and along narrow rock ridges above deep cirques, a wonderful high mountain route that is arguably the finest section of the trail. The scrambling is mostly easy and the situations superb. This is walking to relish.

In complete contrast there follows a forest walk through pines and beech down the Manganella valley and up to l'Onda where there's a refuge and some bergeries (shepherds' summer dwellings) and another camping enclosure fenced against pigs.

A day beyond l'Onda at the end of a long 1200 metre descent lies the small hamlet of Vizzavona, the half way point. Half way in distance but not in time. We took eight days to reach Vizzavona but only another five to reach the finishing line due to the easier conditions underfoot.

High above Bocce di Verdi during the complex traverse of the rocky slopes of Punta Della Cappella the cloud was so thick we could see only a few metres, making the devious twisting route in and out of gullies and around pinnacles disorientating. The wind gusting to 50mph threatened to blow us off the mountain at times and although convinced sometimes that we were heading back the way we'd come we followed the familiar red and white paint marks until the path finally descended to the shelter of a wind stunted beech wood.

The clouds lifted but the wind strengthened and we were blown all over the place on the rough traverse of Monte Formicola that followed. That night we camped below the Refuge d'Usciolu, a wildly scenic site with a splendid view of Monte Alcudina, the last mountain on the route. The wind was so wild that in the middle of the night I abandoned the shaking, rattling tent and crept under a nearby overhanging rock for a more peaceful sleep. High above the sky was fantastically sharp and clear, the stars brilliant, the Milky Way a dense wavy band of glittering points of light.

The wind dropped and the hot sun returned for the entertaining and amazingly intricate scramble along the narrow Arête a Monda, a thin spine of granite pinnacles, steep slabs, stepped gullies and huge boulders. Again I admired the skill of the route makers who had managed to weave a hiking trail through such terrain, constantly switching from one side of the ridge to the other to follow the easiest line. The ascent of 2134 metre Monte Alcudina, a big, bulky mountain with a broad shoulder was easy but the knee hammering descent down awkward slabs and rocks to the Refuge d'Asinau was tricky.

After Monte Alcudina the GR20 has one final day of glory as it rounds the spiky Aiguilles de Bavella and then climbs across the dramatic Punta Tafunta ridge to one of the most scenically sited refuges, Paliri, which lies on a high col. The Refuge de Paliri is also the strangest as the guardian has decorated the area with red and white painted rocks bearing messages, some practical (water sources), some informative (names of plants), some cryptic, some with quotations from poets and philosophers, to create a surreal wonderland.

From Paliri it's a slow descent to the heat haze of *the maquis* and one last pass, the Bocca d'Usciolu. Once through this narrow gateway the journey is over and all that remains is to walk the last few hot kilometres to the little town of Conca.

Walking Sweden's Kungsleden

Whilst southern Sweden is known as a land of forests and lakes, fewer people know that in Lapland in the north there are mountains: 1000 kilometres of them, straddling the Arctic Circle and rising to 2117 metres on Kebnekaise, the highest mountain in Arctic Scandinavia. As well as permanently snow clad peaks, Swedish Lapland has huge lakes, powerful rivers, thundering waterfalls and dense forests of birch and pine, a vast unspoilt wilderness, by far the largest remaining in western Europe.

The sheer scale can be intimidating, but a 450 kilometre long footpath runs south-north through the heart of the mountains. This is the Kungsleden, the King's Way, which passes through four national parks - Pieljekaise, Sarek, Stora Sjöfallets and Abisko - as well as Vindelfjällens nature reserve, at 4,800 square kilometres the largest in Europe.

The trail is waymarked with pairs of cairns and large upright stones, each topped with red paint, that make route finding easy. There are bridges across the deeper rivers and rowing boats or ferries for crossing the long east-west running lakes that lie across the route. At high points there are basic wind shelters and boggy sections have duckboards laid across them, making the Kungsleden a drier walk underfoot than might be expected.

Crossing the grain of the land, the Kungsleden rises and falls as it climbs repeatedly over high ridges and passes only to descend back into forest and lake filled valleys. This makes for a great deal of ascent, but the reward is the variety of scenery the trail encompasses, from deep forest to high mountains.

Dark clouds were shrouding the peaks and rain was falling steadily when I started north along the Kungsleden late one August, incorporating it into a summer-long walk the length of Norway and Sweden. The start, among the ski lifts and snow-free pistes of the Hemavan ski resort, is inauspicious but soon the trail climbs onto open mountainside before traversing into Syterskalet. The walk up this long Glencoe-like valley was exhilarating, the scenery dramatic and mysterious and hinting at big mountains in the swirling mists.

When a small hut loomed up I popped inside for a bit of shelter, a move I soon regretted when the warden appeared and charged me fifteen kroner. This was the day use rate for huts along the trail whether you stayed five minutes or five hours. Although there are many such huts along the Kungsleden I intended camping most nights anyway, and that first evening I pitched the tent at the head of Syterskalet, a wonderful wilderness site. Even in the rain I wouldn't have swopped it for a night in a hut away from the world I had come to be part of.

The trail wound across marshy lakes by way of long boardwalks and twisting bridges, slipped through dense green birch woods, and traversed open fellsides whose slopes faded into grey skies in all directions. In places the bleak scene was enlivened by the fires of bright red rowans. After three days of rain and wind I reached the small village of Ammarnäs and here, I confess, I stayed in a hotel and dried out my dripping gear.

Beyond the village I climbed onto the bleak Pennine-like moorland called Bjorkfjället. All was silent, as if waiting for something: sun? winter? rain? A few cold tarns and long whale-backed hills with small broken crags made up the view. A few reindeer browsed lethargically. There were no people and I was to see only a couple of walkers on the whole 180 kilometre stretch between Ammarnäs and Kvikkjokk. The hut chain is broken here so you have to camp. I didn't mind. It was good to be alone in the vastness.

Solitude is best if you want to see wildlife too. Reindeer were abundant in places, though they aren't really wild, all of them belonging to the native Sami people. Birdlife wasn't prolific but I did see long-tailed skuas, golden eagles, capercaillie, willow grouse and ptarmigan.

Rain fell almost every day and all I could do was keep plodding through it. At the tiny hamlet of Jäkkvik I came on the first of the big lakes. Before setting out I had fondly imagined I would walk round them so as not to break the walk, but doing so would have involved difficult bushwhacking and route-finding and probably double the time. So, I took the ferries, usually just a small boat with an outboard motor run by a local man.

A small wooden sign with 'Polecirklen' scrawled crudely on it marked my entry into the Arctic and reminded me that this land really was as remote and empty as it felt. A long day later I arrived in Kvikkjokk, roughly half way along the trail, which also marked a turning point in the weather when the rain ceased and the sun began to shine. The second half of the walk was a joy.

North of Kvikkjokk the scenery is more impressive, with glacier-clad mountains replacing the bleak flat moorland. The first frosts brought brightness too, the birch woods becoming a magical golden forest that even in dull weather was quite overwhelming. From Kvikkjokk the path cuts through the edge of Sarek national park, a wild and beautiful area I would later return to ski.

At Aktse lake a new problem confronted me. Instead of a phone to ring for a ferry, as at other lakesides, two rowing boats were pulled up on the stony beach. I looked at them doubtfully. I couldn't remember the last time I had tried to row a boat. There was a wardened hut the other side of the lake, three long kilometres away, but whether there was a ferry I didn't know. Reluctantly I climbed into one of the boats and pushed it out into the calm water of a sheltered bay. I wrestled the boat out into the open lake and white capped waves swept down on me. The boat rocked alarmingly and suddenly seemed very small and fragile. I could see the shore I was trying to reach but it didn't seem to get any closer. The red buoys that marked the way had somehow drifted up the lake. No, it was the boat that was drifting, driven down the lake by the wind. I struggled to turn it back on course but to no avail.

Buffeted by waves and wind the boat eventually beached itself, for I had little to do with it, on a headland half a kilometre from where I'd set off thirty long terrifying minutes before. Highly relieved I thrashed ignominiously back along the shore. During the day five more walkers - all of them German – arrived, but none tried their hand at rowing. The next morning a ferry arrived from the far side. Shame-faced I explained what I'd done the day before and the boatman nodded, stone-faced. He had, of course, seen the beached boat as he crossed.

Further on I came to a lake, Teusajaure, without a ferry, and had to row. The water seemed only slightly choppy and it was only half a kilometre. I pushed off and was surprised and relieved to find myself on the far bank twenty minutes later.

Beyond Teusajaure steep slopes closed in around the trail and I felt that I was now entering the heart of the mountains. Ahead lay the long beautiful valley of Tjäktjavagge in which I spent one glorious day, the finest of the walk. The sun shone, the snowy mountains sparkled, the tundra glistened with frost and autumn colour. Reindeer paused to watch me then leapt away. Mountains of every shape and size - spires, domes, ridges, rock walls, snow slopes - lay to either side. A couple of times I glimpsed Kebnekaise and vowed to return and climb it, one day, which I was to do on another ski tour.

I left this magnificent valley by the narrow windswept pass of Tjäktjapasset, at 1140 metres the highest point on Kungsleden. Beyond lay the golden forest of Abisko national park and then, after sixteen satisfying days, the end of Kungsleden on the shores of Torneträsk lake.

Across Scotland on the Southern Upland Way

Coast-to-coast walks are satisfying and full of purpose. There is a sea to reach, a land to cross, a clear destination. Every day you stride out knowing that you are leaving one coast farther behind while approaching another. On reaching that once distant sea you know that you have crossed the country and seen all that lies in between.

Yet despite its attractions the Southern Upland Way, Britain's first official coast-to-coast route which was opened in 1984, is also Britain's forgotten long distance path, seeing little of the numbers who walk the West Highland Way or the Pennine Way. When I followed the route, at the height of the summer, I was surprised to meet only a couple of other end to end walkers and only a few more day walkers. On many days I met no one.

Perhaps it's because the name isn't very inspiring. 'Southern Uplands' hardly stirs the blood or raises the spirits. The route has developed an unjustified reputation for being dull too, for spending too much time in dingy conifer plantations and on metalled roads. Whatever the reason for the low numbers it's not valid. The SUW is a splendid walk.

I confess that I had listened to the stories and ignored

the Southern Upland Way for many years. Indeed, I had rarely walked in the Southern Uplands at all, so it was with a sense of exploration and, yes, excitement that I set off from the little seaside village of Portpatrick.

Before me the trail stretched north east for 340 kilometres (212 miles) from the Irish Sea to the North Sea. The Southern Uplands consist of a series of small hill ranges split by deep south-north trending valleys. In the south the hills fade away to the Solway Firth and the English Border, to the north the Southern Upland Boundary Fault separates the hills from the Central Lowlands. This is moorland country, the hills rolling and rounded, great swells of green and brown rising above steep glaciated valleys.

The land isn't that high, with just six summits rising above 800 metres, but it is lonely and often remote. Lowther Hill at 725 metres is the highest summit on the Southern Upland Way. Nowhere else does the route rise above even 600 metres and much is below 300 metres. This doesn't mean this is a flat route though. My estimate of the total ascent is 9,000 metres (based on calculations from an altimeter watch), which works out at about 800 metres per day on my eleven day walk. In fact I climbed over 1200 metres on two days and the lowest daily ascent was 440 metres. The lack of high summits doesn't mean the SUW is a gentle stroll. It requires stamina and hill knowledge. Mist can quickly cover the higher ground and the route is not all that clear on some moorland stretches.

This isn't a route for peak baggers anyway. Rather it is one for those who love quiet countryside, a complex, changing mosaic of woods, fields, rivers, lakes, moors and hills. It's not wilderness – human activity is apparent almost everywhere – but it is wild. Farming and forestry are the largest and most obvious human manifestations (followed, now, by wind farms). Cattle, sheep and hay are seen in abundance, as are coniferous plantations, but the last are less dull and less extensive than many think though. Forest Enterprise has planted a mix of deciduous species in many places to provide variety and a wider range of wildlife. Riparian restoration can be seen along many of the waterways too, from the Water of Trool in the west to the river Tweed and its tributaries in the east, with new trees and bushes lining the streams. I found it heartening to see this return of nature. As these trees grow both the forests and the riversides will become more attractive and less monotonous, adding to the pleasures of the walk.

Forests may block some of the views but they make excellent habitats for wildlife including Scottish crossbills, goldcrest, siskin and short-eared owls, though they can be difficult to see amongst the trees. On the moors and hills kestrels and buzzards are common and I saw several hen harriers. Red grouse are likely to explode from the heather in many places: some of the moors, especially in the east, are managed for grouse shooting. Smaller birds include wheatear, whinchat, stonechat, skylark and meadow pipit. Dippers live on the rivers, larger water birds such as mallard ducks on the lochs. Animals are less common. I saw a few distant deer and rather more rabbits plus one large adder, lying on the path just a few steps away. Midges were surprisingly few in number, certainly compared with the Highlands, which made the eight nights I spent camping much more pleasant than expected.

There is much history as well as natural history along the way. Historic buildings, relics and artefacts line the route, from prehistoric standing stones to mines, castles, abbeys and Victorian mansions, and even the least historically inclined walker is likely to find some of them of interest. In the west there are many reminders of the bloody history of the Covenanters in the 1680s, when Presbyterian followers of the National Covenant were hunted down and killed by English government troops. Walking down a quiet forest ride it's a sobering shock to suddenly come upon a memorial to Covenanters who were caught at prayer at this remote spot and shot. Some relics are curious and unexplained, such as the Wells of Rees in Killgallioch Forest, small drystone domes built over tiny springs in the hillside. They are guessed to have had a religious purpose as there is said to have been a chapel nearby but no one really knows. In total contrast is the great Victorian pile of Abbotsford on the banks of the river Tweed, built for Sir Walter Scott.

On long walks I usually regard towns as sources of food, showers and perhaps accommodation but otherwise to be left as quickly as possible. On the SUW this is unwise, as there is much to see in the attractive towns along the way such as the castle, the tollbooth and Britain's oldest working post office in Sanquhar, the mining museum and old mine workings in Wanlockhead and the ruined abbey in Melrose.

Starting in the west means the weather is likely to be at your back and the sun won't be in your eyes so this is the way I went, as do most end-to-end walkers. Initially the route heads north along the coastal cliffs but soon the route turns inland through a mix of neat sheep-cropped grassland, rough pasture, low moorland and forestry. Ahead the dark outline of the Galloway Hills draws the eye and keeps the feet moving. Two days from the start and I was there, staying in a B&B in Glentrool Village.

The SUW stays low in the Galloway Hills, running

through mixed woodland beside the dark pools and swirling eddies of the Water of Trool and then above beautiful Loch Trool with the higher heather-clad rugged knobbly hills rising on the far side. All was calm and peaceful, unlike my only previous visit here when I spent two days running round the hills in a storm on the Karrimor Mountain Marathon. Leaving the Galloway Forest Park, in which wild camping isn't permitted, I pitched my tent on the slopes of Shield Rig with a view back over the forest and the Galloway Hills. Rain fell during the night and I woke to see wet grass sparkling in sunshine and strands of mist rising in quivering columns from the damp forest. A glorious morning when you know there is nowhere else you'd rather be.

For eight more days I wandered along the SUW, dipping down into little towns and villages, climbing up through fields and forests to moorland hills and following meandering streams. Highlights abounded: the long shaking suspension bridge over the placid Water of Ken leading into St John's of Dalry; a glowering view of dark hills, dark forest and dark clouds from Benbrack; an exhilarating walk over Cairn Hill and Black Hill to High Countam with a feeling of freedom and escape from the confines of the valleys; the stark ragged ruins of Sanquhar Castle backlit against dark storm clouds; the bleak mining village of Wanlockhead's whitewashed buildings glowing in the dusk on a day of torrential rain; the 'golf ball' domes of the radar station looming eerily out of dense mist on Lowther Hill.

Then there was the real mountain feel of the dramatic landscape of the deep ravine of the Selcoth Burn with the path high on its side and unstable hillsides all around rising into the mist; reaching Phawhope Bothy and settling down warm and snug in front of a roaring fire after a day of heavy rain and a cold wind; watching short-eared owls and hen harriers hunting in the forests and on the moors; wonderful post storm light on the purple heather patched hills across the wind whipped waters of St Mary's Loch; camped below Blake Muir watching the large red dot of the planet Mars appear followed by a mass of brilliant stars.

Then towards the finish the classic Borders country: purple heather, rolling hills, little towns tucked into folds in the hills, winding rivers, woodland groves, the gaunt Gothic ruin of Melrose Abbey.

Eventually the hills slid away and the route reached cliffs above a crashing sea, a mirror image of the start of the walk. Cove Harbour was a final point of interest before the last steps inland to the village of Cockburnspath and the finish. The SUW was a rich experience; a complex, interesting and thought provoking mix of nature, landscape and history. I recommend it.

Trekking to Makalu Base Camp

The path rose through terraced fields fringed with trees to the crest of a broad ridge where, suddenly, the world opened up, expanding beyond cultivated fields and dense forest to the high distant mountains of the Himalaya. And what mountains: the great white wall of 7319 metre Chamlang, over eight kilometres long, the fine pyramid of Peak 6 and the cloud-capped bulk of 8481 metre Makalu itself, the fifth highest mountain in the world rising above green forest-clad ridges and valleys. This was the second day of the TGO Readers' Trek to Makalu Base Camp and our first view of the mountains at whose feet we would camp for three nights. First though, came nine days of trekking that took us from tropical forests and rich farmland across the deep gorge of the Arun River, over high passes into the wild Barun River valley.

For the first four days we walked along steep hillsides on wide paths linking a series of villages and farms. Millet and rice grew in the fields, banana trees overhung the neat bamboo thatched farmhouses. The paths were busy with local people and we passed through many small villages. At times we went through dark and dense subtropical forest, the gnarled tangled trees laden with mosses and ferns, a constant hum of insects and bird calls echoing from the treetops. Cardamom plantations underlay the forest in places, a valuable crop.

Apart from the view of the high mountains the highlight of this section was the steep sided and forested Arun River gorge where the wild glacial-melt grey river was spanned by a narrow suspension bridge.

Beyond the Arun we climbed steep slopes to the last villages on the route, Sedua and Tashigaon, and entered wilder, more remote country where there was little cultivated land and the paths were rougher. This is high steep country. A few lodges with limited supplies were the only facilities. From Tashigaon a steep 1400 metre rocky climb led to Kauma, the first place flat enough to camp, at 3500 metres.

Kauma is beautifully situated, perched high on the side of a steep ridge. From just above camp we could see snowy mountains, including the distant bulky wedge of Kanchenjunga. These mountains remained in view as the path wound along a rocky ridge through rhododendron forest before climbing to the high Shipton La at around 4100 metres. (Different books and maps give different heights, and my two altimeters disagreed with all of them.) The Shipton La and the slightly lower Keke La passes mark the entry into the remote Barun River valley, which leads to Makalu.

Crossing the high passes marked a welcome change in the weather too. During our first five days there were several big thunderstorms with torrential rain and we'd arrived at Kauma in a hail storm that whitened the ground so much that a short snowball fight was possible. For the next week the weather was more settled, each day starting clear and sunny before gradually clouding over in the afternoon. The nights were frosty, with temperatures down to -9°C, and clear, with brilliant starry skies and a waxing moon hanging over pale snowy mountains which gleamed in the faint light.

For three days we walked up the Barun river valley to the pastures of Sherson, at 4500 metres our highest camp, leaving behind the subalpine silver fir and rhododendron forest for alpine tundra. The valley is initially walled by huge cliffs, some with massive caves high on their faces (Rudra, one of our Sherpa guides, told us that two of these were known as Lord Vishnu's Washing Rooms). Long thin waterfalls tumbled down the rock walls. As we climbed out of the forest the landscape opened out into broad glacial rocky tundra with big snow mountains: Chamlang, Peak 6 (so named on the map but called Napo according to Rudra), Hongku Chuli and, finally, Makalu.

Two days were spent exploring the area around Sherson. We climbed the steep ridge north of our camp to a broad plateau, at 5100 metres, that gave magnificent views of the steep, rocky, south face of Makalu. From its western edge we also saw the distant pyramids of Everest and Lhotse, rising above the moraines of the Barun glacier, massive pale wedges of rock and snow. Cloud plumes developed over Everest while to the south mist filled the lower valleys and began to slowly rise and spread upwards as other clouds began to pour over high cols and into the upper valleys.

The dark glacier-spattered rock wedge of Makalu towers over the upper Barun valley, which we ascended from Sherson the next day over rough glacial debris, stony moraines, boulder fields and the rubble covered Barun Glacier. A rickety narrow plank bridge led over the swirling silt-filled river to the main Makalu Base Camp area, where there's a small tea house. Everest and Lhotse came into view again, rising above a tangle of brown ridges, white glaciers and ice falls.

The next day we had to leave. Makalu Base Camp is a there and back again trek and it took a week retracing our steps to Tumlingtar airport for the flight to Kathmandu. The weather deteriorated and we had more thunderstorms, rain most days, snow at Kauma and mist on the Shipton La. The ridge between the pass and Kauma appeared to be floating in the clouds with steep drops into white nothingness either side. Once we'd crossed the Arun river again it felt as though we'd left the wild country behind. We had one more superb view of Makalu and Chamlang, shining in the dawn light, from a campsite in the little village of Gogane, at the start of our last day.

Throughout the trek we were supported ably by our sirdar, Kul, two guides, Rudra and Ramesh, and a superb cook, Amrit. With porters to carry all the camping gear, leaving us with just daysacks, this made for a luxury trek compared with a self-sufficient backpacking walk. This didn't make it particularly easy though. The altitude had its effect as we were at or above 3500 metres for nine days, reaching a maximum of 5100 metres, and the walking was mostly on steep, rough and rocky trails. In total we walked around 200 kilometres. The amount of ascent and descent is more significant than the distance though. We climbed around 7,000 metres to Sherson and another 1300 metres on day trips.

We met other trekkers most days but far less than on more popular treks. The lack of villages and the few teahouses beyond Tashigaon made for a wilderness feel, especially once we'd crossed the Shipton La. From Tashigaon onwards the land is mostly untouched and unspoiled, the dense forests pristine and prolific with bird life. The trek passes through every climatic zone from tropical forest to alpine tundra, giving a fascinating view of the huge range of environments found in Nepal, climaxing with the dramatic surroundings of the highest mountains on earth. It was one of those walks I feel privileged to have done.

4

THE BIG WALKS

Spending weeks and months in wild places brings a joy
and contentment that underpins the whole of my life. I
prefer to call the activity backpacking rather than walking
because the total experience is what matters, the camping
as well as the hiking, the nights as well as the days. This
is what distinguishes backpacking from day walking or
hiking between accommodation, whether mountain huts
or luxury hotels.

The distance doesn't matter. What is key is time. Time
to feel part of nature, time to feel the subtleties and details
of a landscape, time to move slowly yet make progress;
time, crucially, for backpacking to become a way of life
not an escape. Distance is almost a by-product. Walk every
day for week after week and you will cover many miles.
I've never felt that actual distance was important. I've
never set out to do daily big mileages, although hundreds
and thousands of miles accumulate with time. Being in the
wilds, absorbing the intricacies of nature, listening to the
wind, hearing echoes of the past in the rocks, observing
flowers and insects and birds are all important. I need time
to pause and look and listen. I don't want a schedule that
says I have to walk ten or more hours a day with few if
any halts and no time to enjoy my campsites. Backpacking

is about living in nature not streaking through it.

It takes time to enter backpacking as a way of life. On any trip there are niggles and concerns that dominate the first few days or even weeks. Worries about finding the route or water or a camp site; shaking off the last disturbing traces of the life left behind. Some of these, such as fussing over details of gear and wondering if this is the right stove or sleeping bag, perhaps mask deeper fears, hidden doubts about the walk as a whole and whether it really is feasible or wise to attempt it. Together these distractions act as a barrier to being fully involved, but as the days pass they fade away and become inconsequential. Part of this is a growth of confidence, part a shedding of a psychological state attuned to the unnatural hectic rhythms of the modern world – timetables, schedules, deadlines, appointments, fast track this, pay attention to that – be here, be there, be everywhere, now, at once, do this, do that, don't stop, don't relax, pressure, pressure, pressure, go, go, go! Phew!

In the wilds, on foot, this is all put into perspective. Seemingly important concerns become trivial, high pressure essentials seem laughable.

Walks that are too close to what we call civilisation are less satisfying than those that venture into wilderness. I realised this on my first really long backpack, ten weeks walking 2,000km (1,250 miles) from Land's End to John O'Groats. Apart from a few hours in the Pennines the walk only became really fulfilling in the Scottish Highlands where I was away from roads and buildings for days at a time.

Four years later I hiked the Pacific Crest Trail, 4,160km from Mexico to Canada through deserts and mountains that took five and a half months. This walk was a revelation both of the grandeur and power of nature and wilderness and of the rewards and meaning that came from taking on the commitment of spending six months in the wilds. Day after day I travelled through magnificent forests, jagged mountains, spacious deserts and towering canyons, watching as hot deserts and tree-clad mountains gave way to bigger mountains with glaciers and bare granite peaks. The land unfolded, developed, expanded and was revealed. I grew familiar with plants from desert cacti to mountain conifers, with animals from shy mule deer to rattlesnakes and black bears. I grew to know the noises of the night and the forest and no longer woke, as I had in the first few weeks, to sounds that were unfamiliar and potentially threatening.

This is where time came in again. Time to become used to the land and its inhabitants, to its noises and moods. By the time I finished the PCT I felt at home in the wilderness. I also felt fulfilled and ecstatic, full of the glory and power of nature, of the amazing life of this tiny planet, this speck in the unimaginable vastness of the universe. The experience left me so deeply moved, so thrilled and so shaken that I knew I had to repeat it, and I have done so many times. The pleasures have become more familiar although no less intense.

I also felt I had a new understanding of life, that possessions and a frantic urban lifestyle are imposed on us and mask our place in the natural world; superficialities that are dangerous when they persuade us that we are apart from nature not part of it.

I had a desire to communicate the stories of my walks and to share my joy and contentment through my writing and photography. Also, and most importantly, a desire to inspire others to go into the wilds themselves, whether for a weekend or a year. Not just for pleasure, though that is very important, but also because without wild places we are diminished. We came from the wild and it is still within us and without it we are nothing. Understanding this means understanding that protecting nature is vital, and that walking and sleeping in nature is the best way to reach this understanding.

Long distance backpacking also satisfies our ancient nomadic instincts, relics from the time when all humanity was on the move, hunters and gatherers forever traversing the wilds for food. Back then – which covers most of the time humans have existed – there was no possibility of a separation from nature. There was nothing other than nature.

Of course the challenge of long distance backpacking is significant and I do find satisfaction in successfully over-coming difficulties with terrain, route finding, weather and wildlife, but the challenges are not the prime reason for going. They just make the experience more intense and enjoyable. Concentrating on threading a route through dangerous terrain; finding a camp site in steep, dense forest; protecting food against wild animals; and coping with mountain storms all make contact with nature more immediate and powerful.

The planning of multi-week backpacking trips may seem a massive undertaking in itself but, actually, it's not really any different to planning a short trip. There's just more of it. In fact in planning terms a long backpacking venture is simply a series of short trips linked together. Resupply points are the key.

Breaking the walk into sections makes it manageable. I don't set off to walk hundreds or thousands of miles, only to the first supply point, then the next and the next and the next. Supply points may lie on the route or may require diversions. Deciding whether to use the latter or carry more supplies between two of the former is an important part of the planning process.

On my first long walks I was reluctant to leave my route unless absolutely necessary. This led to my setting off through the snowbound High Sierra with 23 days food and fuel plus crampons, ice axe, snowshoes and extra warm clothing in a pack weighing well over 100lbs (44kg). I've never done it again though. Ten days supplies is my absolute maximum (preferably without all the snow gear).

The heaviest weight I've carried since that High Sierra overload was due to the need to carry water rather than food. That was on a six day section of the Arizona Trail through the Sonoran Desert where I started with three gallons of water and a total pack weight of 70lbs (32kg). (These weights may seem ridiculous to light-weight backpackers and my basic gear would certainly be a bit lighter now, but water and food still weigh the same.)

Planning a long distance walk is now much, much easier than in the past, thanks to the internet. In the 1980s it took weeks for letters and packages to travel back and forth as I enquired about maps, routes, supply points and more. Today I can find most of that information in less than an hour and send emails requesting anything I can't locate.

Preparations for hiking an established trail are made easy by almost instant information, although planning your own route for which there are no guidebooks or websites still takes time. This is the part of planning I most enjoy however, spending hours poring over maps, tracing possible routes, working out logistics and getting excited at all the possibilities. I know too that however detailed my planning it won't all make sense on the ground and that I will have to adapt my route to the terrain, sometimes wondering how I could possibly have thought my original idea made any sort of sense.

On my wildest, remotest walks – the length of the Canadian Rockies (especially the northern half) and the length of the Yukon – I often abandoned the red lines I had so confidently marked on maps back home and took what were more logical routes once I could see the terrain. At other times I've deviated from planned routes for aesthetic or emotional reasons – I want to stay high on a mountain ridge or follow a wild river. So I think of my route plans as guides rather than fixed lines. This applies even when I walk named trails. I feel no obligation to stay with the 'official' route. In fact, the long trails I have walked have all been in early stages of development with long sections unsigned and often without actual paths.

Long distance trails

Musing on the attractions these paths have I wondered just what it is about these narrow strips of dirt that seems so magical? The names alone conjure up images of wild landscapes and spectacular camps: Pyrenean Haute Route, John Muir Trail, Cape Wrath Trail, Kungsleden, Appalachian Trail, Annapurna Circuit, Pacific Crest Trail and many more. All have their own special qualities. Each presents enough of a challenge to be an achievement, although none are so arduous that the pain and fear outweighs the pleasure.

107

The first named recreational long-distance path was the Long Trail, which runs for 440km along the Green Mountains in the state of Vermont in the USA and was built between 1910 and 1930. Of course, such long distance paths are in no way essential for long distance walking. Before they existed there were long distance walkers – those, that is, who hiked for pleasure rather than from necessity. John Muir himself, for whom one of the most beautiful and spectacular trails is named, hiked 1,000 miles (1,600km) from Indiana to Florida in 1867 - choosing the 'wildest, leafiest, and least trodden way I could find' – and undertook many long walks in his beloved Sierra Nevada.

Creating your own path like this is very satisfying, but there is a particular delight in following a long distance path, especially if the route has been well-designed. In many areas hiking would be difficult, dangerous or even impossible without long distance paths. Forest routes like the Long Trail would be desperate bushwhacks through dense vegetation while high mountain routes like the GR20 in Corsica would be mountaineering routes requiring technical expertise and equipment. A simple narrow path can open up an amazing wilderness world. Britain's first long distance path, the Pennine Way, was conceived at a time when the Pennine grouse moors were closed to walkers. Writer and rambler Tom Stephenson's 1930s vision of a trail from Derbyshire to Scotland along the Pennine hills was one of freedom and access at a time when attempting such a walk would have meant dodging gamekeepers and risking arrest.

Most long distance paths are a few hundred kilometres in length and can be walked in a few weeks. Some, however, are ultra-long distance and take many months to complete, stretching for thousands rather than hundreds of kilometres. The first of these was the Appalachian Trail running for 3,500km (2,180 miles) along the mostly wooded mountains between Maine and Georgia, which was built between 1923 and 1938.

In Europe there are long distance paths known as E routes, made by connecting shorter trails, such as the 4960 km E1 from Sweden to Italy and the 10,000-plus km E4 from Spain to Greece. These routes sound interesting; the names are not. More attractive and romantic names would make these routes far more appealing. Britain has no waymarked or official ultra-long distance paths but Land's End to John O'Groats can be seen in the same light, especially now there are guidebooks to suggested routes and it's possible to link shorter paths almost the whole way.

The most ambitious long distance path of all is the International Appalachian Trail, which is intended to run through all the landscapes on both sides of the Atlantic Ocean that were once part of the Caledonian Mountain range that split apart as the Atlantic formed. This means a trail running from the south-east USA through Canada, Greenland, Norway and the Scottish Highlands to finish in Spain. As an international endeavour the IAT cuts across governments and nation states and speaks to the shared values of all walkers.

The considerable length of a long distance path means protecting or creating a continuous corridor over a great distance, rather than just an isolated spot. Official government involvement can mean something other than signposts too. Officially designated long distance paths are not necessarily superior in any way to unofficial ones. In fact, they may involve compromises. Because of landowner objections, the Pennine Way follows the South Tyne Valley rather than the northernmost summits of the Pennines. In Scotland the finest long distance path is undoubtedly the unofficial Cape Wrath Trail. But once government has made a path official its agencies are then meant to conserve and promote it, agencies which can be pressured if necessary, for the benefit of us all.

In my view the main value of long distance paths is to open up nature and wild places so people can enjoy them. For many, the human side of long distance paths is as or even more important though: meetings along the way, the sharing of experiences, new friendships and reunions. Today, descriptions of walks along the 4,160km (2,600-mile) Pacific Crest Trail (arguably the finest of all the ultra-long distance paths) can sound like a party on the move. When I hiked the PCT in 1982 there were only a few parties and not many people at them!

Away from the trail long distance paths can act as a shorthand amongst walkers. Establish you have both hiked the same long distance paths and new acquaintances suddenly have much to discuss. Long distance paths are a wonderful resource for dreaming and planning and poring over maps as well as for actual walking, but I think they also have a greater value and significance that reaches far beyond those who walk them. By revealing the beauty and glory of the natural world and the wild land they run through, they create a body of people to defend and protect that land. A named path gives identity and meaning to a landscape, a focus that makes it easier to argue against despoliation and for preservation and restoration. People who love that particular long distance path are motivated to fight for its continued

110

existence, which means protecting the landscape through which it passes.

The Pacific Crest Trail

Some trails linger in the mind. For years afterwards memories of them surface, bringing delight and sometimes intense reflection. Lessons and rewards can still be coming through years later. Such trails can become benchmarks against which other journeys are measured and, for me, the Pacific Crest Trail is one. Running for 4,160km (2,600 miles) from Mexico to Canada through the states of California, Oregon and Washington it traverses the Mohave Desert, the High Sierra, Yosemite National Park and the strato-volcanoes of the southern Cascade Mountains before finishing in the spectacular alpine landscapes of the North Cascades.

For the backpacker who loves wilderness and pristine landscapes it is arguably the ultimate trail, the trail that sums up everything backpacking is about – freedom, adventure, self-reliance, inspiration, beauty and wild nature.

Hiking the PCT is an ambitious and challenging undertaking but not an overwhelming one. It may be rough in places and steep in others but there is an actual footpath the whole way. The trail reaches over 4,000 metres in the High Sierra and remains above 3,000 metres for many miles. Temperatures can range from well below freezing at night to over 40°C. Snow may be lying in the mountains at the start and fall again at the finish. Thunderstorms can crash round the peaks and rain lash down. Mostly though, the weather is benign with warm sunny days, light winds and little rain. The window for hiking the trail is six months at most however, unless you want to deal with winter conditions. Take four to five months and there's less chance of encountering snow at all.

My PCT journey lasted from early April to late September, a walk that took me from a desert spring back into winter in the mountains and then spring again and summer in the forests before finishing in the colours of autumn and the first storms of winter. *En route* I would watch a vast wilderness unfold and see black bears and rattlesnakes, moose and coyotes, strange Joshua trees in the desert, giant firs and pines in the mountains, smoking volcanoes and bubbling mud pots. I would experience searing heat, deep snow, tremendous thunderstorms and dangerous fords. I would learn to carry a gallon and more of water in the desert, the hassle of hanging my food to protect it from bears and the need for snowshoes or skis when hiking through deep, soft snow. My pack would be heavy, my feet often sore and my skin burnt and frozen but at no point would I wish to be anywhere else. The beauty, tranquillity, power and magnificence of the landscape would overwhelm all difficulties and discomforts.

With all this still ahead I shouldered my new pack at the Mexican border and walked into the dusty desert scrub. Tense with anticipation and excitement, in the first few days I learnt two quick lessons. Deserts are hot and dry even in April and just half a litre of water was inadequate for a day's hike. Drinking deeply at every water source and carrying several litres was essential. The second lesson was that my hot and heavy mountain boots were more comfortable in my pack than on my feet and that my light, cool running shoes, brought as camp and town wear, were much better for hiking.

I did need the boots eventually though, as it was a

late snow year. The snowfall pattern is something that prospective PCT hikers watch with trepidation in the months building up to their hike. In many years most of the snow in the High Sierra is gone by late May, when hikers starting in early April usually reach the mountains. In 1982, though, heavy snow fell late in the spring and lasted well into June.

There was snow lying in the Transverse Ranges that the PCT crosses in southern California too and I had my first taste of the laborious and slow activity of postholing in the San Bernardino and San Gabriel ranges. I was clearly not going to make it through hundreds of miles of snowbound High Sierra like this so I bought some snowshoes and also teamed up with three other hikers for safety. Even with snowshoes and skis it took us 22 days to traverse the highest section.

With 23 days food plus snow and ice gear my pack weighed over 100lbs (45kg) when we set off. It must have been horrendous to carry yet I have no such memory. Instead, thinking of the High Sierra conjures up images of spectacular and beautiful mountains with lovely pristine natural conifer forests round their flanks and frozen lakes nestling below rocky ridges and jagged peaks. I remember wonderful camps on the edge of the forests and in remote corries with nothing but the wilderness all around. I remember climbing with crampons and ice axe up hard steep snow and staring down at more lakes, more forest, more mountains. On snowshoes I crossed dazzling white meadows and even forded open streams. Day after day this glory continued, the wild beauty seemingly endless and perfect. The wonder and adventure, the gloriousness of being in this snowy wilderness, has remained. Any pain I felt from the heavy pack is long forgotten and was well worth suffering.

Crossing the snow was arduous but not difficult or particularly risky until the thaw began and for six days in the backcountry of Yosemite the going was extremely tough and hazardous. Those days are probably the most dangerous backpacking I have ever done. Every creek was a deafening mass of white water. Some we crossed on precariously balanced logjams, others we forded roped together, struggling to keep our feet in the freezing, sometimes chest-deep waters. Surviving was enough, and my memories of this section are all of fear and relief. I can recall little of the landscape and my photographs of the mountains don't stir any thoughts.

After this excitement the snow-free walking in the gentler more rolling hills and dense forests of Northern California and Oregon was welcome. After 2,400 kilometres the PCT left California for Oregon, where the walking is perhaps the easiest of the whole route, with many level forest trails. The volcanic landscape was still impressive though: the pristine blue waters of Crater Lake; the spiky rock fangs of Mount Washington, Mount Thielsen and Three-Fingered Jack; the rippled peaks of the Three Sisters; and the bigger volcanoes of Mounts Jefferson and Hood, the former set in beautiful timberline meadows. Oregon ended with a descent to the Columbia River via spectacular Tunnel Falls where the trail is cut into the side of a gorge and passes behind a tremendous waterfall.

From the Columbia River the PCT enters Washington, the last and most rugged state. Fine grey dust coating the trail in southern Washington came from Mount St Helens, which had erupted two years previously. This is not a stable landscape. Beautiful Crater Lake lies in the caldera of a once-massive volcano that long ago blew itself away. One day Mounts Adam and Rainier will erupt again.

The PCT finishes with a flourish in the alpine North Cascades where it dives and swoops over steep ridges below a tangle of savage glacier-clad rock peaks. The climate is less dry than further south and I endured many rainy days and the first snow of winter. There were also glorious days in bright sunshine with open slopes red with autumn colours and the larches in the forests glowing gold. Rain and mist accompanied me on the final day and I reached Monument 78 marking the border with Canada in a storm.

I didn't mind. I'd been privileged to spend nearly six months backpacking through some of the most magnificent landscapes imaginable. I couldn't imagine a better way to spend the time. I still can't. Since the PCT I've hiked many trails in many places from Arctic Norway to the Himalaya, from the Yukon to Corsica, and all have been worthwhile in different ways, but none compare with the PCT for sheer magnificence over such a long distance. It really is the backpacker's ultimate trail.

The Continental Divide Trail

Watersheds have always fascinated me, whether little ones with the water running away into two different valleys or big ones dividing mountain ranges and countries. I really love the idea that two little rivulets starting close together can end up in different oceans. When I followed the watershed of the USA, the Continental Divide, from Canada to Mexico I was fascinated to discover that, for a short section, the trail followed a little creek along the watershed in the Teton Wilderness to a spot called the Parting of the Water. Here North Two Ocean Creek splits into Pacific Creek, which runs 2,177 kilometres to the

Pacific Ocean, and Atlantic Creek, which runs 5,613 km to the Atlantic Ocean. Standing by the creek high in this remote wilderness I watched the water divide, the place symbolising the complexity and structure of the landscape.

On the Continental Divide Trail (CDT) I also discovered that watersheds are nothing like straight lines. At one point in the Never Summer Wilderness in Northern Colorado I was walking north while following the watershed south as it makes a double hairpin bend here. That watersheds stay high and follow the crest of the land is a main reason they appeal to me. That they writhe and wriggle and don't follow obvious lines also appeals.

For 4,800 kilometres the CDT follows the watershed of the USA, down the Rocky Mountains from Canada to Mexico. The idea for a trail on or close to the Divide was developed in the 1960s and 1970s, primarily by a hiker called Jim Wolf, who founded the Continental Divide Trail Society and wrote the first guide books. Even today the trail is not complete, but when I hiked the trail in 1985 it was in its infancy. Guide books only existed for the northern half and even these gave only a suggested route. For the southern half I just had some sketchy ideas from Jim. With just four parties completing the Trail in the five years before my hike, it was a challenging venture. Much of the route I planned from maps, but adapted on the ground.

The Rocky Mountains are an overlapping series of different ranges rather than a single continuous whole. Indeed, in central Wyoming they fade away altogether, leaving a hot dusty desert basin to be crossed. The beauty of the mountains means that much of the route is in national parks and wilderness areas where the landscape is unspoiled. In the north, in Montana, Idaho and Wyoming,

116

there are few people and the CDT runs through some of the remotest country in the lower 48 states. Colorado is more populous but people disappear again in the southernmost state on the route, New Mexico.

I first heard about the CDT when hiking the Pacific Crest Trail and the idea of spending many months on another long trail in spectacular wilderness country immediately appealed, as did the idea of walking the watershed of the USA. As I'd walked from Mexico to Canada on the PCT walking back to Mexico on the CDT seemed the obvious thing to do. The length of the route and the height of the mountains meant snow would be encountered somewhere along the way. By starting in the north in late spring I hoped to have a snow free trip after the first month or so, even though I would encounter the highest terrain in the Colorado Rockies in autumn when it might be falling again, as indeed it did.

A companion from the PCT, Scott Steiner, accompanied me for the first 350 miles after which I hiked alone, meeting few others, sometimes no-one for many days at a time. Scott's company was welcome at the start as we tackled the snow and steep terrain of Glacier National Park and the Bob Marshall Wilderness. High avalanche danger and several fords of deep rivers made this a dangerous beginning and I was grateful to reach the stony slopes of the arid Scapegoat Wilderness. There are grizzly bears in these mountains and for half a day we followed fresh tracks in the snow, tracks that had started just a few hundred yards from our camp.

The trail through the Northern Rockies is a glorious procession of pristine forests and magnificent alpine mountains. The remote, little-known Bitterroot Mountains in Montana, where I often hiked cross country, still hang in my memory as tremendously wild and exciting. Completely different is the Yellowstone backcountry, away from the popular tourist spots, where quiet forest is punctuated by thermal basins with bubbling mud pots and splashing geysers.

The Northern Rockies terminate in the glorious Wind River Range, and here I abandoned the suggested route for a higher one that stayed above timberline, a wonderful walk below the dramatic summits past a series of beautiful alpine lakes.

The Great Divide Basin, which separates the Northern Rockies from the Colorado Rockies, is curious because water that runs into it does not run out again but disappears into the arid heart of this semi-desert. The Continental Divide splits and runs down each side of the basin.

For nine days I followed the eastern edge, a hot, dusty walk in flat sagebrush country that made me glad to reach the cool forests and the mountains of southern Wyoming and northern Colorado. Not many days back into the mountains and the snow began however, making the walk through the southern Rockies difficult and slow, especially as initially I was hiking in running shoes without ice axe, boots or gaiters. Even so the hike was spectacular, especially in the Front Range where I followed the Divide over the summits of many 12,000 and 13,000 foot (3,650-4,000m) mountains.

Blizzards and a ford of the Rio Grande saw me out of Colorado and into the lower, drier country of New Mexico. Here the Rockies dwindle away and the Divide makes its way across rocky mesas and stony deserts. Just north of the Mexican border I climbed into the frozen, icy Mogollon Mountains to stand on rocky summits and camp in high pine forests for the last time. My very last

118

night, though, was spent under the stars on the desert floor, a peaceful camp where an owl watched me from a yucca plant. At the border I remember touching the fence and pausing, sad that my adventure was over. I'd been in the wilds for 179 glorious days, my longest ever walk and an experience I have savoured ever since.

Walking the Munros and Tops

The Munros and Tops (separate 3,000 foot (914 metre) mountains and subsidiary summits as listed in *Munro's Tables*) have been part of my life since I climbed my first one in 1977. Quickly hooked I then undertook my first round of the Munros, which took five years and involved several long backpacking trips including two 800 km ones and the first two cross-Scotland TGO Challenge walks. Fifteen years after completing that round I set out on a continuous round of the Munros and Tops.

My inspiration for these walks came from *Hamish's Mountain Walk*, the story of Hamish Brown's 1974 continuous walk over all the Munros, the first time this had been done. I'd always intended following Hamish over the Munros, though not by his exact route as I wanted my walk to have some degree of uniqueness to make it interesting and unpredictable. Then I read in Andrew Dempster's 1995 book *The Munro Phenomenon* (it's really time for a revised edition) that although a dozen or so people had done continuous rounds of the Munros no-one had included the Tops as well. I had a goal and a challenge.

When I set out on this venture as well as the long Munros walks I had done six backpacking trips of over 1,000 miles (1,600km) so I was quite an experienced long distance walker. Even so I hadn't really grasped just what linking 517 summits in one walk would involve. My other 1,600 km plus walks had been linear , didn't include many summits and the routes could be varied to allow for stormy weather. The most Munros I'd climbed in one walk was 92 on an 800km 35 day trip from Corrour station in the Central Highlands to Ullapool in the Northern Highlands. That June walk was tough with clouds down on the tops on 23 days, though it rained only on eleven, but it was barely over a month long. With over four and a half times as many summits to climb, the Munros and Tops walk would be much longer. Including the Tops was to have more of an effect than I realised as they are often a fair distance from the parent Munro and many require out and back trips. Including them increased the interest and intensity of the walk along with the difficulty.

My planned route, which I mostly followed, looked like a child's scribble or a tangle of thread thrown on to the map as I joined up the 517 dots. The logic of a linear route from A to B was lost and during the walk I would head in every direction of the compass whilst slowly progressing northwards. Ben More on Mull was my first summit, chosen to get that awkward (in terms of a continuous round) island Munro out of the way, and Ben Hope in the far north my last. There were no options for taking easier routes in stormy weather or more direct routes if I was running out of time. Every one of those dots had to be visited.

On the 18th May I set off up Ben More on a bright cold day with a strong south-west wind. 118 days later on the 12th September I reached the summit of Ben Hope on a bright cold day with a strong north-west wind. In between I'd covered 1,770 miles (2,850km) and climbed 575,000 feet (175,250 metres). The weather had been mixed with rain on 64 days and cloud down on 174 summits. The longest period of sunny weather was just six days. Given the popularity of the Munros a surprise was the lack of people. I had 463 summits to myself, though I did meet people on the way up or down. This unexpected (and to me welcome) solitude was a result of this being a back-packing trip in the long daylight hours of summer. I was often on summits before day walkers had set out or long after they were off the hill.

The walk proved to be one of the most strenuous and challenging I've undertaken, even though it was in the accessible Scottish hills rather than the remote wilderness areas of North America. In the Highlands the difficulties came from rugged terrain and the weather rather than remoteness. Averaging 5,300 feet (1,650 metres) of ascent per day (leaving out my ten rest days) was far more than on any walk I had done before (or have done since). Having to reach summits even in strong winds and rain made for many arduous days, and camping was often a challenge as I searched for pitches that weren't too waterlogged or windswept at the end of long tiring days.

My recollections of the walk are not of aching legs, storm swept summits or disturbed nights though. These fade with time, leaving the high points, the bright moments, the great joys of a summer in the hills. With any long walk I find that many of the rewards come afterwards as the experience deepens and becomes part of me. To spend a summer in the mountains is a privilege I will never forget but there are specific memories that have become important. Some are fleeting momnents - the otter I watched by a burn in the woods above Loch Lomond, a brilliant sunset over Rannoch Moor. Others, such as the day I traversed the seventeen summits of the Mamores, are days when I just seemed to flow over the hills and it seemed to be so right, so natural, to be there.

Many camps, splendid and wild, hang in my memory too. Pitched not far from the summit of Glas Maol in the southern Cairngorms I watched mist fill Caenlochan Glen and send white tendrils crawling up the hillside towards me. Many weeks later I was camped near the lip of the Cadha Dearg between Eididh nan Clach Geala and Seana Bhraigh in the north-west Highlands watching the sun set over the Coigach hills. That's what the walk was really about.

An 800-km walk in the High Sierra

Yosemite Valley. Shining golden cliffs. Great waterfalls pouring from invisible heights. Tall pines. A winding placid river. Green meadows. Mule deer. Black bears. The spiritual home of John Muir. So far, so good, but also: roads, cars, buses, crowds, campgrounds, hotels, cabins, shops, restaurants, bars, visitor centres. The roar of engines, the smell of petroleum, the hustle and bustle of a busy holiday resort. Wilderness this isn't.

The first sight of the huge cliffs rising into the deep blue sky is always inspiring and exciting, but if you want to experience the real High Sierra you have to leave the valley floor and head into the forests and mountains.

The Sierra Nevada range stretches 650 km up the centre of California, a mountain barrier rising high above the desert lands of the Great Basin to the east. The highest peaks and most rugged terrain lie at the southern end of the range. For a distance of 150 km the main crest never drops below 3,350 metres. Unsurprisingly, no roads cross the mountains here. Indeed, south of Highway 120 in Yosemite National Park no roads cross the Sierra at all, leaving a vast wilderness made up of three national parks – Yosemite, Kings Canyon and Sequoia – and several designated wilderness areas including the John Muir and Ansel Adams Wildernesses. The range here is from 30 to 100 km wide with an abrupt escarpment on the east that drops precipitately to the wide semi-desert of Owens Valley. To the west the range gradually fades into wooded foothills.

The classic walk is the John Muir Trail (JMT), 340 glorious kilometres through the heart of the High Sierra. The JMT stays close to the crest of the mountains, often at or above timberline, winding across high passes and through lake-dotted rocky basins. It's undoubtedly one of the best and most challenging backpacking trails in the world. There are few resupply points and much of it is over 3,000 metres. Despite this it's very popular and in high summer you'll meet many people every day, and it is only one thin line threading its way through the wilderness. There is more, much more, to the Sierra.

After hiking through the High Sierra on snowshoes and crampons on the Pacific Crest Trail I felt I just had to return and in the following years made several two week trips: ski touring in the John Muir Wilderness and backpacking in Yosemite National Park. I still felt as though I'd only touched the edge of the wilderness though. Wanting to go more deeply into the nature of the High Sierra I decided to really see the area by making a roughly 800 km circuit starting and finishing in Yosemite Valley. *En route* I would visit some of the huge forests and deep canyons not seen on the Muir Trail or on my previous high mountain trips.

The aim of my walk was to experience everything the High Sierra had to offer, a rather ambitious undertaking but the area is conducive to bold thoughts. *Experience* was a key word too, not to 'complete a challenge' or to 'actually get anywhere'. That's why I planned a circular walk. I wanted literally to be going nowhere and to finish where I began to emphasise the experience rather than the statistics. I wanted to enter and feel part of the wilderness rather than treat it as the backdrop to a long walk in which completing the route was the most important factor. Speed and distance were irrelevant and I had only a rough plan, as I wanted to be free to explore as I chose and to take in all the different environments.

After spending half a day with the crowds climbing out of the Valley to see spectacular Nevada Falls I suddenly found myself alone. With the hordes and the manicured trails went the feeling of being held away from nature, of being an outside observer. Now I was following a narrow trail into a wooded valley with no signposts, guard rails, water stations, outhouses and the other paraphernalia of the managed outdoors.

That night I slept under the stars, as I would most nights to come. The only sound was the gentle trickling of a creek. A bright half-moon shone briefly before descending behind a wedge of trees so black it seemed to suck in the light. Above I could see stars through the foliage of a huge ponderosa pine. The night was calm and peaceful yet charged with an intense reality. Sierra Nevada is Spanish for Snowy Range, a name given by the first Spaniards to reach California and a name they gave to almost any snow-capped mountain range. I prefer John Muir's description – 'the range of light' – for the quality of the light in the Sierra does seem exceptional and somehow

124

sharper and with more variations over the course of a day than elsewhere.

On the first few days I was captivated by the way the rocks changed colour with the passing of the hours – black, dark grey, deep red, gold, pale yellow, cream then darkening back to black- and the way shafts of sunlight lit up the shaggy red bark of an incense cedar, the way the creeks sparkled as they slid over speckled granite. Streaked pink dawns expanded into deep blue skies, the white-hot sun pounding down hard, harsh and heavy then fading into a subtle red sunset before moonlight streaked through the trees illuminating almost colourless ghostly bushes and rocks.

There is a touch of the desert in the Sierra light, a touch of that uncompromising clarity and starkness that speaks of vast space and emptiness, of an inhuman beauty and power. It's a reminder that not far away lies the inhospitable stony wastes of Death Valley. It's only a touch of the desert though, tempered by the flowing creeks, the myriad lakes and, above all, the throbbing green life of the forests.

The highlight of those first days was the canyon of the North Fork of the San Joaquin River where the trail runs high above a tangle of cliffs, hollows and tree groves, a complex mosaic of wild nature. Far below, the river twisted through boulders, a streak of white, blue and grey, with the Ritter Range forming an impenetrable looking backdrop.

Red-tailed hawks – a close relative of the common buzzard – wheeled in the sunlight, their tails gleaming gold and red. High above them a larger raptor soared, a golden eagle.

The trail crossed the river below a group of Western Hemlock, delicate yet massive trees with lace-like foliage and distinctive drooped tops. A bridge spanned the river between two falls, the higher a perfect curtain falling, seemingly without movement, into a deep green pool, the lower a wild rush of white water twisting down a narrow rock chute. The banks were lined with magnificent conifers – stocky red-barked incense cedar, huge stately red fir, towering Jeffrey pine with cracked yellow-edged bark.

Glorious light, glorious colours, delicious water – it was magnificent and beautiful. Here, I felt, I had truly entered the wilderness. I knew now, already, that the walk was a success, and it took on a rhythm, a sequence that felt natural and inevitable, the rhythm of a journey in the wilds. A few times I dipped down to remote settlements to pick up supplies – Red's Meadow, Vermilion Valley Resort, Cedar Grove, Lodgepole then Vermilion and Red's Meadow again on the way back north plus, finally, Tuolumne Meadows. Of these Vermilion stood out as one of the most walker friendly places I've visited, with a free soft drink and a night in a tent cabin on offer to long distance backpackers. There's also the opportunity to scavenge through the 'hiker barrels', large metal tubs containing supplies abandoned or never collected by John Muir and Pacific Crest Trail hikers. None of these places interrupted the flow. I was never in any of them long enough to feel more than a touch of the outside world.

In places I followed the John Muir Trail and was amazed at the sudden increase in the number of walkers but also impressed by the sublime scenery, especially Evolution Basin with great rippling rock walls towering above the cold blue waters of a chain of lakes. I never felt lonely, the wilderness was more than enough to occupy and involve me.

The canyon of the Middle Fork Kings River was a wild

rock wasteland with a crashing raging creek calmed by intermittent cool green pools. Broken granite walls soared high above; the trail a narrow thread through the boulders and along cracked slabs. This exciting passage was followed by a slow calming ascent, 4,700 foot to Granite Pass. As I climbed I watched the trees change. Oak, incense cedar, ponderosa pine and great sugar pines with cones dripping with resin giving way to the dark mountain fir forest with massive red and white firs rising like temple columns. Then the gradual dominance of smaller lodgepole and western white pines and, finally, wind sculpted foxtail pines at timberline, seeming to almost crawl across the ground.

Once up, as so often on this walk, it was down again, down steeply into the great cleft of King's Canyon. During the 33 days I was in the wilderness I crossed 23 high passes, this constant rising and falling providing a three dimensional view of the landscape, a grasp of how it fitted together.

Staying mostly on the western side of the Sierra I progressed south to Giant Forest, named by John Muir for its groves of Giant Sequoias. Even when looking at them I found it hard to accept them as real. I had grown used to big trees on the walk but these were dwarfed by the Sequoias. The biggest of them all, dubbed General Sherman for this short period of its, so far, 3,500 year life, is probably the largest living thing in the world, weighing some 6,000 tons and being 272 feet (83m) tall and 36.5 feet (12m) thick at the base. The Sequoias are not just massive and ancient they are also beautiful, the fibrous bark glowing a soft rust red in the sunshine.

Walking, awe-struck, through the Sequoias I came upon a black bear, ambling round a corner. Trees forgotten I froze, as did the bear, momentarily, before it scrambled a few feet up the nearest tree, hung there a few seconds, slid back down and raced off into the undergrowth. I saw other bears during the walk, including one racing away with a food bag in its jaws chased by two semi-naked half-awake campers, but this was the only close encounter.

The superb High Sierra Trail, which runs for 115 km from Crescent Meadow near Giant Forest to Mount Whitney, the highest peak in the Sierra, took me south and east to the southernmost point of the walk, in the deep straight trench of Kern Canyon. Here I turned north, following the John Muir Trail over a series of high passes. The only storm of the walk hit on 3,650 metre Glen Pass, a narrow notch in a steep rocky wall, making for an exciting crossing. Suddenly rain and hail was bouncing off the rocks, visibility was down to a few yards and the wind threatened to blast me off the cliffs. For the next few days clouds swirled round the peaks although little rain fell.

By now I was hearing stories of a big forest fire in Palisade Valley. Notes from rangers started appearing, warning that the trail was closed. I made rather sketchy alternative plans but then met a ranger who told me that a fire crew was escorting hikers through the fire every morning, if it was safe.

Palisade Valley was wreathed in smoke and occasional bursts of flame shot into the sky as I descended to meet the fire crew. Johnny and Todd carried shovels and wore yellow fireproof jackets, hard hats and bulky belts hung with an array of heavy tools. I was escorted four miles through the smouldering forest, a surreal experience with a fire fighter immediately in front and behind me, the forest hazy and heavy with smoke, the air hot and strong with the smell of burning. The fire was being left untouched, the fire crew told me, they were there to monitor it and escort hikers. At one point we passed a blazing tree stump hanging over the trail.

Further north I left the JMT at times for higher diversions onto the rugged Mammoth Crest and the narrow rock ridge of Cloud's Rest, both giving superb views. From the latter you can look down on the curving summit of Half Dome, an unusual experience as this massive lump of rock is more usually viewed from the floor of Yosemite Valley. One night below Mammoth Crest I watched the sunset and saw the golden granite walls darken into impenetrable blackness as a bright sliver of moon rose into the star filled sky. It was nearly over, the Sierra wilderness had worked its spell again.

The Arizona Trail

The desire to go for a long walk in the desert Southwest of the USA had been with me many years. Partly it was the thought of sunny days with little rain that appealed but, on a deeper level, I'd been inspired by the writings of Colin Fletcher and Edward Abbey. Mainly though, it was because the desert remained an alien place that I didn't understand or even know how to understand. I'd walked through desert and semi-desert lands in southern California on the Pacific Crest and New Mexico on the Continental Divide, but these had been small parts of much bigger walks and I felt that, though I'd walked through the desert, I hadn't connected with it, hadn't felt any sort of rapport or closeness. Maybe I never would, but I felt that a walk with the desert at its heart was the most likely way to learn.

After a two-week venture into the Grand Canyon I

wanted to immerse myself in a desert landscape over a period of many weeks. From the North Rim I had looked south to the hazy, distant San Francisco Peaks. Walking to those summits was an appealing idea. Then I discovered the Arizona Trail, which not only linked the Canyon and the Peaks but also traversed a series of desert mountain ranges, the Sonoran Desert and the Grand Canyon itself. Even the names on the maps were exciting, redolent of the American Southwest and hot, dusty, desert landscapes. Back then the Arizona Trail was more of an idea than an actual path, which I also found attractive as it meant a more self-contained and adventurous walk than one along a well-signed, well-built trail. Also, it mostly runs through national forests, wilderness areas and national parks where the land is fairly pristine and there are few restrictions on walking and camping.

'Think water'. This short and pithy statement from an experienced desert hiker was the wisest advice I received before the walk. For safe desert walking it's essential to know how far it is to the next water source, how reliable that source is and how far it is to the next one should the first one fail. Planning water supplies well in advance is the key to a successful walk. If in doubt, carry extra. Planning on collecting water in the afternoon and having a dry camp before walking to the next source in the morning proved a good way of reducing how far I had to carry, and I often walked the last few hours carrying up to eight litres. A few times where water was really scarce I carried twelve litres all day and on one 60 km plus section of open, shadeless Sonoran Desert I put out two water caches.

I don't like knowing too much about new places I am going to walk through, preferring to learn about them when I'm there, entering with an open mind rather than preconceived views. So, although I read a little about the land, and somewhat more about the logistics of the walk, I started without much knowledge of what lay ahead. I shouldn't then have been too surprised at what I found, but I was.

Despite my intentions I did have one fixed idea, that the Arizona Trail was basically a walk in the desert. It isn't. Desert does feature large in the landscapes along the trail, but so do mountains, grasslands and, in particular, forests.

The first surprise came within hours of leaving the Mexican border when I found myself breaking trail through knee deep snow surrounded by tall conifers on Miller Peak in the Huachuca Mountains. At my first camp, at nearly 3,000 metres, I had to stamp out a platform and heap snow round the edges of my tarp to keep the cold wind out.

As I progressed north I slowly learnt the form of the land along the southern section of the trail. A series of small but steep mountain ranges - the Huachucas, Santa Ritas, Rincons, Santa Catalinas - rise abruptly from the desert. They are known as 'sky islands' and when they are seen from a distance, soaring above the pale desert, it's clear why. The route crosses each of these ranges, climbing through a series of different environments *en route* - Sonoran Desert up to 1,100 metres, semi-desert grasslands dotted with cacti and small shrubs between 1,100 and 1,600 metres, pinyon pine-juniper-oak forest between 1,600 and 2,200 metres, subalpine forest with tall pines and firs above 2,200m. Above 3,350 metres alpine tundra is found but only one small mountain range in the north of the state, the San Francisco Peaks, reaches this height. Elsewhere the mountain summits are densely forested and, as you ascend, the vegetation becomes thicker and taller and there are fewer views, a reverse of what is usual in other mountain regions.

It takes a while to realise that the most open landscapes and widespread views lie at the feet of the mountains not on their summits.

The easiest walking lies at the top and the bottom too. In the desert, plants are widely spaced due to the lack of water. On the summits, trails wind between tall conifers whose shade prevents much undergrowth. In between, bushes with long sharp thorns grab and catch your clothing (one is known as the 'wait-a-minute' bush) and tear bare skin. There are cacti too but these I found easier to avoid.

After 350 km of sky islands the mountains fade into a sixty-mile stretch of low, hot Sonoran desert. I'd been warned there was no water so I accepted the offer from Jim Martin of the Arizona Trail Association to drive me round the dirt roads of the area so I could cache some. I hiked this section with Jake Schas, the only other through-hiker I met on the trail, as we both had water cached at the same places. Although fairly flat the Sonoran Desert is fascinating for the wealth of cacti, including huge saguaros that can grow to 15 metres high, and the bird and animal life. The latter includes javelinas, a pig-like animal of which we saw several. Much of the walking was on dirt roads and we had to skirt round private ranches on a few occasions.

Ironically the Sonoran Desert crossing ends with the only serious river ford on the whole trail. The Gila River was deep, fast and muddy where we reached it, full of snowmelt from the far distant Black Range in New

Mexico, and it took an hour or so of searching before we found a wide section where the water rippled over rocks that looked safe to cross. Even so it was thigh-deep and powerful in the middle.

On the far side lay the White Canyon Wilderness, a wonderful desert landscape of red rock canyons and cliffs and a great contrast to the flat lands to the south. The scenery here is some of the most impressive on the trail and it was invigorating and inspiring to thread a way through the canyons and climb over rocky ridges and passes after the plod along the dirt roads.

This area is small though and we went through it in two days to the next supply town, Superior, where I went back to solo hiking. North of Superior lie two very rugged desert mountain ranges, the Superstition and Mazatzal Mountains, which are lower than those to the south but much larger in area so the trail stays high for longer. The scenery here was superb and the feeling of remoteness and solitude great but the walking was the toughest along the trail, both due to the rough steep terrain and the heat and lack of shade.

In the southern Mazatzals I had the hardest days of the whole walk on the approach to Four Peaks Mountain. Between the Superstitions and the Mazatzals the trail dips briefly back down to the Sonoran Desert at Roosevelt Lake. It then climbs steeply back up for some 2,000 metres with no water for about 36km. I started out carrying one and a half gallons of water, having already drunk as many soft drinks as I could in the store-cum-snack-bar at the lake. The sun was high and hot and the trail ran straight up a bare ridge with no shade anywhere. Even with my sun hat on and my umbrella up, I was soon overheating. The water went down alarmingly fast. Eventually trees started to appear; black skeletons as the whole mountainside had been burned. (I later learned the fire had been in 1996 and had burnt 60,000 acres). A sign warned of flash flood damage and sure enough the trail soon became washed out into deep V-shaped ravines or loose scree and earth slopes, making the going very difficult. A tangled mass of bushes, the first regrowth after the fire, added to the arduous nature of the climb. After 21km and 1200 metres of ascent I camped for the night with just one and a half quarts of water left.

When I left the next morning on the ascent of the 2,015 metre summit of Buckhorn Mountain I had just a pint. The climb was a desperately hot sweaty scrabble up steep, loose ground and through sharp spiny undergrowth that scratched my legs and tore at my clothes. It took one and a half-hours and a great deal of water loss. My mood was one of aggravation and worry when I reached the top but this was swept away as a magnificent bald eagle, its white head shining in the sunlight, flew over the ridge just 15 metres away.

From the summit the remnants of the trail were easier to follow as they ran along Buckhorn Ridge towards the impressive face of Four Peaks Mountain. Finally, late in the morning the trail improved and I speeded up and, soon afterwards, unexpectedly and wonderfully, found a tiny flowing creek, snowmelt from the north face of Four Peaks Mountain. The feeling of relief was enormous and the water tasted marvellous.

Beyond the Mazatzals the nature of the trail changes again as it reaches the Mogollon Rim, a long rocky escarpment that stretches for hundreds of kilometres across northern Arizona. The Rim is the southern edge of the vast Colorado Plateau, which stretches north into Utah. Most of the Plateau in Arizona is between 2,000 and 2,500 metres high and forested, mostly with Ponderosa Pine. With a good trail in the trees, little ascent and fewer views I sped through this area, soon reaching the town of Flagstaff and then the San Francisco Peaks, the highest in Arizona. These were still snow-covered and I abandoned my attempt to climb Mount Humphreys, the highest summit at 3,850 metres, when I reached 3,290 metre Fremont Saddle as the snow was deep and the slopes were getting steeper.

Further forest and open grassland walking led rapidly to the stupendous, awe-inspiring Grand Canyon. The trail crosses the Canyon by way of the popular Bright Angel and North Kaibab Trails. To camp in the Canyon a permit is required. Permits are limited and, unsurprisingly, those for campsites along the trans-canyon trails had long been taken. However, I was able to get a permit to camp along the Clear Creek Trail on the Tonto Platform on the north side of the Colorado River. This involved 500 extra metres of ascent and eight more km of distance but it meant I could camp alone and wake to the silence and glory of dawn in this magnificent place.

The 1,800-metre climb out of the Canyon through Bright Angel and Roaring Forks Canyons is long and steep but the overwhelming beauty and grandeur of the scenery makes every step worthwhile. On this crossing the hardest walking was on the more gentle trails at the bottom of the Canyon, as it was 35-38°C in the shade. In the late afternoon it became cooler.

Beyond the North Rim of the Grand Canyon the trail returns to the forest for the last 85 miles, finally leaving the trees as it descends into beautiful Coyote Canyon with the red rock cliffs of Coyote Buttes rising above, a superb finish to an excellent walk.

135

Did I learn about the desert? To some extent but, more, I learnt that convenient labels don't fit the ebb and flow of the natural world. Cacti and conifers grew together in places, ribbons of bright green deciduous trees traced the line of creeks while cacti rose from the arid slopes just above. The Arizona Trail passes through a wide variety of landscapes and habitats and it is fascinating to see how these merge into each other.

The Pacific Northwest Trail

The Northwest USA is a land of mountains and forest, a wild land where bears and wolves roam. Through this magnificent country a route threads its way from the Rocky Mountains to the Pacific Ocean, passing through three national parks and seven national forests along the way. The Pacific Northwest Trail is a 1,900 km mix of signed footpaths, abandoned old trails, dirt roads, animal tracks and cross-country hikes. Eventually a complete signposted trail may exist but it was a long way from that situation when I hiked the PNT in 2010, making it an adventure requiring route-finding skills and the ability to deal with difficult terrain. The PNT guidebook doesn't lay out a detailed route that is easy to follow but rather advice and suggestions. The author says conditions range from perfectly built and groomed paths to 'hellish jungles' and warns that 'you are going to have to work to enjoy the Pacific Northwest Trail', which is just the sort of challenge that appeals to me.

One of the newer long distance trails in the USA, the PNT was conceived in 1970 by hiker, conservationist and writer Ron Strickland. Since his initial exploration it has developed into today's network with new sections of trail being constructed every year. In 2009 the PNT became an official National Scenic Trail.

Ron's idea was for a trail running from the Continental Divide, the watershed of the USA, to the Pacific Ocean. As such the PNT begins on the Continental Divide in Glacier National Park in Montana, just south of the Canadian border. Having already walked south and north from this point on the Continental Divide Trail and my length of the Canadian Rockies walk the idea of beginning a third long walk and heading west from the same spot was really appealing. The route also crosses the northern end of the Pacific Crest Trail (and in fact follows it for a short distance) in the Pasayten Wilderness in the North Cascades and the idea of linking that trail with the Continental Divide Trail was also attractive.

I planned on starting the trail in early July, when the snow should have mostly gone. I began the Continental Divide Trail in late May and struggled through deep unstable snow in Glacier National Park. This time travel should be much easier, there was more likelihood of sunnier weather and I hoped to fully appreciate the glorious mountains of Glacier National Park. The autumn weather in the North Cascades on the Pacific Crest Trail had also been stormy. This time I'd be there in summer.

Between the Rockies and the North Cascades the PNT runs through the Purcell and Selkirk Mountains, the Kettle River Range and the more arid sagebrush country of the Okanogan in the states of Montana, Idaho and Washington. From the Cascades the trail descends to sea level at Samish Bay to the east of Vancouver Island and then follows the coast round to the Olympic Mountains before crossing this range to the shores of the Pacific Ocean and Cape Alava, the westernmost point in the 48 contiguous states.

Neither the start or finish of the trail are actually accessible by vehicle so any hike of the PNT involves extra mileage at both ends, though it's only 6 km from Cape Alava to the nearest road. The start is in remote wilderness however and it takes a day and half over a high mountain pass just to reach it.

As well as dealing with complex route finding and difficult rough terrain hiking the PNT also involves much ascent, with altitudes ranging from sea level to nearly 2,500 metres. The terrain is mostly forest and mountain, with some coastal and more open drier sagebrush landscapes. . Temperatures can range from below freezing in the mountains to over 35°C in the Okanogon country so it's necessary to be able to deal with these extremes. Rain is likely, especially in the Olympic Mountains, which records the highest rainfall in the continental USA and where there are rain forests, and snow is possible in the highest areas of the Rockies and North Cascades while in the Okanogon and the east side of the Olympics hot dry weather is likely.

Creating a long distance trail like the Pacific Northwest requires a phenomenal amount of work, energy and commitment. Routes have to be explored, trails constructed, signs erected, information provided and amenities checked (natural campsites, water sources, viewpoints). The volunteers of the Pacific Northwest Trail Association, founded in 1977, have spent thousands of hours on this work. Without them there would be no trail so every backpacker who loves long walks in wild country owes them gratitude. Providing a trail for walkers is only a starting point however. The real value of long distance trails is in the protection they give to the landscape through which they pass. As Ron Strickland says at the end of his guidebook to the trail 'saving it for others is the ultimate challenge'.

I successfully completed the Pacific Northwest Trail in 2010 and described the walk in my book Grizzly Bears and Razor Clams.

139

5

●

VISIONARIES OF THE WILD

In his classic book *Desert Solitaire*, Edward Abbey writes that the earth is 'the only paradise we ever need if only we had eyes to see'. As well as the outdoors we can find those eyes in the words of writers on wilderness and landscape, including Abbey himself. These 'visionaries of the wild' are walkers, climbers, thinkers and philosophers who set out to inspire and educate with their love of the wild, and who, to a great extent, have built our view of the nature and value of landscape and wild places. I've been inspired by these writers for many years and re-read their works regularly, often lying in a tent or under the stars far from the noise of roads and the bright lights of the city.

Writings on wilderness go back thousands of years but our modern visionaries really begin around two hundred years ago with the Romantic Poets, especially Wordsworth, who greatly shaped the way we see the landscape of the Lake District. British poets continued to write about landscape, Ted Hughes being the best late twentieth century example, and it appears as a backdrop in many novels. Direct, non-fiction British writings on wild landscapes are rare though, and it is to the USA we have to look to find a tradition of wilderness writing

The first major literary figure in this movement for

wilderness is Henry David Thoreau in the mid-nineteenth century, living and writing beside Walden Pond in Massachusetts and exploring the forests and rivers of the North-Eastern States. Thoreau put forward the idea that 'it would be well perhaps if we were to spend more of our days and nights without any obstruction between us and the celestial bodies' and, most famously, 'in Wildness is the preservation of the world'. Thoreau saw human beings as part of nature, not apart from it, and wilderness as having great value to humans. It was the beginning of a revolution in thinking about wild places.

Although most noted for his contemplative sojourn at Walden Pond Thoreau also saw the value of walking. Indeed, in his essay entitled *Walking*, he wrote 'I think that I cannot preserve my health and spirits, unless I spend four hours a day at least--and it is commonly more than that--sauntering through the woods and over the hills and fields, absolutely free from all worldly engagements'.

Six years after Thoreau died in 1862 John Muir, an immigrant from Scotland, arrived in the Sierra Nevada mountains of California, a seminal event in the history of landscape and wilderness preservation. Whilst Thoreau had bemoaned the destruction of nature he did little to prevent it. Muir however used the power of words to describe, praise and defend the great landscapes of the Western USA, especially the Sierra Nevada.

Muir was a long distance walker who walked a thousand miles from Indianapolis to the Gulf of Mexico by the 'wildest, leafiest, and least trodden way', a mountaineer who made many first ascents in the Sierra Nevada, a scientist who showed that glaciers had carved the landscape of the Sierra Nevada and a campaigner who founded the Sierra Club and wrote articles that led to the creation of

Yosemite National Park. He also wrote a vast number of books and articles from which many quotations are regularly pulled, perhaps most often, 'do something for wildness and make the mountains glad'.

Muir revelled in every aspect of wilderness, climbing trees in storms to experience them swaying from side to side, edging to the brink of waterfalls to feel the shaking of the ground and the roar of the water, and sleeping out on snowy mountain sides with just a coat to cover him. One of my favourite quotes, which I try to remember as more rain sweeps across the Highlands, is 'when I heard the storm and looked out I made haste to join it; for many of Nature's finest lessons are to be found in her storms, and if careful to keep in right relations with them, we may go safely abroad with them, rejoicing in the grandeur and beauty of their works and ways'.

After Muir a succession of American writers wrote in praise of wilderness, the most significant of which in the first half of the twentieth century was Aldo Leopold, an ecologist and forester and founder of The Wilderness Society. Leopold developed the ideas of an 'ecological conscience' and a 'land ethic', major parts of current environmental thinking, writing that 'conservation is a state of harmony between men and land' and *'we abuse land because we regard it as a commodity belonging to us. When we see land as a community to which we belong, we may begin to use it with love and respect'.*

Leopold saw wild land as being necessary for human beings saying 'wilderness areas are first of all a series of sanctuaries for the primitive arts of wilderness travel, especially canoeing and packing' in his classic book *A Sand County Almanac*.

At the same time as Leopold was writing, a Scottish

climber by the name of W. H. Murray was writing an equally important book called *Mountaineering in Scotland,* a book written twice in prisoner-of-war camps, the first version being destroyed by guards. Through the 1930s Murray had made many first ascents on rock and ice in the Scottish Highlands and was one of the premier mountaineers of the time. However, his climbing came out of a joy in wildness and his book is packed with wonderful descriptions of the mountains and the effect they had on him.

After a night-time winter ascent of Buachaille Etive Mor he wrote: 'We had set out in search of adventure; and we had found beauty. Thus we had found both in their fuller sense; for in the architecture of hill and sky, as in great art and music, there is an everlasting harmony with which our own being had this night been made one. What more may we fairly ask of mountains?' Realising that his beloved Highlands were threatened by development Murray became an active conservation campaigner, his greatest victory, for which we should be very thankful, being the prevention of a hydro-electric scheme in Glen Nevis. Of industrial developments in the Highlands he wrote in *Scotland's Mountains* that 'they could invariably be sited elsewhere than the regions of outstanding landscape quality; sometimes at a greater cost in money, which civilized man should be prepared to pay' and lamented that 'to find a wholly wild scene, unmarked by man's building, one has to go ever farther into the hills'. That is even truer today.

Much of Murray's prose is evocative, romantic and emotional. In this he is more in accord with American wilderness writers such as John Muir or Edward Abbey than most British outdoor writers. And here I think lies one reason for the lack of passion about wild land, the lack of a tradition of landscape writing. British writers tend to be more detached, more cool about their subjects, more reticent about their feelings, which results in work that may be descriptive and informative but which isn't inspiring or visionary, which lacks intensity. British writers can be divided, crudely, into two camps: nature writers and adventure writers. The former give intricate accounts of plants and wildlife, the latter factual descriptions of climbs and long walks. Neither usually presents a vision of wildness. Some nature writers, like Gavin Maxwell, approach this but none succeed like Murray or the Americans. Adventure writers still tend towards the cliché of the stiff-upper lip, eschewing feelings towards beauty or the wonder of wild places.

In the USA the 1960s saw the emergence of two very different writers who have been a major influence on wilderness thinking and wilderness travel, Colin Fletcher and Edward Abbey. Fletcher is the walkers' writer, the backpacker who wrote about walking 1,000 miles through desert and mountain in California and, for two months, solo along the Grand Canyon. No one has captured the spirit of what it is like to walk and camp in a wild landscape better than Colin Fletcher. Here he is on his 1,000 mile walk: 'High above the West Walker River, I climbed the final snowbank into a 10,000 foot pass ... Beyond the snowbank the mountainside dropped away again. And there below me lay the valley of the Silver King. Timbered slopes plunged down to a twisting V that held the creek. Two miles downstream, a meadow showed emerald green. Beyond, peak after Sierra peak stretched away northward to the horizon. There was no sign that man's hand had touched a single leaf or a single blade of grass.'

Whilst not a major campaigner Fletcher does make it clear that we have a responsibility to preserve wilderness. At the time he walked through the Grand Canyon this amazing cleft in the earth was threatened with being dammed and flooded. Horrified by this Fletcher wrote that it was 'vandalism' and that we had 'to shield from the blind fury of material 'progress' a work of time that is unique on the surface of our earth', finishing 'and we shall be judged you and I, by what we did or failed to do.'

Fletcher's account of his walk through the Grand Canyon, *The Man Who Walked Through Time,* was published in the same year as another book that was to have repercussions for decades to come and introduce the world to the iconoclastic, controversial and distinctive voice of Edward Abbey, *Desert Solitaire.* For the next 21 years until his death in 1989, Abbey was to be a provocative and challenging writer on wilderness and many other topics. Abbey's love was for the deserts of the South-West USA where he walked, camped and paddled down rivers. His view of wilderness was that it was essential for human sanity and that preserving it came before anything else, writing 'I come more and more to the conclusion that wilderness, in America or anywhere else, is the only thing left that is worth saving', and 'Wilderness is not a luxury but a necessity of the human spirit.'

Fond of disappearing into the desert for days or weeks Abbey noted that 'a journey into the wilderness is the freest, cheapest, most non-privileged of pleasures. Anyone with two legs and the price of a pair of army surplus combat boots may enter'.

Having regretted the lack of a British tradition of writing about wild land and landscape I have been delighted with the work of Robert Macfarlane. In his book *The Wild*

Places Macfarlane explores the idea of the wild through wild places, large and small, in Britain. Macfarlane walked and slept in his wild places and at times his writing has the same intensity and power as Murray, Fletcher or Abbey. Of a camp on a November walk across Rannoch Moor he writes 'we stopped there, for dusk was spreading over the Moor, and pitched a small tent. We lay talking in the dusk: about the ground we had covered, the ground still to go, about the odd mixture of apprehension and awe that the Moor provoked in us both. Our sleeping-place was cupped in a curve of the river, on a miniature flood-plain that the winter spates had carved out and flattened: a shelter in the middle of the Moor's great space'.

Macfarlane ends his book with the important insight for our small, crowded island that wild places don't have to be vast and that small pockets of wildness exist almost everywhere – 'there was as much to be learned in an acre of woodland on a city's fringe as on the shattered summit of Ben Hope'. And that whilst wild places are under 'multiple and severe threats', these are temporary in the history of our planet and the wild will return – 'the ivy will snake back and unrig our flats and terraces' – an image that reminded me of The Handsome Family's wonderful song *Peace In The Valley Again*, which contains the lines:

> Empty shelves will swarm with bees,
> cash machines will sprout weeds,
> lizards will crawl through the parking lot
> as birds fly around empty shops.

Somehow I find these sentiments comforting and optimistic, and I am sure that Edward Abbey would agree.

Visionary writers on the wild are important, especially

when we are far from wild places, both physically and spiritually. Read these authors, relish their words, turn over their ideas in your mind, let their visions inspire you. But above all go out into the wild and let it envelop you as it did them.

Discovering John Muir

2014 was the centenary of the death of John Muir, arguably the most influential defender of wild places ever and whose legacy is still relevant and important today. Born in Dunbar in Scotland, Muir emigrated to the USA when he was eleven and lived there for the rest of his life. In America he is regarded as the 'father of National Parks'. The Sierra Club, which he founded in 1892, is one of the USA's leading conservation organisations and does much to keep his memory alive. Scotland is slowly catching up with John Muir's Birthplace, a statue of the young Muir and the John Muir Country Park in Dunbar plus the 215 kilometre John Muir Way across the Central Lowlands. And, of course, the John Muir Trust, founded in 1983 to campaign for wild land.

I discovered Muir many years ago, not with a sudden revelation but slowly, as I came across the name every so often. I didn't really pay him much attention though until I hiked the Pacific Crest Trail and found his name recurring again and again in the High Sierra

From signs and leaflets and talking to other hikers I began to learn a little about the man. A few years later I came across a second-hand copy of *The Mountains of California* (books by Muir were hard to find in the 1980s) and began to read him in his own words. Immediately I was taken with his passion and devotion to nature. I went on to read his other works, some several times. The language can be flowery for modern tastes but his eye for detail and his love of everything natural shines through. I also read books about Muir, wanting to know more about this iconic figure. I think the best of these is Michael P. Cohen's *The Pathless Way: John Muir and American Wilderness*, which goes more deeply into Muir's dilemmas and contradictions than other biographies.

Muir is to be admired not just as a conservationist, not just for his love of nature, key though these are to his greatness, but also for his outdoor adventures and experiences. Long before any of the equipment we take for granted, or guidebooks, maps and paths, Muir would head off into the wilderness on long solo treks. From a boy scrambling on the cliffs and castle walls of Dunbar to the adult mountaineer making a daring first ascent of remote Mount Ritter in the High Sierra, described superbly in *The Mountains of California*, he revelled in exploring wild places. He walked long distances as well, *A Thousand-Mile Walk To The Gulf* describes his journey from Indianapolis to the Gulf of Mexico in 1867. When he arrived in California he walked from San Francisco to Yosemite Valley. There followed many trips into the then little-known Sierra Nevada and in later years further afield, especially Alaska (as told in *Travels in Alaska*).

He was not just concerned for the conservation of wilderness for its own sake and the sake of the animals and plants that lived there. He was also concerned for the sake of humanity. Not being a conservationist who wanted to exclude people he wanted to share his joy in nature with everyone. He led trips for the Sierra Club and his writing was aimed at encouraging people to visit wild places as well as calling for their protection. He wrote in

The Yosemite, 'Everybody needs beauty as well as bread, places to play in and pray in, where nature may heal and give strength to body and soul alike' and in *Our National Parks*, a book intended to encourage visitors to the parks, 'Thousands of tired, nerve-shaken, over-civilized people are beginning to find out that going to the mountains is going home; that wildness is a necessity; and that mountain parks and reservations are useful not only as fountains of timber and irrigating rivers, but as fountains of life.'

John Muir's vision of the necessity of wildness and nature is as valid now as it was 100 years ago, maybe more so.

Tracking the spirit of John Muir

'We are all, in some sense, mountaineers, and going to the mountains is going home.' John Muir

Muir Station Road. Best Western John Muir Inn. Muir Family Dentistry. Muir Lodge Motel. John Muir Medical Center. John Muir Elementary School. Muir Heritage Land Trust. Muir Station Shopping Center. Spend much time in the small town of Martinez (population 37,000) in western California and it's hard to avoid the name of John Muir, though the use of it seems to have little to do with the great conservationist.

The reason for the rash of Muir names is because Martinez is where Muir lived for the last 34 years of his life, 24 of them in a rather grand house built by his father-in-law and now the centrepiece of the John Muir National Historic Site. The house gives interesting insights into Muir but there's not much feel of his presence and what little there is suggests a desire to be elsewhere, in the wilderness. His bedroom lacks curtains, as he wanted to be woken by the rising sun, and a downstairs parlour has a massive fireplace, put in by Muir after the original one was damaged in the 1906 San Francisco earthquake, so he could have a 'real mountain campfire'.

His study is scattered with books and papers and it is easy to imagine him sitting here writing about the mountains and forests, his mind and spirit far away in what he regarded as his true home.

From Martinez I travelled to Yosemite Valley, where he lived from 1868 to 1873, and which lies at the heart of his inspiration and philosophy. 'Incomparable', he called it. Whilst the Valley is beautiful and inspiring it's also a holiday resort, crammed with cars, coaches, campgrounds, cabins, cafes, visitor centres, shops, hotels and hordes of people. The sandy banks of the Merced River look like a seaside beach in summer. Yet somehow the grandeur overcomes all this, the beautiful trees, the magnificent rock walls, the feeling of harmony dominates the works of humankind and makes them seem small and transitory.

It was like this in Muir's day too, when Yosemite was already a popular tourist destination and he wrote 'the tide of visitors will float slowly about the bottom of the valley as a harmless scum, collecting in hotel and saloon eddies, leaving the rocks and falls eloquent as ever and instinct with imperishable beauty and greatness'. Walking round the Valley in the evening on quiet trails away from the crowds and looking up at the massive rock face of Half Dome I shared the wonder and inspiration he felt.

Beyond Yosemite Valley lies the vast High Sierra, Muir's 'the range of light' which he spent many years studying and exploring, discovering the evidence that the glorious landscape was created by glaciers and making many first ascents. Now a large swathe of the Sierra bears his name as the John Muir Wilderness and the magnificent John Muir Trail threads a way through the places he loved. There's a Muir Pass, Muir Gorge, Muir Lake, Muir Grove and Mount Muir too as well as lakes named after his daughters, Wanda and Helen. These names seem appropriate here, unlike those in Martinez. This is the land that inspired Muir and that he knew intimately, describing it in detail in many books and articles. If his spirit is to be found anywhere it is in the Sierra wilderness.

Leaving Yosemite Valley I spent five weeks exploring the High Sierra, without once crossing a road, though I did dip down to remote resorts to resupply. Like Muir I slept out under the stars most nights and appreciated daily why he wrote 'How glorious a greeting the sun gives the mountains! To behold this alone is worth the pains of any excursion a thousand times over'. I visited the deep trench of King's Canyon, where Muir gave talks to Sierra Club members, and Giant Forest, named by him for the Giant Sequoias, which he called 'Nature's forest masterpieces'. These trees are so massive – the largest living things – that I found it hard to believe in them even while looking at them.

Travelling from the depths of the canyons and forests to the high passes and the mountain summits I found it easy to understand his feeling for this land. His words meant so much more to me once I had walked in his footsteps.

Whilst John Muir's spirit can be found in the High Sierra it can also be found in wild places everywhere and also, and importantly, wherever people fight for nature and wildness and are prepared to speak out against those whom he described as 'temple destroyers, devotees of ravaging commercialism, (who) seem to have a perfect contempt for Nature, and, instead of lifting their eyes to the God of the mountains, lift them to the Almighty Dollar'.

His legacy is found in the John Muir Trust, the Sierra Club and other wilderness conservation organisations as well as in the mountains and forests of the Sierra Nevada. However while continuing John Muir's campaigns for nature we shouldn't forget his advice to 'keep close to Nature's heart... and break clear away, once in awhile, and climb a mountain or spend a week in the woods. Wash your spirit clean'. Renewing our inspiration is important.

Colin Fletcher: the man who walked through time

'I stood for a while looking at the mountains and listening to the silence. Then I walked slowly out into the desert that for six hundred miles would be my world'. Colin Fletcher, *The Thousand-Mile Summer*

Few people in Britain have heard of Colin Fletcher, yet he is in my opinion the finest of all writers on backpacking and wilderness walking. Every time I read the words above a shiver runs through me as I know I am at the start of a literary adventure. Although living in California for half a century Colin Fletcher, who died in June 2007, was British, born in Wales in 1922. Fletcher inspired thousands of American backpackers and an appreciation of his work in Britain is long overdue.

Before reaching California and the start of his writing life Fletcher served in the Royal Marines in World War Two, then farmed and built roads in East Africa before working as a prospector and road builder in Canada. Shortly after moving to California from Canada in 1956 he decided 'that what I wanted most in life just then was to walk from one end of California to the other ... I knew, of course, that the idea was crazy; but I felt almost sure I was going'. And go he did, within a month, on a journey that resulted in his first book, *The Thousand-Mile Summer*, which captures superbly the nature of wilderness walking and camping.

I have to admit to a bias here as this book changed my life. I first read it in the late 1970s and it had a profound and inspiring effect on me. Fletcher's descriptions of the deserts and mountains, of walking through real wilderness and camping under the stars started in me a hunger to do the same and resulted in my walking the Pacific Crest Trail and long distance walking becoming my passion and my life.

Many people have written about long walks and backpacking but none have captured the experience so fully, intensely and personally as Colin Fletcher. He walked alone, and indeed shunned the company of others, coming across as quite a curmudgeon in some of his writing, but what he sought was 'the gigantic, enveloping, including, renewing solitude of wild and silent places' (*The Complete Walker*). His books are mostly about nature and his thoughts and feelings rather than about groups or other people. Indeed, he says little about his private life or relationships outside of his journeys. But the reader learns much about his relationship to nature and wilderness. Here he is describing dusk in the California desert after going down to a lagoon to wash:

'I stood still, waiting for the light to go out over the mountains.

'But the mountains were not yet ready. A line of golden peaks caught fire. Black canyons gouged their slopes and pierced the iridescent red with deeper hints of hell. The iridescence deepened, the hints broadened. And then – on

153

the very threshold of revelation – the shadow reached out and quietened everything, and the world was only shades of grey.

'I found myself shivering on the edge of the lagoon, still clutching a cake of soap'. *The Thousand-Mile Summer*

Colin Fletcher wasn't bothered about distance or speed. His concern was with experience. Camping was just as important to him as walking and he described many camps with a loving detail that every backpacker will recognise. Perhaps the book that describes this best, along with the intensity of feeling his walking engenders, is *The Man Who Walked Through Time*, which describes his walk the length of the Grand Canyon, the first time it had been done. Fletcher gives a long description of his first camp on that walk, covering every detail, even down to where he places every item. Here is a sample:

'I unzippered the mummy bag part way, pushed my feet down into it, pulled the bag up loosely round my waist, and leaned back. It was very comfortable like that, with my butt cushioned on the pillow of the air mattress and my back leaning against the fully inflated main section, which in turn leaned against the now almost empty pack. I sat there for several minutes, content, relaxed, drifting – hovering on the brink of daydreams without ever achieving anything quite so active'.

Doesn't that just make you want to be out in the wilds sitting there almost daydreaming?

Fletcher's best known book is *The Complete Walker*, which has gone through four editions (though the last one with a co-writer. I recommend one of the earlier editions for the full Fletcher approach and the pleasure of his delightful prose). Subtitled 'the joys and techniques of hiking and backpacking' this is the most detailed and

the most readable guide imaginable. Fletcher covers everything entertainingly and, in places, with humour. It's a
very personal book, describing what he did and what he
used, with the idea that others can learn from this. The
detailed descriptions of equipment are now out of date
but this doesn't matter. They are only examples and it's
the overall approach to walking and camping that matters.
This timelessness is also why *The Thousand Mile Summer*
and *The Man Who Walked Through Time* are fresh and
relevant many decades after they were written.

Throughout his work there is a deep respect and love
for nature and a strong desire for it to be protected. He's
not an out and out campaigner like that other great writer
of the desert Southwest, Edward Abbey, though *The
Man Who Walked Through Time* does contain a moving
epilogue about the threats to dam the Grand Canyon in
the 1960s. Fletcher warned that 'unless we do something,
you and I, we may soon find this book has become a
requiem for Grand Canyon'. The depth of his feeling is
shown when he writes 'I suggest that we little men have
no damned right even to consider such vandalism – for
any reason at all'.

The same feelings surface in *The Secret Worlds of Colin
Fletcher*, a collection of essays on different walks. In the
chapter entitled 'Among The Redwoods' in which he is
horrified by the destruction of ancient redwood groves
and writes of the logging of old growth forests that it 'left
you ashamed ... of belonging to a species that for personal
gain waged war on its own planet.'

The four books I've referred to above are the key works
for walkers interested in Colin Fletcher. Perhaps the most
interesting of his other works is *River*, which tells the
story of his trip, mostly by raft, down the length of the

Colorado River at the age of 67 in 1989, another first, in which his journey also stands for his journey through life. The book contains one of my favourite Colin Fletcher quotations:

'I knew, deep and safe, beyond mere intellect, that there is nothing like a wilderness journey for rekindling the fires of life'.

His final two books, *The Winds of Mara* and *The Man From The Cave*, are both quite obscure and long out of print. Devotee that I am, I hunted them down in second-hand book shops on visits to the USA long before the Internet made finding such books easy. *The Winds of Mara* describes a return visit to Kenya on which he camped, with a vehicle, in the bush. He describes well the wildlife and the landscape and his interactions with people but it lacks some of the drive of his wilderness journey books. *The Man From The Cave* is a real oddity, a fascinating book that tells you more about its author than its subject. Fletcher discovers a cave in a remote part of the Nevada desert with some old possessions that showed someone had once lived there. The book is the story of his research into who the person was and why they were there.

Colin Fletcher writes mainly about the Southwest USA. His heart lies with the Colorado River and the surrounding landscape, but don't let this put you off reading him. His backpacking tales are about the experience as much or more than the place and thus of interest to all who love walking and camping in the wild, whether the Scottish Highlands or the Grand Canyon. Be warned though the books might just stir a desire in you to go and walk in Fletcher's country, as they did in me.

6

PERCEPTIONS OF WILDNESS

A wide belt of Corsican pines runs along the coast at Formby in Lancashire. These were the first large woods I ever saw as a child; mysterious and inviting and promising excitement and adventure. Beyond the pinewoods lay marshes and then sand dunes - the highest hills I knew for many years - and finally the sea. Wandering this landscape I discovered the joys of exploration, solitude and nature. To me it was wild and vast. As a child the concept of wilderness didn't really exist. I just accepted what was there and assumed it was as it should be and always had been.

As a teenager I discovered, via school trips, Snowdonia, the Lake District and the Peak District. These national parks were a real revelation. The mountains seemed huge, the wildness almost infinite. Although I read natural history books I didn't grasp anything about ecology or natural systems. I wanted to identify what I saw but didn't understand how little I knew about how it all related. It didn't occur to me that these wild mountains could be anything other than natural and untouched. I saw sheep - plenty of sheep - but had no idea of the effect they had.

Once I'd discovered the hills my outdoor desires changed from woodland exploration and bird watching

157

to climbing to the summits and striding out along the ridges. I discovered wild camping and started carrying a tent into the hills, revelling in nights out in the silence and splendour of the mountains.

My second revelation came with my first visit to the Scottish Highlands. I wandered up onto the Cairngorm Plateau and stood there amazed at the scale of the landscape. I can still remember the sense of shock. I didn't know anywhere this big existed. All those hills to climb! All those wild places to camp! Suddenly the English and Welsh hills didn't seem so big after all. I set out to climb all the Munros in what I again assumed was a pristine wilderness. I read Fraser Darling and Morton Boyd's *The Highlands and Islands* to learn about the natural history of my new favourite place, but the words about deforestation and the degrading of much of the landscape didn't sink in. I didn't 'see' it when I was in the hills. The bare glens looked natural so I thought they were.

A change in my thinking came not in the Scottish hills but in the High Sierra. Here, in John Muir's heartland, I discovered real forests and real wilderness when hiking the Pacific Crest Trail. Already impressed by the small transverse ranges and the deserts of Southern California I was now faced with hundreds of miles of roadless wilderness. The rugged alpine mountains were magnificent but it was the forests that really impressed themselves on my mind. Many of the individual trees were magnificent but it was the extent and naturalness of the forest as a whole that most affected me as the trail rose and fell, climbing high above timberline and then dipping down into dense forest.

Timberline! There was a new and magic word. I fell in love with timberline, with that band between the bare mountains and the forest where the trees grew smaller and more widely spaced until they faded away completely. I noticed how timberline varied with the aspect of the hills - higher on the warm southern slopes, lower on the colder northern ones. No straight lines here.

The forests continued all the way to Canada. I had never spent so much time in the woods. Back home after the walk I missed the trees and started to wonder why our forests were so small or else were block plantations that didn't look or feel like the woods of the High Sierra and the Cascade mountains. The Pacific Crest Trail had changed me. I started to think about the tree stumps I saw sticking out of the peat in those bare Scottish glens. I started to wonder why in so many places the only trees were on steep slopes in ravines or on islands in lochs. I noticed the lack of a timberline like that in the High Sierra. Once I started to ask these questions the answers appeared quite quickly and I began to properly understand the concepts of deforestation and overgrazing. I didn't though, think that anything could be done about it and my growing interest in protecting the hills was still solely about preservation. Restoration was a concept still to come.

My second American long walk, down the Rocky Mountains from Canada to Mexico on the Continental Divide Trail, reinforced my love of big forests and big wilderness. I was reading conservation writers now - John Muir, Edward Abbey, W. H. Murray - and thinking about their words. In the USA I read about restoration projects in wild areas. Back home developments in Scotland helped my thinking develop. The year I hiked the Pacific Crest Trail the Scottish Wild Land Group was founded, a year later the John Muir Trust came into being. I joined both. The year after I hiked the

Continental Divide Trail the then Nature Conservancy Council bought the Creag Meagaidh estate and began the process of forest restoration by reducing grazing pressure. The forest could return.

My eyes open I could no longer walk the bare Scottish glens without thinking of the forest that should and could be there. Sometimes I regret this. It was nice being innocent and thinking this an unspoilt wilderness. More often I look for any signs of recovery and relish them when I see them, whether it's a single sapling poking through the heather or a fenced enclosure of planted native trees intended to create a natural forest. Overall I prefer not to have fences or planting but if they are the only option I don't object. Eventually I moved to the Cairngorms, to the area where there is the largest extent of wild forest remaining, and one of my greatest joys is to see this forest regenerating and spreading.

I still return to North America every so often to experience again the vast wilderness areas. Each time I see these glorious forests I think that with will, determination and effort Scotland's wild areas could be so much more natural and wooded.

Backpacking and wilderness

For me backpacking and wilderness go together. Backpacking is all about venturing deep into wilderness and experiencing nature at its most pristine and perfect, but what exactly is wilderness and how do you know when you are there? The answers may seem obvious but legislators and conservationists who have tried to define wilderness have found this surprisingly hard.

Generally the conclusion is that wilderness is land

without human habitations and little sign of human activity.

In the USA there are designated wilderness areas, deemed to fit the definition of the Wilderness Act: 'An area where the earth and its community of life are untrammelled by man, where man himself is a visitor who does not remain'.

As there is little land "untrammelled by man" (and what a lovely word untrammelled is) in the UK we prefer to talk about wild land rather than wilderness though the distinction is unclear.

According to the John Muir Trust wild land is 'uninhabited land containing minimal evidence of human activity' while the National Trust for Scotland is rather more expansive, saying 'Wild Land in Scotland is relatively remote and inaccessible, not noticeably affected by contemporary human activity, and offers high-quality opportunities to escape from the pressures of everyday living and to find physical and spiritual refreshment'.

There is a problem with these definitions. They leave out large areas of Britain beloved by backpackers, including much of the Lake District, Snowdonia, Peak District and Yorkshire Dales, not to mention many coastal areas. Popular long distance paths like the Pennine Way, West Highland Way, Offa's Dyke and Cleveland Way don't run through much wild land by these criteria either. Yet surely they do. The land in these national parks and along these trails doesn't feel tame, which it must be if not wild, but feelings don't come into official designations. Camp high on Cross Fell on a night of storm and wind, with the clouds racing across the moon and heavy showers hammering on the tent, as I have, and tell me this is not a wild place.

Many years ago I came up with my own explanation of wilderness: 'If there is enough land to walk into, enough room to set up a camp and then walk on with that freedom that comes when you escape the constraints of modern living, then it is wilderness, in spirit if not by definition'.

For backpackers I think this still holds. Trying to classify wilderness precisely doesn't work, as it shouldn't. The wild cannot be contained, defined and corralled into a neat box. If it could it wouldn't be wild. As well as having a physical reality, wilderness is also an idea, a feeling, a set of concepts that come together to shout 'this is wild'. This idea is especially important in Western Europe where we do not have the huge areas of pristine land found in the Americas. Yet we do have many pockets of wildness that fit my description, places where you can feel you are far from civilisation even if it lies only a few miles away.

Camp deep in a wood with the only sounds those of wild life and the wind in the trees and you are in the wilds despite the nearby roads and villages. Climb into the Lakeland fells to camp by a high tarn and you are in a wild place though you could be back down in the pub in a few hours. The distance doesn't matter; it's the situation that says where you are. Strolling country lanes to camp on a crowded roadside campsite only touches the edge of the wild. Walk just a few miles on and camp in solitude beside a hill stream and you are part of it. In distance and time you are almost in the same place. In feeling and experience you are in a different world.

I realised this when I camped in the Grand Canyon on the Arizona Trail. I was crossing the Canyon on the popular trails, which are spectacular but crowded and with strict regulations about where you can camp. I had planned on camping at the Bright Angel Campground at the bottom of the Canyon, a lovely but organised, safe and tame campground with picnic tables, neatly laid out tent sites, toilets and fees. However the site was full so I followed a ranger's suggestion and walked a few miles away from the campground along the Clear Creek Trail to an area where I could camp wild.

Leaving the somewhat tempting lights of the campground and nearby Phantom Ranch with its bar and restaurant I followed the narrow winding trail below great cliffs as darkness fell. The instant the lights of Phantom Ranch vanished I felt back in wild country. Camp was on a flat stony platform just off the trail, where I simply threw down my foam pad and sleeping bag. The walls of the canyon rose above me, a hard blackness darker than the soft black of the sky, in which a myriad stars sparkled. There were no lights, no sounds, no sign of people. Phantom Ranch and Bright Angel Campground were just a few hours away but no longer existed in my mind. For this night the Grand Canyon felt it belonged to me. At dawn I woke to the sun slowly lighting the colourful cliffs as the Canyon came back to life. I lay and watched the light and the glory return and felt incredibly grateful to be there rather than at Phantom Ranch. It was the finest camp of the whole walk.

Similar feelings of excitement, wonder and wildness can be found all over Britain by walking that little bit further away from bright lights and warm indoor cosiness.

Once wilderness is seen as a feeling and a concept, an ideal perhaps, then various factors can change how wild a place seems. The weather and the time of year are significant here. A storm adds wildness to any place, as I found on Cross Fell, while winter changes the nature of the land. Under snow tame domesticated land can become like the

Arctic. One February, after exceptionally heavy snow, I set out from my front door and camped not far away on a rounded undistinguished hill, exploited for grouse shooting with heather burning and shooting butts. I could almost see my house from the summit, but all around spread a white wilderness, almost every sign of humanity hidden by the snow. It looked wild, it felt wild; it *was* wild. There are many such places that are transformed by storm or winter into wilder places that echo with what they once were. And many more that feel wild under blue skies and warm sun. Seeking them out is a large part of the joy of backpacking.

Rewilding the hills

How wild and natural should the hills be? Do you want them tame and docile so the walking is easy and secure? In an online comment one walker said they liked sheep in the hills because they make walking 'very pleasant'. Now, sheep-cropped grassland certainly is easy to walk across but it's also an artificial and biologically degraded landscape. Natural landscapes are wilder, more diverse and, for the walker, more challenging. Where the terrain is impossibly tough - dense forest, tangled bushes - the answer can be a path. I'd rather see a narrow trail through a wild and natural landscape than sheep-cropped terrain where it's easy to walk anywhere. And if there's no path then I'd rather find a way through the difficulties than have them tamed.

A bigger question is how to achieve more natural and diverse wild lands. Just what does that involve anyway? Ideally I think it means leaving land alone, leaving it to be 'self-willed'. However, whilst that's fine for pristine and near-pristine places it may not be for more damaged ones. The question then becomes: 'how much interference and management is acceptable?' In turn this raises the question of how long you want to wait and whether the rewilding of a landscape can be speeded up. The answers vary depending on your outlook and aims. Aesthetically I think any management should be as unobtrusive and unnoticeable as possible. I also think such management also produces a more natural landscape in the long run. However I accept that in some places it just isn't possible, at least at present.

In Eskdale in the Lake District some extensive tree planting is being undertaken by the National Trust. Because this is sheep country the planted areas are fenced and the trees are caged. This looks highly unnatural. In time I guess the cages and fences will be removed and the forest will look more natural though it will still have straight lines dividing it from the bare land outside. Less obtrusive is the work being done by Trees for Life in Glen Affric. Again planting is involved but the trees are not caged. The new forests are simply fenced in to keep out deer. Again the line between the rich vegetation inside the fence and the sparse boggy vegetation outside is stark.

Contrast these schemes, both of which I support, with that of the RSPB in Abernethy in the Cairngorms, a huge nature reserve that stretches from the forests around Loch Garten of ospreys fame to the summit of Ben Macdui. Having heard that the RSPB was to plant areas that as far as I knew were already regenerating and pretty natural anyway, I contacted the RSPB to find out what was going on and was invited on a field trip so I could see for myself (thanks to Regional Director George Campbell for organ- ising this and also to Senior Site Manager Jeremy Roberts and Ecologist Andy Amphlett).

Before we headed out to look at the area the scheme was explained and I was shown detailed maps of the forest divided into different types of area. No planting was going on in the mature natural forest or in areas where there was good regeneration I was told. Overgrazing isn't a problem in Abernethy now as deer numbers have been reduced and sheep removed. However, there is a wide band of higher ground where the sheep used to graze, that runs up to what should be the natural treeline of 650 metres, where there are no trees at all and so no seed source for regeneration. There are also areas of previously felled and then planted forest where many tree species are absent. It's in these areas that the RSPB is planting small groups of trees to provide a seed source. The planted areas won't be extensive, just small clumps, and there will be no cages or fences.

Out in the field I was shown some aspen that had been planted on heather moorland. I would never have known they weren't the product of natural regeneration. Higher up, we found the last tiny pines still well below the 650 metre line. It was clear that there would be no natural regeneration here for a very long time. The RSPB has set a 200 year goal for the return of the forest so even with the planting it will take a long time. For walkers there will be no discernible sign of this management, unlike in Eskdale and Glen Affric. That's because the RSPB owns the land and has control of grazing, which takes us back to the start of this piece and the question of what sort of landscape we want. For myself the idea of the returning forest is exciting and inspiring. I'll only see it beginning but that is a joy in itself.

Across Scotland with pylons (and fences, roads and plantations)

This is the story of a walk across the Highlands in search of ugliness. It was my twelfth coast-to-coast

TGO Challenge but on this occasion I approached the event from a slightly different and, it must be said, less positive viewpoint. I'd been impressed by David Jarman, speaking at the public inquiry into the Beauly-Denny power line (a string of huge pylons running down the Highlands that has now been built), when he painted a picture of the slow attrition wearing away the wild character of the Highlands. In an email he said 'amazing how difficult it is to get hold of 'ugly Highlands' images - I don't take them, others I have asked don't' in the context of producing a presentation showing the effect the proposed Beauly-Denny pylons would have.

As I was soon to set out to walk from Strathcarron to St Cyrus I thought that maybe I would take some 'ugly Highland images'. I too had never taken many of these in the past and I knew full well why. When in the hills I want to appreciate the beauty and wildness that remain and try and block out any ugliness or intrusions. For that reason I've always planned high level routes, keeping as far as possible to the relatively unspoilt summits and passes and away from the degraded glens. I did the same this time but once I'd started photographing intrusions and damage I found that I couldn't ignore it as easily as in the past. In fact I found myself looking for opportunities to include fences and bulldozed roads in photos rather than ways to cut them out. I can't say I enjoyed this different mindset but it did make me very aware again of just how damaged some of our hill areas are. And I did return with a collection of 'ugly Highlands' images.

The first intrusion came in the form of a deer fence above Strathcarron complete with high stile and gate through which I could look across the strath to the harsh angular lines of a forestry plantation above which rose the dark outlines of the Achnashellach hills. Soon afterwards, a rusty old iron gate between two tall fence posts reminded me that such intrusions are not new. Over the Bealach Alltan Ruairidh a bulldozed road led to Bendronaig Lodge, an old road that was not too horrible compared with some I was to see. The ugliness faded as I crossed the boggy wastes between Loch Calavie and the Allt Coire nan Each, noting the old tree roots sticking out of the peat showing this area was once wooded, and then traversed the An Riabhachan – Sgurr na Lapaich ridge, finishing with a splendid wild camp on the col with Carn nan Gobhar. Up here the sight of the bathtub rings on the reservoirs either side of this ridge didn't really impinge on my joy.

The next day I descended to the fake loch called Mullardoch with its bleak, bare shores and crossed Glen Cannich below the massive concrete ramparts of the dam. A blizzard on Toll Creagach cut out all views of ugliness and beauty, then it was down to always attractive Glen Affric, though I was more than acutely aware of all the deer fencing and the straight unnatural lines between the protected and unprotected land. Crossing to Glen Moriston I passed through some really nasty clear-cut forest on the way to Cougie before leaving the glen on the old military road and marching to Fort Augustus with a double line of pylons that looked like H. G. Wells' Martians and were just as alien. This brought me to the start of the climb to one of the most trashed places in the Highlands, the Corrieyairack Pass, noting how ironic are the signs saying that General Wade's road here is a protected historic monument. Maybe one day we can keep just one pylon – in a city park - as a historic monument and reminder. Warning signs told of the construction of the dam in Glen Doe just to the east, a huge intrusion into what was a vast wild area.

The Corrieyairack is a tangle of pylons, power lines and bulldozed roads and I was happy to escape it for a walk east over the misty, rain-strewn hills to the Monadh Liath. A short section of Strathspey with its main road and railway led to Glen Feshie, one of my favourite places but where I was horrified to discover that the bulldozed road in the upper glen, built without planning permission some years ago, had been renewed in places while in others 4WD vehicles had very recently gouged great ruts in the ground. Escaping the despoiled glens again I climbed lonely Carn Ealar and An Sgarsoch, then returned to tracks and roads at White Bridge from where I walked to Braemar.

Lochnagar was magnificent on a wild day of high winds, hail, rainbows and flashes of sharp sunlight. I circled round high above the Dubh Loch to Cairn Bannoch and Broad Cairn. A reminder of the fragility of this seemingly tough landscape intruded on the descent of the latter, the wide eroded track up its south eastern flanks being in sore need of repair. The bulldozed roads at the head of Corrie Chash are depressing too as are the gouged tracks on Sandy Hillock. From the latter I crossed the rolling heather and peat bog moorland to Glen Lee, where a bulldozed track runs deep into the hills almost to the head of the glen. Once on the track I was on the downhill slope to the coast and stuck on roads the rest of the way. One and half final days of striding out saw me on the beach at St Cyrus staring out at the sea. It had been a good walk, despite all the damage, but someone really ought to do something about it. I guess that means us.

A *fragile freedom*

The great corrie spread out far below, glistening as the early morning sun touched the rocks that were wet from the overnight rain. A thin white line split the topmost cliffs, the rushing water looking solid and immobile at this distance. Beside where this water slowed and spread, forming pools in the flat peat and heather bottom of the corrie, I'd camped the night before, looking out across the deep cleft of the Lairig Ghru to the bulky mass of Ben MacDui. Now I was high on a rocky ridge that soared upwards into the sky. The dark black oval of Lochain Uaine lay beneath my feet with the soaring spire of its namesake peak rising high above in a sweep of jagged, broken rock.

I went on up the rough slopes, revelling in the sunshine, the beauty of the mountains and the freedom to be here and the freedom of being here, of being able to wander freely in the hills, going where I wished, seeking out what lay round enticing corners, peeking into hidden niches and exploring everything offered by this glorious wild country.

The ridge ended suddenly and there, just a few metres away, lay the summit of Cairn Toul. Here, unsurprisingly, the solitude of the day was broken and I was soon joined by two others, ascending from their camp in Glen Geusachan. Talk initially was of the wonderful landscape of the Cairngorms that spread out all around us but it soon turned darker as the shadow that lay over all walkers in the spring of 2001 was mentioned: the foot and mouth outbreak. My companions had come up from England to escape the closures still prevalent down there. Yes, they said, you could walk in some places, as long as you used certain access points, stuck to certain footpaths and returned to designated points. Regimented, controlled walking was not what they wanted so they'd come to the Highlands to walk in freedom.

Understandably the debate over the foot and mouth closures concentrated on regaining access, driven mainly by the need to bring visitors back and rescue the hard pressed economies of the hills. Why people go to the hills, what it means and why it is necessary tended to be forgotten. I think it's important to look beyond the economic arguments and consider the less tangible reasons for access rights and why they should never be lost again.

Over a hundred years ago John Muir wrote 'thousands of tired, nerve-shaken, over-civilized people are beginning to find out that going to the mountains is going home; that wildness is a necessity.' For many of us that last phrase resonates with truth and meaning. 'Wildness is a necessity'.

Not a hobby, not a casual pursuit, not a fashionable activity. A necessity. Necessary in order to feel whole, to feel free, to feel able to cope with the complexities and restrictions of the modern world. One of the great insults of the foot and mouth debacle was the dismissal of walking and climbing as unimportant, trivial, just hobbies that people could abandon for something else. No mention here of mental and spiritual renewal or physical wellbeing.

An essential component of wildness is freedom; freedom to go where and when you like, freedom from the rules and regulations that govern the world of work and urban living. Take that freedom away and the wildness disappears with it. That's why disinfection points, controlled access, a plethora of notices and all the other attempts to regulate access to the hills during the foot and mouth outbreak were so objectionable. They destroyed the freedom of the hills, the sense of adventure and the sense of responsibility that goes with mountain exploration even for those who stick to footpaths.

My two companions on Cairn Toul needed that freedom, that's why they were in the Cairngorms and not the English or Welsh hills. The absence of visitors even in villages and other 'permitted' places at the height of the crisis showed that others felt so too, even those who don't walk far or venture high into the hills. For them, as interviews and letters in the press made clear, the countryside, even farmed lowland countryside, represented a freedom that was lacking in cities. So when the country roads were lined with Keep Out notices people stayed away. Just knowing that they couldn't stop for a picnic or to wander a few hundred yards to a riverbank or into a forest meant they no longer felt free and no longer wanted to be there.

Days in the hills are a restorative, a way of slowing, relaxing, unwinding, and shedding the stresses of daily life. Watching a buzzard wheeling overhead, figuring out the next move on a rock climb, gazing into a rippling burn, navigating carefully across a mist-shrouded hillside all set you firmly in the present where nothing matters beyond the moment and where you are responsible for yourself. This I think is far more conducive to health and well-being than any amount of happy pills, sleeping potions or other chemical substitutes. A day in the hills, even a physically exhausting one, can lead to feelings of energy and renewed confidence in your ability to cope with everyday life.

Indeed, perhaps it is the physically exhausting,

physically challenging days that are the most beneficial because they provide something not usually found in most people's daily lives. Facing real challenges in uncontrolled wild country can have a marvellously recuperative effect. Just how good can be seen from the results of a two-week wilderness trip in 1972 on which 51 patients from the Oregon State Hospital all suffering from serious mental illness were taken backpacking, river rafting and rock climbing. Some of these people had been in the hospital for over ten years; all were felt to be incurable. However it was hoped that the trip would help them to come to terms with themselves and feel at least some degree of achievement and self-fulfilment. The results were astonishing and far beyond what was expected. Over half the group improved so much they didn't need to return to hospital.

As well as helping you stay mentally well-balanced going to the hills is also of course a superb way to keep physically healthy. It will never be known just how many individuals suffered in mind or body because of their forced absence from the hills or how much it cost the health service.

Yet how easily the hills were 'closed', how suddenly we were told to stay away, as though going to the wilds was an irrelevance, something that mattered little to individuals or society. Most land managers, including some of those who were believed to hold land on behalf of everybody but who proved to be no better than private owners, gave no thought to the needs of those who use the wilds. Farming became the only activity worthy of support or even consideration, even though it was clear from the outset for those who bothered to look into the matter that keeping people off the hills would have no effect on the spread of foot and mouth. The knee-jerk reaction was to shut the land, claiming that walkers and climbers could spread a disease they had no contact with.

To prevent this happening again, to ensure that wild country is always available as a necessary counter to Muir's 'over-civilized' world, the hills need to be viewed as belonging to everybody, to being there for everybody and not as the private playthings of the rich or the property of empire-building conservation bodies. The rights of access to wild land should be absolute. The freedom of the hills has proved to be alarmingly fragile. We need to ensure that it is strengthened.

In 2003 the Scottish Parliament passed the Land Reform (Scotland) Act, which gives access rights to virtually all land.

Woods and wolves

I was crossing a big meadow when the feeling came over me that I was being watched. I stopped, looked towards the forest a few hundred yards away and froze with a mixture of awe, excitement and, I must admit, slight fear. On the edge of the trees a pack of wolves was watching me. There were six of them, ranging in colour from pale grey to almost black, all silent, alert, magnificent. I stayed still and after a few seconds the wolves began to slowly move away in single file, one of them always staying stationary, watching me. When the watcher fell to the rear of the line another would stop and the pack would continue. After several minutes they vanished into the trees and I breathed out and relaxed. Later in the evening I heard them howling, a wonderfully wild sound.

That incident, far away in the Yukon Territory, remains

a highlight of all my days in wild places. I saw wolves once more on that trip and heard them howling many times more. How I would love to hear that sound in the Scottish Highlands! That thought occurred to me several times on my Scottish Watershed walk. The Highlands are wild but could be so much wilder.

During rainy evenings on the Watershed, cooped up in my shelter, I read three excellent books on rewilding and the reintroduction of wildlife. Two were by Jim Crumley – *The Last Wolf* and *The Great Wood* - and one, *Feral*, by George Monbiot. Crumley's books are about wolves and forests in Scotland and discuss the history of these as well as proposals for the future while Monbiot's book is more general, though centred on Wales. The message of these books is that for our wild places to become wilder, for their ecosystems to become healthier and more robust, extinct species, especially predators, need to be reintroduced.

Crumley particularly wants wolves, which he sees as being the key to the renewal of the Caledonian Forest. Monbiot spreads his suggestions more widely and accepts that wolves are unlikely in the near future. Lynx however, could be brought back now. Both authors mention the results of reintroducing wolves into Yellowstone National Park, which has led to far more positive changes than expected. As well as keeping deer numbers down the wolves have kept the deer moving, reducing grazing pressure. The deer now completely avoid some areas where the wolves could easily trap them, so in those places there is no browsing at all. This has allowed many plants to flourish and with them a host of birds and animals. It is a fascinating and inspiring story.

Realistically wolves are unlikely to be reintroduced in Scotland in the near future, due to the opposition of estate owners and the false picture created about them over the centuries (well described in *The Last Wolf*). Other less controversial species could be reintroduced though such as lynx while beavers, already present both officially and unofficially (the latter seem to be doing best), could be released in more places. Cairngorms National Park is considering this.

In the meantime the main way for rewilding to take place is to allow natural forest regeneration, which means reducing deer numbers as overgrazing prevents new trees growing in many parts of Scotland. In the absence of large predators this can only be done either by increasing the numbers shot or by fencing deer out of forests. Where deer numbers have been reduced and sheep removed the results are startling as can be seen at the Creag Meagaidh National Nature Reserve where a new forest is springing up. I have seen the results much closer to home, though in this case due to abandonment of rough pastures rather than intentional removal of animals. There are wet meadows close to my home that are rapidly reverting to woodland now there are no cows or sheep grazing them. There are roe deer but not enough to prevent the new trees springing up.

The new forests that appear when overgrazing is ended will not be the same as the old Great Wood of Caledon (Jim Crumley reckons there were actually four separate 'Great Woods'). It would be impossible to achieve this and anyway what period would you pick as the model to try and emulate? 5,000 years ago? 8,000? A new forest will be just that, new, and it will include introduced species such as European larch and even the much-maligned Sitka spruce. The latter, now the commonest tree in Scotland, would be impossible to eradicate anyway, and Sitka spruce not grown in regimented lines in dense plantations are magnificent trees. Ending the plantation system and the clear-cutting that leaves areas devastated would greatly improve forests. On the Watershed I often saw self-seeded spruce and larch growing outside of plantations and I delighted in seeing these free trees.

Rewilding would result in a more diverse landscape with a greater variety of plants and animals. It could be done very easily if the will was there.

7

THE JOY OF WINTER

It is late November, and snow lies deep across much of Britain. Winter has set in hard with record low temperatures. The weather has brought the usual chaos to the roads but, once it settles, the hills and wild places should be superb for winter backpacking. For me this snow has brought a feeling of excitement and desire that never comes with grey skies and rain, the norm on too many winter days. I have visions of climbing pristine white slopes with a perfect mountain world spread out all around to camp beneath a star-filled sky with a crisp frost sharpening the senses and making every sound ring. I relish the prospect of lying in my warm sleeping bag with a mug of hot chocolate, watching the snow drifting gently across the landscape. Winter camping can be a joy, and when the wind picks up and rattles the tent, sending swirling snow into every crevice, I love the feeling of being secure inside while listening to the storm thrashing the land.

Before snow closed the Lowlands there was already snow in the hills and I had made two overnight trips into the frozen mountains. Both brought the pleasures of winter backpacking, but also the pains. The first trip was to a favourite spot of mine, the great cliff-ringed bowl at the head of Loch Avon, arguably the finest corrie in the

Cairngorms. The forecast was for clearing weather but the hills were shrouded in dense cloud and drizzle when I set off. The wet summer and autumn and recent heavy rain meant the lower ground was saturated and the streams full. I climbed up the Fiacaill a'Choire Chais into the wet mist, crossed below the invisible summit of Stob Coire an t-Sneachda and descended into boggy Coire Domhain from where a badly eroded stony path led steeply down to the corrie and long Loch Avon (this path has since been improved).

As I dropped out of the cloud the loch appeared, grey and windswept, while whitewater streams roared down the hillsides. The floor of the corrie was sodden and I had to pitch on damp ground, choosing a spot that didn't squelch too much under my boots. I was soon inside the tent in my sleeping bag with a hot drink wondering what had happened to the drier, clearer weather.

During the early part of the night gusts of wind shook the tent and rain rattled on the nylon. Awake before dawn I noticed whiteness around the edge of the porch, a light dusting of snow. The temperature was below freezing and there was ice on my water bottles. Looking out I could see stars. Daylight came with a bright sky, hazy sunshine and dappled clouds. The mountains were spattered with snow, stark and dramatic, the tent was frozen to the ground.

Next day, and back up on the Cairngorm plateau, the sky was blue and I could see far out to the west. The fine weather didn't last long though and by the time I reached the summit of Cairn Gorm the clouds had rolled back in and all I could see was the weather station, plastered with frost and snow. The rain returned as I descended to the car. I didn't mind. The glorious morning had made the trip worthwhile.

My second trip was to Creag Meagaidh and another favourite spot, Coire Ardair with its little lochan nestling under huge jagged cliffs. Again the forecast suggested fine, cold weather. Again it was only partly correct. I camped beside cold, dark Lochan a'Choire with the rock walls, shattered pinnacles and stony gullies rising above me into grey clouds. There was only a smattering of old snow on the corrie floor but, not far above, the slanting slabs were white. Venturing into one of the wide stony gullies I could see long icefalls spreading over the cliffs high above.

During the night there were flurries of snow and when I woke the ground was frosty and crunched underfoot. Clouds still hung over the summits and a chill wind blew. Not wanting to move camp higher in these conditions – especially as the tent was a previously untried test model – I made a round trip to Creag Meagaidh, a real winter excursion requiring ice axe and crampons. I kicked steps up the crusty snow filling the wide steep cleft leading up to the notch called The Window. Above this the snow was thinner and icier so I used crampons for security on the slope up to the huge gently tilted plateau of Creag Meagaidh. I was in the cloud now and found it hard at times to distinguish between the air and the ground. Both were white and hazy with only ripples in the snow and the occasional rock giving me anything to focus on. Compass bearings led me to the summit and a sharp cold wind. Chilly though it was I welcomed this wind as it sometimes tore apart the whirling clouds to give brief views of the surrounding peaks and down to dark glens. A silver sun pulsated weakly through the clouds. The light and the clouds changed every second and the world felt very unstable. Only the snow-encrusted rocks of the summit cairn seemed solid and fixed.

180

Following my steps back across the plateau I dropped below the cloud and returned to camp. My little grey tent looked tiny and fragile against the immensity of the landscape, but it had kept off the wind and snow and now provided a warm shelter for a hot drink before I packed and descended out of the mountains.

As with many winter trips there were only short periods of clear weather on these ventures and the tops were often in cloud. However, one of the delights of winter backpacking is being out there in the wilds during times of magical light, clearing skies and frosty sunshine, even if these are brief. This is very much the time of year to welcome any sunshine, any abatement of the wind, any clearance of the clouds. It's also a time to enjoy the comforts of camp.

In summer I resent spending much time in the tent, impatient to be outside and walking. In winter I'm happy to lie inside, warm and snug, listening to the wind, watching the snow fall, staring out at the ice-bound landscape. I don't close the tent unless the weather is really stormy, unlike in summer when midges often force me to zip myself in, and so don't lose my contact with the outdoors. When storms do mean closing the doors then I'm happy to lie and read a book and make endless brews and mugs of soup. Even in bad weather winter backpacking can be fun.

The Cairngorms in winter

Combine the largest area of high ground above 800 metres in Britain with the highest snowfall and the coldest and stormiest weather and you have the Cairngorms in winter, a challenging and spectacular mountain landscape. Snow falls on over 100 days a year on the summits and winds over 160kph (100 mph) occur every winter. The highest wind speed in Britain, a frightening 278kph (173 mph), was recorded by the weather station on the summit of Cairn Gorm in March, 1986. Blizzards and white-out conditions are not unusual.

At the same time the Cairngorms in winter are wonderful and magical, a real mountain wilderness. When the snow lies deep the paths, cairns and other human artefacts disappear. The world is renewed and the mountains are pristine again. The vast areas of high ground can hold the snow for months at a time, a frozen glorious winter landscape. Indeed, wintry conditions can last a long time in the Cairngorms with the first snow arriving in October and big snowfields lasting through May. The snow isn't guaranteed though and can thaw at any time, leaving the hills wet, grey and chilly. Sometimes freezing temperatures arrive when there's no snow and the land is covered with hoar frost and rime ice, creating a ghostly unreal landscape of sparkling rocks and white-sheathed grasses. Tumbling streams flash freeze into bubbles and corrie lochs become sheets of cracked ice. When the land is frozen hard any snow that falls lasts well, bonding to the cold beneath. However if the temperature rises, even a little, rain may fall, chilling bare skin and creating a hazardous coating of thin ice on rocks as it freezes.

Snow and ice change the landscape not just once but many times. Every day in the winter Cairngorms conditions can be different. Snow that falls on windless days forms a gentle blanket over the land, smoothing out ridges and hollows. More commonly snow comes on strong winds that blow it into great drifts and furrow the surface into ridges. Where there are steep slopes or cliffs the snow can be blown into great cornices that curl over the drops below; beautiful to look at but hazardous for walkers. More wind moves the snow again, packing it down in hollows, scouring exposed areas down to bare ice, sculpting it round rocks and boulders. The sun, weak though it is in winter, can thaw the surface of the snow, only for it to freeze hard overnight. A winter walk up here can involve crossing hard-packed icy snow where crampons are needed, sinking into deep soft drifts, and skidding across patches of bare ice (crampons again). The effort needed can be great, but then so are the rewards.

The Arctic-like feel of the Cairngorms in winter is enhanced by the light, which is that of a northern landscape. The low sun and short hours of daylight - barely more than six hours around the solstice - make for deep shadows and emphasise the shape of the hills. Even at noon on clear days the slanting sunlight gives depth and form to the mountains. Old snow, often refrozen after the surface has thawed, glimmers in the sunlight, dazzling the eyes. The mountains look magnificent, real snowy giants shining in the bright light.

Wildlife is rare in this harsh frozen land. Only the hardiest creatures can survive on the high ground. Of these some turn white to camouflage themselves against the golden eagles that may be seen sailing high above in search of prey, a wonderful sight. Ptarmigan stay close to the ground, scuttling over the snow or flying low when disturbed. Often they keep still until you are almost on top of them, relying on their white plumage to hide them. White-coated mountain hares are more wary and will dash away long before you are near, their presence betrayed by their movement. On summits small black and white snow buntings peck around, happy to take scraps that fall from walkers' snacks. The red deer often seen high in the hills in summer are gone in winter, sheltering in the glens where there is still food. In the Northern Cairngorms you may see the semi-wild reindeer from the Cairngorm Reindeer Centre down in Glenmore. These arctic animals roam freely across the hills and can scrape through snow to the moss below. They are at home in the winter landscape.

The Cairngorms are made up of a series of high plateaux split by deep passes and glens and bitten into by deep cliff-rimmed corries. The plateaux consist of rolling tundra-like terrain, stony and featureless. Under snow there is a feeling of the Arctic as the white landscape rolls away to the far horizon. Distances can be hard to judge even in sunlight. In mist and snowstorms navigation can be very difficult. The cliffs and steep, avalanche-prone slopes ringing the plateaux mean that good route-finding is essential for safety.

Each plateau is different, but they share the same characteristics that make them instantly identifiable as part of the Cairngorms. Let's take a trip over the Cairngorm Plateau itself, which stretches from Cairn Gorm to Ben Macdui and includes the subsidiary tops of Stob Coire an t-Sneachda and Cairn Lochan. This is my favourite winter trip, which I've done many times, sometimes on skis, sometimes on crampons. It takes the walker right into the heart of the Cairngorms and there are many possible variations.

Whatever the route it always starts with a steep climb up onto the Plateau, which is rimmed by big corries and long ridges, some broad and stony, some narrow and rocky. As height is gained the views below stretch out across the dark swathes of Glenmore and Rothiemurchus Forests surrounding the waters of big Loch Morlich, which may be a shining patch of brightness when ice-covered or a light-absorbing black hole when not frozen. Beyond the forest and the loch the distant tiny buildings of Aviemore can be seen with the rolling hills of the Monadh Liath on the horizon. Already the world is expanding and there is a feeling of leaving the mundane flatlands far behind. Then a final pull up stony slopes and the Plateau is reached. The world now explodes and is suddenly vast. Snowy hills rush away in every direction. This moment is always magical, always astounding. Initially the view is overwhelming and confusing in its complexity. Pause and absorb the scene to make sense of this immense mountain landscape.

Crossing the Cairngorm Plateau keeps you high above the world. Once away from the rim the lowlands vanish. All that exists is a snowy wilderness. Venture onto the edges - beware of cornices! Now look down the ice and snow clad cliffs to frozen lochans far below. Across the Lairig Ghru pass rise Braeriach, Sgor an Lochain Uaine and Cairn Toul, a magnificent trio of peaks. Between them the great slash of the Lairig Ghru can be sensed. Ben Macdui, oddly, is the least distinctive peak in view, just a big rounded hump in the distance. Slowly it comes closer and an awareness grows that you are now far from roads and buildings and fully committed to a big mountain adventure.

Eventually the last slopes lead up to the summit cairn, a huge mound of stones with a trig point on top. When the snow lies really deep even the latter may be buried. Here on the summit of the Cairngorms it feels like the top of the world, a world of nothing but mountains and snow. Wander away from the cairn towards Cairn Toul until you can see the great east face of that mountain dropping precipitately into the Lairig Ghru, through which snakes the tiny dark line of the infant River Dee. Turning south the edge of Ben Macdui's summit dome can be followed round to a view down the Lairig Ghru past the gateway sentinels of Bod an Deamhain and Carn a'Mhaim and out over great snowfields to the rippling peaks of Beinn a'Ghlo.

Ben Macdui is only half way though. Now there is the return over the Plateau, unless you are camping out overnight (and nothing beats a night high in the winter Cairngorms with a vast starry sky above and pale mountains all around). Here the route can be varied, perhaps along the edge of the Lairig Ghru and over the shoulder of Cairn Lochan with tremendous views of Braeriach and then the cliffs of Coire Lochain, or else round the head of the great trench holding the long twisting waters of cliff-hemmed Loch Avon. Either way it's a long return but a wonderful one. The Cairngorms in winter are always inspiring.

During the early months of 2013 film maker Terry Abraham and I made a film in the Northern Cairngorms. This was Terry's first full-length feature and the first time I'd been the presenter of one, my previous filming experience limited to very short snippets in various TV programmes, so this was a big challenge for both of us.

When Terry approached me to appear in the film he'd never been to the area at any time of year either. An initial week alone on the high tops in January shooting landscape scenes soon showed him just what a difficult challenge he'd undertaken. Filming is slow patient work with much standing round, not easy when the wind is bitter and the temperature below freezing. Camera equipment, especially batteries, doesn't deal well with the cold either and Terry had to take great care to keep it all working. While making the film we had to deal with blizzards and white-outs, once retreating from the Lairig Ghru in the face of a ferocious storm. I was impressed that Terry kept on filming despite the wind constantly covering his lens with snow and threatening to blow him and his tripod over.

Progress is slow when filming as sections are repeated from different angles and words said again and again. Often I walked more slowly than usual so I didn't sound too out of breath. I reckon it took at least twice as long to cover the same distance as it would have done normally. Given the short hours of daylight this restricted what we could do and where we could go. Our longest day, across the Cairngorm Plateau to Ben Macdui, did end with a descent in the dark during which we lost each other for a while as I was on skis and Terry on crampons so we took different routes.

An answer to the short days was to camp out of course and we did this often, sometimes high up, sometimes in the glens. One camp stood out, a magnificent night on the summit of Mullach Clach a'Bhlair above Glen Feshie when there was nowhere else in the world I'd rather have been. Ironically the stormiest camp, which resulted in bent tent poles for both of us, was down in the forest on what we thought was a sheltered site. There is no footage of that night!

Snow shelters

Sleeping in the snow seems unusual but it is actually the warmest and safest way to spend nights out in the winter mountains. Snow has amazing insulation properties and snow shelters are warm, windproof and quiet. They don't blow down, keep you awake by rattling in the wind or snow inside as frozen condensation falls from the roof. They are much roomier than backpacking tents too as you can dig out sleeping platforms and kitchen shelves and have room to sit up and spread your gear out.

I first discovered snow shelters on a winter mountaineering course. Setting out with overnight gear, but no tent, we found a steep snow bank high on the slopes of Aonach Beag, and dug into it to make a roomy cave. Once inside we spread out our bedding, set up the stove and made dinner. It all felt very civilised, and after spending a comfortable night inside I was hooked. The weather was fine though so I didn't gain any particular sense of security. I was just impressed by the space.

Later that same year, on a ski tour in the Cairngorms, I was to learn the big advantage of snow shelters when I woke after a night in another snow cave. Pushing my way through the surprising amount of snow that had built up against the rucksack that was acting as a door, I climbed out into a blizzard. Visibility was almost nil; the ground and sky a swirling mass of snow. The wind almost blew me off my feet and I soon retreated to the calm and quiet of the snow cave. The storm lasted all day and, apart from one short venture out when we almost failed to find the cave again (this being before the days of GPS) even though we didn't leave the corrie it was in, we spent the day in the snow cave reading, making hot drinks and relaxing. I knew from experience that being in a tent in that storm would have been unpleasant to say the least. We would probably have packed up and descended to calmer conditions.

Years later when I worked as a ski tour leader, mostly in Norway, I taught shelter building and realised that many people thought sleeping in the snow was a very strange thing to do. For some it was quite challenging. We built the shelters near to huts so people could choose to sleep in them or not and could retreat to the hut if they didn't like it. Not everyone chose to sleep in a snow shelter. However, I think everyone realised just how useful the skill of building a shelter could be in an emergency.

On all the tours I led this occurred just once, high in arctic Norway, when avalanche danger during a big storm made it too risky to descend to the hut that was our intended overnight destination. We were carrying two small tents as some of the huts were quite small but these could only squeeze in six of our group of ten so we built a snow dome for the rest of us by heaping up a huge pile of snow and then hollowing it out. That night the temperature fell to -25°C as the storm faded away and the sky cleared and we emerged to sunshine and an easy ski down to the hut for breakfast.

My enthusiasm for snow shelters was rekindled on a trip to Yellowstone National Park with Ed Huesers, inventor of the Ice Box igloo building tool. With this ingenious device igloos can be built from any type of snow including powder. On our five day trip we built two igloos, which we used as bases for exploring the surrounding wilderness. Night temperatures were all below -20°C yet the coldest temperature in an igloo was -7°C. On the coldest night we stood outside as light snow fell and the moon rose, listening to the crack of branches snapping as the sap in them froze. The temperature was below -30°C. Yet whenever we felt chilly we could nip back in the igloo and warm up. On further trips I've explored Yellowstone again and the Wind River Range to its south, using igloos throughout. On none of these trips did we even carry a tent, just the Ice Box and snow shovels.

Now I always look forward to the first igloo, the first

snow shelter in which I might live comfortably even with a blizzard raging outside. I love igloos. I love building my own shelter and knowing that I can be snug and safe inside regardless of the weather. No need to look for a sheltered site or to get up in the dark to shovel snow off the tent. All that's needed is enough snow and, even when there's not all that much around, deep drifts can be found that are suitable.

In Scotland I've built igloos on the Moine Mhor in the Cairngorms with members of the Inverness Backcountry Snowsports Club. One January we constructed two igloos on the slopes of Carn Ban Mor. The sun was out and the weather, though cold and with a brisk wind, was pleasant and we were hoping for a good long ski tour the next day. However, after a comfortable night, we woke to a white-out and a strong wind. Instead of swooping across the white expanse of the Moine Mhor we struggled to pack up our gear and then navigate to the edge of Glen Feshie. Only when we were part way down to the glen did we escape the blasting spindrift. Yet in the igloos we had been warm and comfortable. Tents would have been uncomfortable, if indeed they had stayed up.

On another trip one January, in a winter that was one of the most snow free on record, I set out with two others to build an igloo above Glen Affric. Initially we had to carry our skis as the snow was patchy and soft with too many tussocks and boulders poking through. The walking was difficult, not just because we were carrying skis as well as all our overnight gear, but also because we were constantly plunging through the snow into bogs and stumbling over hidden rocks while the heather tore at our gaiters. In the distance we could see a denser white streak, a thick ribbon of snow in a deep stream gully. We staggered across to it and were relieved to find it wide and solid enough to provide a good line for a ski ascent.

Above us the bank of snow grew steeper and cornices began to appear above the gully. We climbed a rib of snow onto the top of the bank and found it was deep enough for an igloo. It was a magnificent spot, half way up the hillside with views of cloudy, snowy mountains all around.

Building an igloo is not something to hurry, unless the weather is really stormy. In between the shovelling and snow block construction we stopped to make hot drinks and revel in the location and the wild surroundings. Night comes early at this time of year and it was a few hours after the sun set before we put in the final horizontal roof blocks and moved into our spacious home to cook dinner. Inside all was peaceful and calm. In an igloo there is no sound of the wind, no rattling of tent fabric, no showers of condensation. We slept well, waking to a cloudy day with poor visibility. We skied a little further up the mountain but turned once we reached the cloud level and skied back down. No one felt a need to reach a summit. The aim of the trip had been the igloo and that had already been a success.

I'd hoped that igloo would be the first of many that winter, but it was not to be. January's snow melted and February and March were snow free. By the time it returned in late April it was too late for igloos (they don't go well with hot sun!) though I did have the best ski tour of the season across the Cairngorm Plateau to Ben Macdui on May Day.

Every year when the first snow falls I'm excited at the thought of building igloos and the thrill of anticipation is sharp. There are many places in the Scottish hills I'd like to build igloos, some of them where I'd be wary of camping in winter unless the weather was very settled. I plan on snow camps as well, for those times when the snow isn't deep enough for igloos or I want to move on each day – igloos take so long to build that you want to use them for more than one night.

Whilst building an igloo takes several hours and requires at least two people, simple snow shelters can be made quite quickly by one person. If there's much snow on the hills I always carry a snow shovel and have occasionally dug a small slot in a bank for a lunch stop out of the wind. One day I'll hollow one of these out a bit more and spend the night there.

8

ADVENTURES WITH SKIS AND IGLOOS

Deep snow looks lovely, bringing a sense of freshness and rebirth to the land, but try walking in it and the beauty soon loses its lustre. Once snow is more than ankle deep walking becomes hard work, and when it approaches knee deep progress slows to a crawl with every step an effort. Walking a mile becomes an exhausting marathon. In North America such 'walking' has the graphic and appropriate name of post-holing. I love snow. I hate post-holing. The answer of course is to stay on the surface or at least close to it, which means using snowshoes or skis. Suddenly moving becomes much easier and the snow can be enjoyed again.

I first encountered snow like this many, many years ago in the English Lake District on an astonishingly arduous ascent of Great End. At times we waded through seemingly bottomless thigh-deep snow. Continuing to Scafell Pike was out of the question and it was with relief that we plunged back down our track, still stumbling and falling in the soft snow.

Soon afterwards, on a December trip in the Highlands, I turned back on an ascent of Stob Coire Easain above Loch Treig due to snow that was thigh-deep in places. These were day walks. If I'd been backpacking I'd probably have never got far uphill because of the weight I was carrying. This was brought home to me later, on the Pacific Crest Trail. There had been heavy snow that winter and spring, and the mountain ranges the trail crosses in Southern California were all deep in snow. Struggling along their crests with a heavy pack was slow and tiring. However, each range could be crossed in a day or so and the lower slopes were snow free, so I never ploughed through snow long enough for it to be too gruelling.

Up ahead though was the High Sierra, 800 kilometres of snowbound mountains, much of it above 3,000 metres. Post-holing that distance was unthinkable, and probably impossible. A hiker I met was using snowshoes and staying on top of snow that came up to my knees. Impressed, I took a day off from the trail to buy a pair. Two other walkers joined up with us for the High Sierra section, and they were using Nordic skis. Watching them glide across meadows and swoop down steep slopes while I plodded along behind on my functional but slow snowshoes I suddenly understood that real skiing wasn't being hauled up a slope by a metal contraption in order to slide back down but was a superb way to travel over snow-covered wild country. I vowed to learn how to ski and the very next winter I did so, courtesy of my friend, writer and broadcaster Cameron McNeish, then a ski instructor.

The freedom of snow-covered forests and hills now opened up. Instead of fearing deep snow and hating the restriction it placed on my outdoor activities I relished it and looked forward to seeing dark clouds piling in and the first thick white flakes falling on the brown land. Now it was a lack of snow that I disliked. My ideal conditions became ones when the snow was deep enough to ski from my front door. One of my favourite ski backpacking trips was when I did just that, skiing from home to the top of a nearby hill where I camped overnight.

Since learning to ski I have done many ski backpacking trips from such overnights to two and three week long expeditions. For a decade I led trips, taking groups on wilderness skiing and snow camping trips in remote places like Svalbard, Greenland, and the Yukon Territory. Many of these ski trips, whether as group leader, with friends or solo, are amongst my most memorable. The landscape changes dramatically under deep snow. Wild places become wilder. Tamed and half-tamed places shake off some of the controls and revert to wildness, becoming vaster and more magnificent. Being able to travel easily through a snow-covered land means it can be appreciated fully. It's hard to delight in beauty when you're soaked in sweat, your legs are throbbing with pain and you're plunging in knee deep with every step. Gliding over the snow on skis is a totally different experience that feels natural and in tune with the white wilderness.

The ultimate way to enjoy the snow is to stay out night after night, either in a tent or a snow shelter. Skiing with a big pack may seem challenging but with a stable load (skiing is a good way to find out just how secure a pack is) it's not as difficult as you might think. However, snow provides a means that is unavailable for much of the year and that is to pull the load on a sled. On reasonably gentle terrain this is much easier than carrying it on your back. Skiing steep slopes with sleds does require some practice. Downhill isn't too difficult as long as the slope is wide as the sled actually helps with balance – though in trees life can be exciting if the sled decides to wrap itself round one. Steep ascents are the real difficulty as sleds tug you backwards or slip sideways on rising traverses, but it's still easier than post-holing with a big pack. Much more can be comfortably hauled than carried, two weeks food is a burden in a pack but no problem with a sled.

A *ski tour on Spitsbergen*

Watching two blocks of rock-hard snow-ice sitting in a pan above a roaring paraffin stove and failing to melt is a disturbingly surreal experience. This is especially so when you are the chief cook for a group of ten (as well as the leader) and it's the first night of a two week expedition. After an interminable wait the snow began to thaw but even with four stoves working full blast it took three hours to melt enough snow to cook dinner and make hot drinks for everyone.

While I was fretting over how long the snow melting was taking, other members of the group were more concerned about the risk of meeting a polar bear. The previous day I had watched faces grow more and more serious as we were given a lecture on bears and how to use the rifle we were hiring. Concerned that everyone might want to go home immediately I enquired as to how often rental guns had been used to shoot bears. 'Never,' came the reply. 'What's the real risk?' I continued. 'Not much where you're going at this time of year.' With that reassurance we had set off to ski down the wide frozen wastes of Adventdalen for ten kilometres before setting up our first camp. We never saw a bear.

Our plan was to explore the mountains of Nordenskiold Land, which lies to the south of Adventdalen, and ascend some peaks if the weather permitted. This area had been chosen to maximise our skiing time as we could start and finish at Longyearbyen, the capital of Spitsbergen, outside of which is the only international airport.

Spitsbergen is the largest island of the archipelago known as Svalbard that lies far to the north of Norway in the Arctic Ocean between latitudes 74° and 81° degrees (Longyearbyen is 78° degrees) so it's not surprising that nearly 60% of Svalbard is permanently covered by snow and ice. It's 1300 kilometres to the North Pole and 930 kilometres south to Tromsø in northern Norway. Spitsbergen has many large valleys that are snow-free in summer though, including those we skied through, but there are many glaciers and some of these are gently angled and wide with few crevasses, making them excellent highways into the mountains.

The mountains of Nordenskiold are not very high, rising to 1145 metres on Moysalen, but you do climb them from sea level. The highest summit on Spitsbergen is 1717 metre Newtontoppen, named after Sir Isaac Newton, in the north-east of the island. Skiing on Spitsbergen isn't difficult. Indeed, much of it is on flat or gently sloping terrain. It's the cold and the wind that are challenging. The stark landscape can be mentally daunting too. Although it's inhabited all year round it feels an alien place, a land where human beings can barely survive.

Our route led for two days down huge Adventdalen, past some of the coal mines that are the reason Longyearbyen exists. Being close to the town Adventdalen is laced with skidoo tracks so, although the scenery is wild and Svalbard reindeer can be seen, there's no real feeling of remote country. The third day though, we left the valley behind and climbed up the Dronbreen glacier to camp surrounded by fine peaks with steep faces linked by sharp arêtes decorated with pinnacles covered with rime ice.

To the north of our camp lay Moysalen and we took a day off from hauling pulks (low sleds) to climb this peak. The ascent was quite easy, the only steep section, where it was easier to walk and carry the skis, being near the top. The sun that had shone throughout the trip so far began to fade as we climbed and we reached the summit just in time for some last hazy views before a thin dry mist swept over us. A quick descent, swooping down the snowfields, saw us back at camp just as snow began to fall.

The light layer of fresh snow made for good skiing the next day as we crossed the gentle col at the head of the glacier and traversed the Rugastonna Icefield on which we met a party of Norwegian skiers, the only other party we saw all trip. A long, straight, fast, exciting run took us down the Kokbreen glacier to Reindalen, a wild valley walled by splendid mountains. We had seen no sign of water and it had been very cold, well below freezing all day every day, so I was startled on reaching the toe of the glacier to go through the ice into ankle deep water. Aware of the dangers of wet feet in such cold conditions I was out of the water very fast, before it could get through my boots and gaiters.

For camping the water was a boon though, as it meant a break from the long, tedious chore of snow melting, so we camped not far away. Because of the bitter cold the camping was much harder than the skiing. It took a long time to set up and strike camp wearing thick gloves and mitts but if these were removed hands became numb with cold very quickly. Snow melting and cooking took several hours every morning and evening. My admiration for polar explorers increased significantly during this trip. It takes a taste of harsh conditions to gain some understanding of what months on end must be like.

198

Our plan was to ski into the mountains to the south of Reindalen. However, the changing weather meant we ran out of time. The first morning in Reindalen we woke to a cloudy day with very poor visibility and a strong, gusty wind so, rather than move camp, we just skied up the valley to Reindalenspasset at its head. Near the pass we found a pingo, which is a small rounded hillock formed by water being forced up under pressure through the permafrost from below, pushing up the topsoil. The water then freezes to leave a curious-looking cracked mound of soil and gravel with ice beneath.

During the next night the weather worsened with much swirling spindrift that filled the tent porches and showers of heavy wet snow. Moving on in this storm would have been unpleasant and possibly hazardous so we spent the day in camp. Two days of no progress meant we now hadn't time to safely venture further from Longyearbyen. Improved weather did allow us to move on our third day, when we skied down the valley to camp in the mouth of the side valley of Gangdalen. This was marked as a danger spot on the map due to weak river ice and open water but, for us, it meant having water close to camp again. Above us the mountains shone white with new snow and there were fine thin cornices on east-facing ridges. Gangdalen led to a pass beyond which lay a valley that led back to Adventdalen, a route we thought we could ski in all but the worst weather.

That belief was put to the test two days later as we skied over 431 metre Gangskardet pass in an increasingly strong wind and blown snow that quickly transformed into a complete white-out. Moisture from our breath froze almost instantly on hair, beards and exposed skin, and care had to be taken to stay in touch with each other as visibility dropped to just a few metres. The map showed fairly gentle slopes on the descent from the pass into Todalen, which was a relief as we could see nothing. Camp was again in the partial shelter of a corniced bank and again gusts of wind shook the tents and filled the porches with spindrift.

By morning the wind was dying and the skies clearing. The fleshpots and warmth of Longyearbyen, now only a day's ski away, were too tempting for three of the party who chose to head back. By doing so they missed the best day of the trip, a day of sunshine, amazing clarity, spectacular views and excellent skiing. With no need to move camp we set off for the summits, climbing a steep narrow gully to an unnamed glacier below the peak of Karl Bayfjellet. After crossing the glacier we abandoned our skis and climbed to a narrow ridge that led to an unnamed top that gave tremendous views.

Continuing looked difficult so we returned to our skis and traversed to another glacier, Svensenbreen, which we followed to the col at its head, a col through which the wind roared so strongly we were barely able to stand up. Unable to go further we turned and had a wonderful run down a twisting series of bowls and gullies. The snow was so perfect our skis seemed to turn on a twitch of the ankles. We hadn't come to Spitsbergen for such skiing but it was a joy to find it and it was a satisfied group that plodded back to Longyearbyen the next day.

A ski tour in the Tombstone Mountains

It was August and I was camped alone beside Talus Lake in the heart of the Tombstone range just south of the Arctic Circle in Canada's Yukon Territory. Across the lake the huge curving amphitheatre of granite walls and spires glowed gold in the rising sun. The great black wedge of Tombstone Mountain towered above the ring of rock peaks, soaring some 600 metres into the sky. It was a glorious dawn amidst scenery of unsurpassed grandeur in remote wild country and one of the most memorable camps I've ever had.

Seven years later I stood beside the gravel Dempster Highway, the only road in the northern Yukon Territory, and stared up the North Klondike River towards Tombstone Mountain. I was going back. Could it really be as splendid, as awe-inspiring, as I remembered? Would years of looking at the photographs I'd taken, of giving slide shows and talking and writing about the area, have dulled the reality?

I shivered in the cold air and turned away. There was little time to ponder such things now. I had a group to look after, for this time I was leading nine others on a ski tour. Our plan was to ski through the mountains to Dawson City, which lay to the south- west on the edge of the fabled Klondike goldfields. This should take only five to six days, leaving at least four for side ventures. I knew though that this could only be a tentative aim.

Much would depend on the state of the snow. Would it be deep and soft, making travel slow and arduous or would we be able to glide rapidly over a firm, wind-packed surface? Would we be able to follow the rivers, which should still be frozen, or have to find a way through the dense bush that filled the lower valleys?

By the end of the next day we had the answer. After a few kilometres of relatively easy skiing on river ice swept clean by the wind, plus some old snow scooter tracks, we plunged into deep, sugary, unbroken snow and breaking trail became extremely difficult. Every step involved

201

wrenching a ski tip high out of the snow then thumping it back down. This quickly proved exhausting with our heavy packs and we soon realized we could make slightly faster and certainly less tiring progress if the leader broke trail without the added burden of a pack. Even so, ten to fifteen minutes was the longest most people could manage. Progress was very slow. Going back for the pack was easy and fast of course, as the trail was well broken.

Even on the frozen river the snow was knee deep, though in places moose had made bits of trail that were slightly easier to follow. On the banks the tangles of springy willows added to the difficulties so we often followed the loops of the river rather than a direct line. Higher up we found intermittent thin strips of hard snow along the lower edges of south facing banks where the snow had thawed slightly and then refrozen, and linking these made skiing a little easier and faster. Even so, after two days and around fourteen hours of skiing we were only seventeen kilometres from the start. Our heavy loads didn't help. As well as packs, containing winter camping gear and clothing along with ice axes and crampons, we had two sledges packed with ten days food and fuel.

Hazy granite peaks appeared at times in the mist. Light snow fell. We were skiing up the North Klondike River valley towards Tombstone Pass, which separates this valley from that of the Tombstone River. To the north of these valleys lay the shattered scree slopes of the Cloudy Range, to the south the massive granite walls of the Tombstone Mountains. The first is the higher, just, though peaks in both rise to well over 2,000 meters, but the Tombstone Range is by far the more impressive with 900 meter pinnacled cliffs that curve round vast cirques, unbroken for many kilometers.

Shedding our loads for a while we spent two nights at our second camp, spending a day finding a route up to Tombstone Pass and down the far side to Divide Lake. As we'd hoped, the snow on the mountainsides above the willow clogged valley was firmer and made for good skiing. Even so it was hard work hauling the sledges up the steep slopes to the pass the next day.

The gentle run down the far side came to an abrupt halt when we reached the Tombstone River valley. Here the willows were even thicker and there was a thick crust on the snow that gave way beneath us and made trail breaking even harder. The river, which I'd hoped to ski down, was open in places so we had to smash a way through the willows. We learnt later that the thaw had started early.

Exhausted and frustrated, we ground to a halt. A choice faced us. If we went on it would probably be like this or worse all the way to Dawson and it was possible we wouldn't meet our deadline. There would certainly be no time to explore the high cirques of the Tombstone Range as we'd planned. Alternatively, we could abandon the through route and spend the next six days in the high mountains, returning along the trail we had so laboriously made. This was the more attractive option by far so the decision was quickly made. We would stay in the mountains. How we would tell our pick-up of the change of plan would be my problem.

Our camp that night was below Tombstone Mountain itself and we spent the next day touring the three great cirques that lie directly east of the 2192-metre peak. The weather had remained hazy for the last few days but now clearing skies gave us our first good views of the mountains. We also had our first real downhill runs, mostly in deep, heavy powder snow. Skiing without heavy packs and on reasonable snow was a great joy. I was aware too that lifting the burden of concern about getting to Dawson had liberated my spirits and I was now enjoying the trip.

That evening the final clouds faded away and there was a wonderful golden light over the jagged peaks. In the middle of the night I stumbled outside to a brilliant display of northern lights. Bright white spots on the horizons suddenly turned into dazzling searchlights while ragged white sheets of light rippled and swayed as if in a celestial wind. Once a twisting red and green coloured band sped from horizon to horizon. With the sky rimmed with the ragged black outline of the peaks and all around a vast expanse of pale snow there was a feeling of immensity and grandeur. This was a glorious place.

Two hours easy climbing took us to Talus Lake, where I'd camped seven years before and where we'd decided to spend a couple of nights. The scene was as exciting and dramatic as I remembered it. Although the lake was frozen and snow-covered and the shoreline unclear the view showed me where I'd camped. We pitched our tents on the same spot, but this spectacular site had one disadvantage; no water supply. We'd been close to rivers up until now but here at 1500 metres there was no running water.

Attempts to chop through the hard ice on the lake with our ice axes came to nothing. It was well over a metre thick. Melting snow was a process we wished to avoid, especially as we were using butane/propane cartridge stoves due to the airline refusing to carry petrol or paraffin burners. These stoves were just about adequate in temperatures above −10°C but agonizingly sluggish below that. When only half empty the cartridges had to be changed because of the cold. Luckily we had plenty.

Two search parties went out to seek water. Both

were successful but the farther source, away down the Tombstone River, was the better one and throughout our stay pairs of skiers set off regularly to fill our motley collection of water bottles and vacuum flasks.

Above our camp lay a great cirque of granite peaks, the most distinctive being Mount Monolith, a huge granite wall topped by a giant boulder. Below Mount Monolith ran a wide flat shelf, high above the floor of the main cirque. We spent a day skiing up to this platform and then along it below the sheer cliffs. There was no wind away from the lake and the sun reflecting off the rock walls and the vast snowfields made it very hot. The sky was deep blue, the granite cliffs gold in the sun. Far above an eagle circled over a distant spire. The grandeur was awe-inspiring yet at the same time there was a peaceful, relaxed feel.

The hot sun turned the surface of the snow soft, making for good downhill skiing as we returned to the camp. When it set behind the mountains a soft pink alpenglow spread across the peaks.

Tombstone Mountain was shining in the sunshine early the next morning but the camp was still in the shade and the temperature was down to minus 20°C. Once the sun reached us though, it was soon very hot as again there was no wind. We began the slow journey back to our starting point, following our tracks back over Tombstone Pass to the North Klondike River. This time the mountains were sharp and clear and the views beautiful and spectacular. Back down by the river, which was now much more open than before, we found many tracks of grouse, fox and hare and saw several of the first. Spring was coming and the world was waking up. For the first time we sat outside the tents, warm in the sunshine.

We had the sun early in the morning, although there

were clouds to the east, small white fluffy cumulus with more solid grey behind. With just one day left for exploring the mountains we decided to try to climb a minor peak in the Cloudy Range, none of the Tombstone summits being feasible without rock climbing gear. Leaving the skis in a gully high on the mountain as the terrain was too rocky for them we climbed steeply through deep soft snow amongst boulders to a broad ridge up which easier walking, sometimes on scree though mostly on snow, led to the neat little summit. As we climbed, the sky clouded over from the south and the peaks grew hazy. A cold wind swept the top so we soon turned back, stomping down the ridge back to the skis then making fast descending traverses across the crusty, bumpy snow above the camp.

A final day was spent following our tracks back to the Dempster Highway. As we sped along it was hard to believe how difficult it had been to make this trail. At the road I started walking towards a highway maintenance depot we'd seen when we arrived. Using the depot's radio-phone I called the charter bus company. The driver had already left for Dawson, where he was expecting to pick us up the next day. 'I'll try and reach him,' I was told. He turned up at lunchtime the next day. We loaded our gear and said farewell to the Tombstone Mountains. It had been a difficult trip, but a satisfying one.

An expedition to Greenland

Huge rock walls rose silent and grey to either side as our tiny boat chugged up the Tasermuit Fjord. We stared, overawed and somewhat intimidated by the spectacular and inhospitable Arctic landscape that was opening up around us.

This was our third day of travel, days that had seen us go from transcontinental airliner to passenger helicopter to small fishing boat; from the inhuman confusion of vast urban airports to the friendly atmosphere of the small fishing port of Nanortalik on Greenland's south-western coast. Ahead, at the end of the fjord, a jumbled mass of smashed and cracked ice poured down some 1300m from the inland ice. The height of Ben Nevis, I thought, trying vainly to sense the scale. I knew that the rock walls lining the east side of the fjord were up to 1500m high but I couldn't grasp what that meant.

My emotional reaction was strong. The scene was wild, fantastic, intense, but also in some way, uncaring. No, not uncaring, rather indifferent, alien; a world not for people but for what? Itself?

Mountains can feel friendly, welcoming and reassuring. At other times they may seem hostile, threatening and dangerous but always there is a human dimension, a sense of relationship between you and the mountain. I felt none of that here. This land existed apart, in another world. Entering it was going to be exciting if, indeed, possible. Even the maps added to this feeling of disconnection with few features named. At a scale of 1:250,000 with 100 metre contour intervals many do not appear at all.

The purpose of our group of ten was to find a way through the coastal ring of defending peaks onto the permanent ice and to ski as far out on this as we could in the short time available, hopefully climbing some of the easier peaks along the way. At home this had seemed almost without ambition, here it seemed immensely arrogant.

We had come well prepared with winter climbing gear, Nordic ski touring gear, winter camping gear, food and fuel for ten days. Too much by a long way for even the biggest packs (and I'd brought a huge 115 litre capacity one) so we also had three pulks (low sleds), each capable of carrying 50 kilos or so.

Late in the afternoon the boat chugged in towards the land and we ferried our loads ashore in a dinghy. Finally the boat turned and slid away, and we were alone. I was acutely aware that although I'd been in places as remote as this before I had always travelled there on foot or on ski and knew I would leave the same way. Here there would be no exit until the boat returned in ten days, although we had both a radio and a satellite distress beacon. I put them out of my mind, aware that they were no substitute for care and experience.

Our first camp in this wilderness, and for once the word is completely accurate, was on the beach, the tents pegged out with ice axes and weighed down with rocks on the loose shingle. Sparse bushes of scrub willow and birch and a few smaller plants were the only life in what was mostly a barren world of stone and ice. Above us lifeless cliffs soared into grey threads of cloud spitting squalls of cold rain.

Although south of the Arctic Circle, we were far enough north for darkness never really to arrive in June, which was just as well; during the night the wind shifted 45 degrees and strengthened until it was a wailing banshee powering down the fjord to seize the tents and shake them violently.

Half the night was spent resetting the tents, putting larger and larger rocks on the pegs only to see them dragged across the gravel. Eventually a frighteningly powerful gust hit the tent I was clinging onto, inverted the poles and smashed it to the ground. More of this and we would lose them all; we took them down and packed. No-one could sleep anyway.

208

Retreating to the partial shelter of a large boulder I set up a stove and surrounded by a windbreak of packs and pulks cooked up a large pot of porridge for breakfast.

Our first day was spent hauling gear across the stony moraines of the beach, through a huge boulder field and up a steep slope of loose scree and earth to a long valley. At its head lay a magnificent wall of cliffs and spires. We camped here for two nights while we ferried gear up the valley to the base of some tongues of steep snow and scree, leading to a traverse around an overhanging frozen waterfall below the glacier we hoped to ascend.

Pulks, we were discovering, may be wonderful on snow but, for carrying over rough mountainsides, they are about the worst things imaginable.

My co-leader John White's mountain rescue experience came in useful the next day. Thankfully not to assist anyone, but to haul the heavily laden pulks up the steep snow by a system of continuous ropes. It was unnerving to hear John refer to the pulks as stretchers! That night we camped at around 650 metres by the iced over meltwater lake at the toe of the glacier, We were ready now, after three days, to actually start skiing.

So far the weather had been very mixed, each day bringing bursts of sun, showers and wind. This pattern continued as we skied up the glacier, finally moving all our gear at once. That afternoon the clouds descended and we finished in a white-out, skiing across a vast white plateau between huge rock walls. Careful compass work took us to what we hoped would be a sheltered site around 1500m below the invisible walls of an 1870m peak. We were to spend four nights in this spot.

Despite building double snow walls to protect the tents, the wind that first night threatened to flatten them and we spent long hours sitting with our backs braced against the poles. Beyond our tiny camp the low sun blazed through swirling spindrift, shining gold and red on the soaring peaks. Such a dramatic scene made up for being outside at 4.30 am, but I noted that the sky had blazed with the same fantastic light during the windstorm on the beach. Clear and windy, cloudy and calm was the pattern for the early morning weather.

As the winds eased the clouds closed in and we spent the morning catching up on lost sleep. With visibility down to a few metres we couldn't risk travel in this potentially heavily crevassed terrain. In the afternoon the best high level weather of the whole trip gave us a few hours respite so we skied, packless and pulkless for once, north and east to look across Lindenows Fjord on the east coast (Greenland is very narrow at this point) to a superb array of rock peaks. The scale was unbelievably vast.

Unfortunately, that glimpse of the mountains was all we were to have. For the next two days we lived in a claustrophobic closed-in world as mist shrouded the tents. Even worse, it rained, steadily and persistently. The snow walls melted, sagged and collapsed, and the skis, ice axes, snow pegs we had used to stake out the tents rose out of the wet snow. Other than rebuilding the walls and resetting the tents all we could do was lie inside having endless brews, ripping up and sharing round paperback books and dreaming of what we could be doing.

A clearance on the fourth evening led to high winds again in the early hours but also to a clear morning. With just three and a half days left we decided, reluctantly, that we had better retreat while we could.

The descent was dramatic with the great rock peaks silhouetted against a threatening black sky. To either side great crevasses split the mountainsides and steep icefalls filled the hollows between the peaks. However, the skiing was quite easy and we were down at the camp site at the snout of the glacier early enough for some people to scramble up the 1230m peak above the camp (ironically 300 metres lower than our highest camp), while others returned up the glacier for a load free descent.

Our route to the fjord now open, we remained for a second day, as the weather worsened and snow started to fall. There was little in the way of views, though below and to the north the pale lines of the massive, heavily crevassed, Semiitsiaq glacier floated in the hazy air.

Wet snow plastered the tents the next morning and with more falling steadily from the leaden sky we packed for the final descent to the beach. The snow kept up throughout the morning as we stumbled and staggered down the rough slopes, lowering the pulks down the steeper snow on ropes, then strapping them to packs for the walk down the upper valley and the last clamber through the boulders to the beach.

Finally, the skies cleared and the sun came out to give us one last afternoon to wander the shoreline and revel in the wildness and beauty.

Being the joint birthday of two of the party, an impromptu celebration was held with balloons and whisky courtesy of their respective spouses. A driftwood fire in the soft light of the sub-Arctic night followed, making a gentle finish to a long, hard day and a tough trip which, in the way that these things are, was a satisfying adventure.

Skiing Yellowstone with Igloo Ed

Cold, icy mist drifted over the Firehole River, a freezing grey wall hiding the land. Crossing the bridge over the

211

river we skied into this dawn mist and my weirdest start to a wilderness trip ever. On the far side lay Biscuit Basin, an area of geysers, hot springs, bubbling mudpots and mineral stained, crusted, smoking ground through which a snow-covered boardwalk threaded a narrow way. Geysers exploded into the air, sending up vast plumes of steam that mingled with the mist. Skiing through the warm clouds of steam dampened us, and when we emerged back into the freezing air the moisture froze, coating us with frost and ice.

Biscuit Basin lies on the main south-north road through Yellowstone National Park, a few miles north of Old Faithful village. You can't drive there in a car in winter though. The roads are snow-covered and closed to non-tracked vehicles. We'd come in the day before on a snowcoach, a noisy, bone-shaking journey made enjoyable by entertaining companions, our informative driver/guide Sarah, the splendid scenery and regular stops to visit waterfalls and thermal features. Our snowcoach friends, like many winter visitors to Yellowstone, were going cross-country skiing on cut tracks. Ed Huesers and I were heading into the untracked wilderness and would see no-one for the next week. Our plan was to live in igloos and explore the wilderness west of Biscuit Basin, a vast, steep sided, undulating region around 2,600 metres high known as the Madison Plateau that contains several remote thermal areas.

Yellowstone, the first national park in the world, is a supervolcano sitting atop one of the largest masses of molten rock lying close to the earth's surface that exists, known with great understatement as a hotspot. The supervolcano last erupted some 640,000 years ago, though there have been smaller lava flows since. The

Yellowstone landscape is formed by the lava and ash spewed out in eruptions and then shaped by glaciers and water. The volcanic forces are still active, as evidenced by over 10,000 thermal features, more than anywhere else in the world. One day the Yellowstone supervolcano will erupt again. One day.

Our immediate concern as we left Biscuit Basin was to find a way up the steep slopes of the narrowing Little Firehole River valley to the undulating wooded plateau above. A deep basin cutting back into the slope looked a possible weakness, though there was a band of low cliffs around the rim, and we headed up this slowly, dragging sleds packed with winter equipment and supplies behind us. The snow was soft and deep among the trees, hard and icy in open areas. Dead trees and boulders lying just beneath the snow caught skis and sleds, bushy young trees snatched at pole baskets and sled straps. At times the sleds slid back down the slope pulling the hauler over. Climbing skins on the skis strained to maintain grip while dragging the sled back up. Finally we breached the cliffs and reached the rim of the plateau and the reward of a splendid view of the Upper Geyser Basin stretching back to Old Faithful, with columns of steam rising into the now mist-free air from a stark monochrome landscape of snow and dark conifers.

Turning away from the views we skied through dense forest, making slow progress in the mix of breakable crust and deep sugary snow, further hampered by the many areas of fallen trees. These were from the great fire of 1988 that burned much of Yellowstone's woods. Many of the dead trees still stood, grey and skeletal, their limbs snapped off, but there were also many young trees, often packed closely together, showing that life had returned.

213

In the late afternoon we selected a spot on the rim of the plateau and started to build our first igloo. To do this shovelfuls of snow are heaped into a form and then pressed down to form the blocks of the igloo. However the sugar snow we had to work with was very slow to consolidate and each block took a long, long time to make. It was well after midnight before we finished and crawled inside to melt snow and make dinner. We finally lay down to sleep at 4.00 am after an exhausting 23 hour day.

Inside the igloo it was surprisingly warm, -3°C, with the stove going, -7°C without. Outside it was -23°C. It was drier and roomier than a backpacking tent too, with no condensation, room to sit up on the sleeping platforms with feet on the floor and a table for cooking. Outside sounds were cut out completely but daylight percolated through the walls.

A slow, leisurely day followed, during which we broke trail through to Little Firehole Meadows then returned to the igloo. After all that effort we weren't going to abandon it after one day. The morning was sunny but clouds rolled in after noon and light snow was falling by evening. There were many tracks of all sizes in the forest. None were clear. Fox, coyote, wolf, moose and ground squirrel were all possible. However, the only wildlife we actually saw were little mountain chickadees (a type of tit) and big black ravens, both year-round denizens of the forest.

The following day our tracks made for a speedy return to Little Firehole Meadows, this time with the loaded sleds. The meadows were extensive, spreading out amongst groves of trees with steep wooded slopes rising all around. The slow meandering Little Firehole River wound its way through the snow-covered meadows, fed by little creeks, all open despite the low temperatures due to the thermal features heating the water.

To continue through the meadows we had to ford the river. This was a new situation to me. I'd skied across many frozen rivers and lakes but had never had to cross open water in such cold temperatures. The day before we'd cleared snow to make a platform on the bank and here we loaded our sleds and skis onto packs ready for the crossing. I went first, barefoot with trousers rolled up, into water that appeared only knee-deep. However a thick mat of green water plants covered the river bed, which consisted of soft, deep mud. The plants gave way disconcertingly under my feet, causing me to wobble under my load, and once through the vegetation I sank into the mud. Soon I was wading thigh-deep, my trousers soaked. I didn't feel cold though. That came when I clambered out again. The shock of freezing air and snow on my wet, bare legs was excruciatingly painful and left me gasping.

Perched on my foam pad I hurriedly rolled my trousers down, pulled on my socks and boots and swigged hot lemonade from my flask. Ed, having observed my struggles, removed his trousers and started across. His load was taller and less stable than mine and it began to lurch to one side almost immediately. He still made it almost the whole way before he started to topple over, desperately trying to get his load onto the bank. I grabbed the nearest object to me, a ski, but it began to pull out of the load so I had to release it and seize the top of the sled itself.

As I did this the load pushed Ed down so that his face was in the water momentarily. Once free of the load Ed had to cross back to collect gear he hadn't been able to manage on the first ford. By the time he'd made his third

215

crossing his feet and legs were numb and I had to help get his trousers and boots back on. Then we harnessed up the sleds and strode across the meadows to warm up. Luckily Ed's load was dry, only the front of his waterproof jacket and his wool shirt were wet.

Out in the meadows we found a lovely situation for our second igloo, on a big snow drift on the edge of a grove of trees looking out across the meadows to the steep slopes of the Madison Plateau. The snow was more powdery here, still slow to form into blocks but better than the coarse sugar snow in the forest. It was after dark when we finished the igloo.

We woke to snow falling and a bitter north wind and spent a few hours breaking trail across the meadows to the slopes lying below an area known as Smokejumper Hot Springs before retreating to the warmth and comfort of the igloo. There was little to see in the swirling snow but some fine big lodgepole pines and some big grey grouse. That evening the clouds cleared and a full moon shone in a cold blue sky. Tree shadows were sharp on the snow and the visibility was greater than it had been during the day. The temperature plummeted. Our boots squeaked in the snow and sharp cracks rang out across the meadows, wood splitting as sap froze in the trees. Later we heard that the temperature in West Yellowstone, some 25 miles away, had fallen to -36°C.

There followed a day of snow and wind and low cloud and a bizarre, weird and eerie mix of thermal features and atmospheric conditions. Heading for Smokejumper Hot Springs we climbed out of the meadows up a steep thickly wooded gully to suddenly emerge out of the trees into a narrow smoky chasm, an unexpected thermal area not on our maps. A steaming stream ran past hot springs and warm pools. The clouds of steam condensed on the trees into grotesque shapes.

Gingerly we picked a way through this fascinating terrain, hoping the ground would not give way and pitch us into hot water or mud, then climbed out steeply through deep, soft snow. Back in the silent forest we climbed on to reach the mist-shrouded plateau. A whiff of sulphur swept by on the cold wind. We sniffed, turned and followed the smell to the hot springs, the first time I've ever navigated with my nose. Snow was falling, mist drifted through the trees and steam rose from the springs, pools and smoking cracks in the earth that faded in and out of view.

Back at the igloo the snow fell and the wind roared, a cold and stormy end to the day. Dawn came with a rising sun and clear sky though the gusty wind was pickup up spindrift and blasting it across the meadows. Leaving our igloo home for the last time we skied into the woods and headed back towards Biscuit Basin. Part way there we picked up the waymarks of the Summit Lake Trail, a path I'd walked on my first visit to Yellowstone on the Continental Divide Trail 22 long years before. Then it had been summer and the forest had not yet burned. No memories came back. It all felt new.

Steep wooded slopes led down to the Firehole River valley, across which we could see the big bulge of Mallard Lake Dome and, far in the distance, the ragged outline of the Beartooth Mountains. A final delight awaited us.

At the base of the slopes on the edge of Biscuit Basin bison and elk were grazing, scraping away the thin snow around the heated ground. We watched them for a while before skiing on to a final challenge, a branch of the Little Firehole River that wasn't bridged. A logjam provided a way across, the main difficulty being sliding the sleds across the snow on a latticework of precarious logs. Then it was through the thermal area, much more visible now without the morning mist.

Back on the road Ed stuck out his thumb. A snowmobile soon stopped and then a snowcoach and soon we were ensconced in the Snow Lodge at Old Faithful having a celebratory drink after one of the most intense and strange ski tours I've ever undertaken.

Another Yellowstone Ski Tour

Yellowstone in winter can be a daunting prospect; sub-zero temperatures, deep snow, freezing winds, blizzards, but there is the other side. The beauty of the snowbound forest, the spectacular mix of hot, colourful thermal features, freezing air and cold white snow, the emptiness of the winter wilderness, a pristine landscape unscarred by trails, campsites, worn ground. By the end of my first trip with Igloo Ed one thing was certain. We wanted to come back.

Planning for a longer trip began on the journey home and continued for the next year. Ed was the driving force, working out a detailed route with various options and recruiting others so it was a group of seven that gathered at Old Faithful in February impatient to head into the wilderness – Ed, myself, Will Rietveld, Mike Martin, Steve Nelson, Dave Knight and Rick Hagar. Then, at the very last minute, Ed was taken ill and had to depart (thankfully he made a swift recovery).

Suddenly leaderless we considered our options. Someone needed to take Ed home to Colorado. Will volunteered. Maybe he could make it back in a few days, but how would he find us? We looked at Ed's route. The start was up the Midway Geyser Basin, some way from Old Faithful. We'd intended taking an early morning snow coach there and skiing a fair distance the first day. However the end of the route was down a groomed trail straight to Old Faithful, which would be much easier for Will to follow. Reversing the route seemed sensible. We already had a permit for the original route but the Old Faithful rangers were happy to change this for us and said it would be fine for our first igloos to be built just beyond the end of the groomed trail near Lone Star Geyser.

Ed and Will gone, six of us were left to pack our sleds, put on our skis (snowshoes in the case of Steve) and set out along the snow covered road to the Lone Star trailhead. Convoys of snowmobiles zoomed past as we plodded up the road but, once on the trail, our journey into the wilds felt as though it was really beginning, despite the neat groomed snow and cut tracks. Gliding through the quiet trees beside the Firehole River had a calming effect after the upsets and dismay at Old Faithful, and arriving at Lone Star Geyser was exciting. The large cone of this big geyser sits alone in the middle of an open area, hissing, bubbling and steaming. Every three hours the pressure builds up and the geyser erupts, shooting some 15 metres into the air. The eruption lasts from 15 to 30 minutes and ends with a towering steam plume.

On the edge of the forest above the geyser we built our first igloo, the success of which was crucial to the future of the trip as we'd never built an igloo or worked together before. Progress was slow and there was an interlude while we watched the geyser erupting during a beautiful sunset, a spectacular scene. It was long after dark when we finished the igloo but there were no problems and five of us soon settled inside, Steve pitching his tent nearby. A day out, an igloo built, the trip was underway.

Igloos take so long to construct that abandoning them after one night always seems a waste of time and effort, especially at such a magnificent site as Lone Star. As we were waiting for Will this was not an issue here. We knew we'd be staying for at least two nights. It turned out to be three. The first day at Lone Star we climbed a little knoll above the geyser from where Steve managed to get a phone connection and received a message that Will would be coming in the next day. A small bowl of perfect powder on the far side of the hill provided entertainment and a chance to practise downhill skills.

Whether it would be easy to reverse Ed's route we found out the next day when Dave, Rick and I reconnoitred the slopes north of the Firehole River that led to the plateau stretching out to Smoke Jumper Hot Springs. Thick trees, deep snow and twisting, steep-sided gullies made route finding difficult and we quickly concluded that hauling the sleds up these slopes would be slow and arduous. Reversing Ed's alternative and longer route up the Firehole River valley to the Continental Divide looked easier, though going this way would make it very unlikely we would even reach the northern part of the route. That evening Will arrived, sounding remarkably fresh given that he'd driven to Colorado and back over the last few days, and we discussed plans. Happily nobody was keen to push on and complete as much of the route as possible, everybody wanted to experience igloo living and the Yellowstone wilderness. Now we knew that it would take 4-5 hours to build an igloo, nobody wanted to move on and build igloos every day or even most days.

While we were at Lone Star a steady stream of day

skiers came up the groomed trail to see the geyser. Amongst them were Roy and Carol Anne Wagner, who Ed and I had met the previous year. Unable to take part in the tour but involved in the planning and with a keen interest in the trip, he was delighted to be able to actually visit an igloo. And we were delighted with the hot tea Carol Anne brought for us. Other visitors were not so welcome. Because four in an igloo is a tight squeeze we'd left much of our food and spare gear outside. Early on the first morning Dave was thrilled to see a fox outside the igloos but not so thrilled when he discovered that a bag of sausage had disappeared. Despite a hunt around, following the myriad fox tracks, there was no sign of the food. The next night food was hung from branches or brought inside.

Steve, who had always planned to leave the trip early, decided to go out from Lone Star so it was five of us who skied through the peaceful forest and meadows of the Firehole River valley for half a day. On the edge of the meadows we found a lovely scenic site. Here we built two igloos. Four of us in an igloo had been a little cramped, with no trench for sitting and access and a small kitchen area that only one person could use at once. Five in an igloo would have been uncomfortable. Two igloos made for plenty of room. Again we toiled long into the evening. I found the rhythmic work of shovelling snow strangely hypnotic and calming. The slow fading of the forest into blackness, eerie moonlight giving a yellow tinge to the snowy meadows, stars sparkling in the black sky - the changing surroundings were magical and caused me to shiver with delight whenever I paused from shifting snow.

Another reconnoitre day followed for Will, Rick, Dave and me. Mike, who had a sore arm, stayed in camp.

221

Upstream from the igloos the valley narrowed and the river ran down a ravine between steep slopes beyond which it widened again into the huge meadows at the headwaters of the Firehole River. Initially we ventured into the mouth of the ravine, an impressive place that closed-in around us, shutting out the world, in contrast to the wide open meadows and spreading forest on the outside. Snow bridges took us across creeks and the river itself.

It quickly became apparent that threading a route through the ravine with sleds would be difficult and maybe impossible, especially as the river was still open. Traversing steep slopes above rushing water with a sled was not appealing. Climbing out of the ravine we skied across cliff-rimmed bowls through tall subalpine firs laden with huge mounds of snow. Here, deep in the snow forest, it was cold and shadowed, even though the sky above was blue and elsewhere the sun was shining.

Eventually we came to Grants Pass between the Firehole River and Shoshone Creek. A summer trail runs through the pass and ski tracks showed that others had been here recently. The trail signs were ankle to knee high, showing the depth of snow. A fast descent down the trail took us back to the Firehole River valley and the igloos. Over hot food and drink and snug inside the igloos we perused the maps again and remade our plans. Just below Grants Pass on the Shoshone Creek side was a small flat area with meadows that looked a good place to build igloos and from where we could descend to the Shoshone Geyser Basin for a day trip.

Rather than haul all our gear over Grants Pass and then build igloos, which would make for a long day, we decided to go up with shovels and the Ice Box igloo building tools on a day trip and start the igloos. The day was hot and sunny and we had the odd experience of building igloos in the heat, sleeves rolled up, ski pant legs unzipped and with shady hats and sunscreen the most important protective items. One igloo complete and the other mostly done we skied back over Grants Pass and down the now icy trail in the dusk.

I took the sled and hurtled down, skidding round corners and using speed to keep the sled stable on traverses where it started to slip sideways. A tree root almost tripped me near the bottom but I managed to stay upright. It was the most exhilarating and exciting descent of the trip, one where being alert and reacting fast were essential and my senses felt sharpened and my mind and body really alive.

Rick and Mike reached the Firehole River igloos first and startled an animal in the igloos. It ran up a tree and they identified it as a pine marten. It had been in both igloos, taking some peanuts from one and nibbling a corner off each one of Dave's stock of chocolate bars in the other. Now the igloos had been found it was probably good that we were moving on the next day.

Hauling our sleds up the now familiar trail to Grants Pass was less arduous than expected, leaving us plenty of energy to finish the igloo. That evening the sky was dramatic and black with an astonishing array of bright stars. The full moon rose and turned a Mars-like dark red – it was the night of an eclipse. Being outside in the dark cold air under this spectacular sky here in the Yellowstone wilderness was joyous and awe-inspiring, a perfect night in a perfect place. There followed the most perfect day of the trip, beginning with a descent of the lovely, narrow Shoshone Creek valley, winding across steep slopes above the open water sparkling in the sunshine.

This led into the Shoshone Geyser Basin, a fantastic

area of steaming pools and vents, bubbling hot springs and erupting geysers. Brightly coloured volcanic rocks set against the bright whiteness of the snow and the dark trees plastered with ice and rime and frost. We wandered on foot through the basin, marvelling at the thermal wonders and the contrasting worlds of ice and fire. Here it felt like the heart of Yellowstone, the mix of forest wilderness and dramatic thermal features that inspired the creation of the national park.

Leaving the smoking basin we skied out onto big Shoshone Lake, a vast expanse of snow beyond which rose the distant peaks of the Absaroka Mountains. While sitting on some bare, sun-warmed rocks on the shore we spoke to the first people we had seen in several days, a party of three ski tourers (unusually on alpine mountaineering skis) on a three-day trip. They would camp in the geyser basin that night then ski out to Old Faithful the next day. We skied back to our igloos, replete with the glories of Yellowstone.

We had no intention of leaving our fine site or building any more igloos but we did want to visit Madison Lake at the head of the Firehole River valley, the furthest point we could now reach on Ed's original route. From Grants Pass we angled up to the big wooded plateau above and then wove a route through the trees to the Firehole River. This was another snow forest, huge Engelmann spruce and subalpine fir heavy with snow soaring into the sky, their amazingly tall narrow spires silently dominating the landscape.

The forest opened gradually into the vast and wild meadows of the upper Firehole River, stretching for over two miles into the distance, walled by steep wooded slopes. We skied up the meadows in a cold wind as huge clouds built up, edged by the searingly bright sun, a vast skyscape that enhanced the grandeur of the meadows. There were no thermal areas here and the river was hidden under the snow as was Madison Lake, its location only evident in consultation with the map.

The huge clouds and the wind presaged a change in the weather and we woke the next day to light snow and a thick grey sky. We spent the day exploring the upper reaches of Shoshone Creek as it wound through little meadows and narrow canyons and through a small thermal area where Rick was disappointed not to find a hot spring we could bathe in. The snow fell all day and this change in the weather seemed suited to a quiet end to our trip. Heavier snow fell overnight and the last day dawned with the igloos almost buried under the fresh snow. The new soft snow made the descent from Grants Pass with loaded sleds slow and easy. Soon we were passing Lone Star Geyser and skiing the last miles to Old Faithful, a warm cabin, showers and a celebratory beer.

9

NATURE, WEATHER & SEASONS

Backpacking is a year-round activity, there is no 'season' and every time of year has its attractions and rewards. However, one time of year is special and that is spring, the months of March, April and May. If there was a season for backpacking this would be it.

Spring is traditionally the time for journeys. The reawakening of nature, the return of life to the woods and hills with fresh greenness, bird song and the first flowers, the strengthening of the sun, the lengthening of the days all stir the desire for adventure and travel.

'Thanne longen folk to goon on pilgrimages' ('then folk long to go on pilgrimages') as Chaucer wrote in *The Canterbury Tales,* before his travellers set out in April for Canterbury. My pilgrimage is to go into nature, to watch the spring develop and restore the world to life.

The short days of winter, the blizzards and storms, the bitter cold, the long dark nights, the monochrome landscape are all fading and the prospect of warm sunshine, endless daylight and the bright colours of summer are approaching, soon to arrive. This is an exciting time, full of anticipation for the joys to come, of days spent enjoying the weather rather than fighting it and time in camp spent sitting watching the world rather than huddled in the tent away from the snow and cold, days where an eye no longer has to be kept on the time for fear of being caught in the early dark, days where you can walk for hours over the hills free from fear of avalanche, ice and blizzard.

Spring days can often be wet, windy and cold. Snow may fall and night frosts chill the air, but in my head the winter has gone and there is a feeling of lightness and freedom. I know the dark cold is fading, I know the sun is growing more powerful. The hills may still be snow clad but they shine in the sun brighter and sharper than in the dead of winter. The sun is now high in the sky, rather than creeping along not far above the horizon, and there is warmth in its rays not felt earlier in the year. Winter is retreating even if frost and snow linger on.

Long winter backpacking trips are challenging and arduous. Most people make short forays into the wilds, a night or two here and there, before retreating to the warmth and security of solid walls. Long dark, stormy nights in a tiny tent eventually lose their attraction, while in spring there is always the hope that tomorrow will be sunny and dry and an awareness that the hours of darkness are shrinking day by day. Even snow camping is more enjoyable as winter weakens and spring takes hold.

Once summer is in full possession of the world and the days are so long that darkness is slept through, once the concern is that nights might be too hot rather than too cold, the excitement and anticipation fades. Summer is fulfilment, satiety even. And at the back of the mind is the tiny but growing thought that from now light and warmth will diminish as the year moves towards autumn and winter. Summer is fine but spring is finer. The energy-sapping heat of hot summer days and nights is absent. There is still a sharpness and bite in the air that encourages striding out.

New life is burgeoning, and the fecundity of nature is everywhere to be seen but biting insects are still to come and you can sit outside the tent on calm evenings without head nets, insect repellent, mosquito coils and tightly woven clothing – paraphernalia that usually drives me into the tent. Sunrise and sunset can be viewed in the fresh air rather than hazily through insect mesh or not at all due to the hordes of midges hovering just outside the tent.

Spring is the ideal time for us, like Chaucer's pilgrims, to undertake a long walk, a pilgrimage to the wilds, to celebrate nature and the eternal turning of the seasons. My first long distance walk was the Pennine Way in April, a walk that saw every type of weather (though mostly wind and rain) including snow at Tan Hill but which always had that promise of more warmth, more sunshine. A few years later I followed the spring north from Land's End to John O'Groats, keeping pace with the fresh growth, the first flowers and the increasingly vocal birds from the wild Cornish coast to the even wilder Scottish Highlands.

Others have felt spring is the right time for long walks too. Two of the books that inspired me when I began backpacking tell of spring backpacking trips: John Hillaby's *Journey Through Britain* and Hamish Brown's *Hamish's Mountain Walk*. Both started in April and walked through the spring, Hillaby from Land's End to John O'Groats, Brown over all the Munros. Neither gives a clear reason for choosing spring. I guess it just seemed the natural thing to do. A later inspiration, John Muir, reckoned spring was the best time to visit his beloved Yosemite Valley. And Henry David Thoreau says that one reason he went to Walden Pond was 'to see the spring come in'. The power of springtime is great.

The real joys of spring can be summed up in two words:

warmth and light. In northern countries it's not surprising that the return of the sun has always been marked with festivities and celebrations. It is a sign that the world is not ending, that the growth of plants and wildlife will begin again, that there will be food. Today we no longer live so close to nature. Winter is not a time for food shortages or fear that crops will never grow again, but it is still a time of darkness and cold and we carry memories stretching back to the dawn of humanity. We still feel the excitement, relief and joy when spring arrives and the power of nature still surges through us.

For walkers this can be celebrated in long backpacking trips, in feeling close to, perhaps part of, the new life and brightness of the soaring sun. Spring is a wonderful time to be in the hills and the woods and to glory in the beauty of life renewed.

Down to the woods

When the UK government proposed selling off the state-owned forests in England there was a huge outraged reaction that not only forced the government to abandon their plans but also showed the deep feelings that many people have for woods. The massive outpouring of concern took everyone by surprise, including those of us for whom forests have been important for many years. We didn't know there were so many of us.

For me, forests have been an important part of my outdoor life since I was a child. Brought up on the Lancashire coast, the first woods I encountered were the Formby pine woods. Too young to be allowed to venture into them I can remember staring into the dark forest and longing to wander down the sandy paths I could see vanishing beneath the trees into mystery, adventure and the unknown, a secret, hidden world where anything could lie behind the next tree.

When I was finally allowed to enter, I found them just as exciting as I'd imagined. Much of my early route-finding and outdoor skills were begun amongst those pines. I carried no map or compass. I had no waterproof clothing, just wool and cotton garments that soaked up rain (and bog and pond water as I discovered). I often returned home wet to the skin, but I learnt how to find my way in the woods, how to recognise and remember subtle changes in the terrain and understand the landscape.

From the first day I loved walking in the forest, loved the silence, the solitude, the patterns of light and shade, the coolness, the wildlife, the whole 'other world' feeling of being in the midst of thousands of trees. Then there were the storms, the winds shaking the tops of the trees so they sounded like the surging sea and bringing down cones and needles and twigs and occasionally branches and even whole trees. Then the woods were stimulating and energising and it seemed as though the whole rain-lashed forest was alive, a single sentient being responding to the gale. When snow lay on the ground and the trees were white I tracked squirrels and foxes and other rarely seen animals, tracing their signs in the snow and working out what they were doing. Bird song was important too, a musical background to the silent trees that came and went as invisible flocks passed through the branches seeking seeds and insects. In the woods only nature existed.

My first camping experiences were in forests too, not backpacking but with the Scouts at Tawd Vale Scout Camp (which I'm pleased to see still exists) where I learnt about camp fires, building shelters and other stuff now called 'bushcraft'. Mainly though, I learnt to love camping in forests though at Tawd Vale that meant sleeping in a big canvas tent with a dozen and more others. Putting together the camping and the walking made for 'backpacking', for moving through forests day after day, waking every morning surrounded by trees and the sounds and smells of the woods.

Many decades later when I hiked the Pacific Northwest Trail I was in forests much of the time, sometimes for weeks without a break. There were clearings, big meadows, views across lakes, and rocky summits but all were contained in the forest and were part of it. It is a glorious feeling to move through vast unbroken forests every day and sleep under the trees every night. The Pacific Northwest forests are not all magnificent old growth forests of giant trees, though some are, such as the western red cedar forests of the Cascades National Park and the lichen-draped Douglas fir rain forests of Olympic National Park. Many are young, the old woods having been felled or burnt by lightning fires. Most are regenerating naturally but a few have been replanted. Yet they still have a 'presence', stimulating the same deep emotions that all forests do. I relished being in them.

Only in fresh clear-cuts, where the felling was so recent no new trees had started to grow, and in active logging areas did I feel I would rather be somewhere else.

The pleasure taken in forests is a major part of the public's positive feelings towards the Forestry Commission, despite all its regimented conifer plantations, which make up most of Britain's woods. Even these plantations are still forests and bring forth the same feelings. It's easy to denigrate them, but they can still be pleasant to walk through and camp in. Just being surrounded by tall spruce trees is relaxing and there is a feeling of safety in their dark confines. Hearing people talk of their intense feeling

231

for forests that are not 'heritage' or 'old' or any other special designation, but just local woods to wander in and connect with the natural world in, has made me rethink my views of conifer plantations and realise that they are better, much better, than no woods at all.

Sadly, there is nowhere in Britain where you can walk for weeks through woods as I did in the Pacific Northwest. Linking forests to create woodland corridors that enable longer backpacking trips would be wonderful. In the meantime there are forests big enough for trips of several days and more, especially if circular routes are taken. The Cairngorms has some of the finest remaining native woods and it is possible to walk through the Abernethy, Glenmore, Rothiemurchus and Glen Feshie forests for several days enjoying many excellent wild camping options along the way. Wild camping is of course a legal right in Scotland so there's no concern about whether you can camp or not. In many English forests it's different, though that never stopped me when I lived in England and I was never discovered. It is, after all, easy to hide in a forest!

For the future of forests and wild land and natural places to explore and camp in and enjoy and for the health and sanity of humanity it's important that children have the same opportunities to visit woods that I had, and to have adventures in them and develop a love for nature. If changing the ownership of forests made it even harder, by restricting access even more, it would be detrimental for all of us now and in the future.

Forests

On days when the wind drives the rain against you and the very air roars and howls, descending from the hills into the shelter of a forest can bring relief and safety. Suddenly there is calm. The air is stilled. The wind may still whistle in the tree tops but once inside the wood only stray breezes drift across the forest floor.

I've used woods as shelter many times, sometimes even descending in the dark to escape a storm, as I did when I came down from the Moine Mhor into the pinewoods of Glen Feshie on a wet black autumn night and pitched behind a gnarled, half-dead, ancient tree that gave a primeval feel to the forest and, more importantly, cut the bitter wind.

Forests have far more to offer the backpacker than just a place to hide from the weather though we have only traces of the old wildwood that once covered much of the land. Mere hints of the glory that once was, these remnants are splendid and inspiring and a joy to walk through and camp amongst, and are expanding where the forests are being restored.

Fragments of the old forests can be found in many places in Britain, adding wildness and a feeling of raw nature. I have memories of wandering through the ancient oaks of Wistman's Wood high on Dartmoor and the lovely woods along the River Wye on the Offa's Dyke Path and feeling that within these forests lay an older untamed country. In the Highlands the same emotions are stirred by the Caledonian Pine forest fringing the Cairngorms and the oakwoods of Loch Lomond and the Trossachs. I also take pleasure in the regenerating forest: in seeing the young trees spreading out in Coire Ardair in the Creag Meagaidh National Nature Reserve or up the slopes of Meall a'Bhuachaille above Ryvoan Pass in the Cairngorms, or the Carrifran valley in the Moffat Hills in the Southern Uplands.

Far larger unspoiled forests exist abroad, where you can walk for days amongst mighty trees, beautiful groves and delicate woodland meadows. Among the most glorious I have seen are in the Sierra Nevada in California where a profusion of magnificent trees grow, including the biggest of them all, the giant sequoia. It was in the Sierra Nevada that my pleasure in backpacking in a forested wilderness deepened and became more intense. The high granite mountains of the Sierra are spectacular but my strongest memories are of the trees, of walking through the solemn silence of the dense and dark red fir forest (known as the snow forest as it holds so much snow), across open sunny slopes of ponderosa pine and over the stony terrain of the subalpine forest where the trees grow smaller and slowly fade away to contorted, wind-stunted, timberline thickets of whitebark pine known as krummholz, a German alpine word meaning twisted wood.

This diversity is one of the delightful features of a natural forest. There may be big areas of similar sized trees but there are never unbroken crammed-together regimented ranks of the same species stretching for miles. Real forests are places of variety with a mix of species, a rich undergrowth of shrubs and flowers, open clearings, rushing streams, slow meandering rivers and hidden pools. Real forests are places of discovery and enchantment. Trails wind and twist through the trees, paths to who knows where and with what delights along the way. Dense thickets open out into flower meadows, distant peaks appear towering over the trees, sudden views open up as the path reaches the edge of a cliff.

Even when the forest is more uniform and the trees seem to go on forever, with little in the way of views or openings, the feeling is one of peacefulness and contentedness and there is time to notice the details of bark and twig, leaf and needle. Walking in deep forest can be contemplative, a form of meditation, as you lose yourself amongst the trees, hypnotised by the regularity of the walking. I love hiking for hour after hour there, rhythmically striding through the trees, and then camping amongst them, secure in their shelter.

Forest sites may seem dull compared with those out in the open, but there is much that is attractive in a woodland camp. The patterns on the forest floor of fallen leaves, pine cones and moss, wild flowers and shrubs, the trees providing shade and shadows and, if you are quiet and patient, the wildlife. Tents make good hides for watching birds and animals and these are far commoner and more likely to appear at a forest camp than one out in the open. I have memories of watching black grouse displaying at a lek in the Eastern Cairngorms, mule deer grazing outside the tent in the Rocky Mountains, a black bear passing a hundred yards from camp in the Sierra Nevada, red deer stags bellowing during the autumn rut in Glen Feshie and a mass of smaller birds and animals going about their lives oblivious to the human watching them.

To fully enjoy these moments and gain the most from a forest camp I prefer to use as little shelter as I can. I am there to be in contact with nature not hide from it. Trees make good supports and I try to set up camp so I can sit with my back against one. Ideally I sleep out with just the trees for shelter. I love lying in my sleeping bag staring up at the patterns of leaves and branches above me and the little patches of sky and stars far above.

Often though the weather makes this unwise or uncomfortable and a tarp or tent is needed. Then I close myself in only if rain or biting insects make it necessary. Otherwise I lie with my head at the door so I can still watch the forest. Rain in the forest is usually softer and less wind driven than on open sites so being totally enclosed is rarely necessary. At night the dark shapes of the trees are silhouetted against the sky, the branches strange twisted forms hanging high above. The rustle of animals crossing the forest floor is louder and sharper. Owl calls echo through the branches. Occasionally the silhouette of a deer drifts through the trees.

The peace and quiet makes for a good sleep too with no roaring wind and shaking tent to keep you awake. Dawn comes with soft light filtering through the trees and colour gradually returning to the woods. A night in a forest is an intense and wonderful experience.

Encounters with wildlife

Towards the end of an overnight trip, my mind more on thoughts of finding a café than on nature, I noticed a rather odd-looking stick on the track ahead of me. Something about it was not quite right. I approached it cautiously, unsure of why I was doing so. Then it moved, only slightly but enough for the missing word that had been lurking on the edge of my mind to surface. Snake! We both paused. The adder, for such it was, raised its head and flicked its tongue, before slowly slithering off the track to disappear into long grass. I admired its beautiful markings and subtle colouration then set off again, all thoughts of the café gone, recalling other encounters with wildlife I've had over the years and the great pleasure they bring.

I also considered the importance backpacking played in many of these encounters. Sometimes it was simply that long trips allowed me to reach remote areas rich in wildlife that were too far for day walkers. Often it was because I was out at dawn and dusk when wildlife is more active than in the middle of the day when most walkers are about. When camping, my shelter often acted as a hide. My liking for only closing doors when absolutely necessary helps with this too although even when shut in a tent you can still hear sounds clearly.

Once, during my walk through the Yukon Territory, I was wakened by the sound of splashing and opened the tent Ito see a moose high-stepping through the edge of a lake, the huge ungainly beast silhouetted against the pale dawn sky looking like a prehistoric monster. On another occasion, while camped on the edge of a conifer wood during a TGO Challenge crossing of the Scottish Highlands, I was woken by a strange bubbling call. Two male black grouse were displaying in a clearing not far away. Uninterested in my tent the birds circled each other, spreading their white tail feathers, raising their wings and pushing out the bright red wattles above their eyes while continuing their loud calls.

Going solo makes wildlife encounters more likely too. A single person is quieter and less noticeable than two or more even when they are not talking. Alone there is nothing to distract you from noticing signs of wildlife either. In Britain wildlife observation is for enjoyment. We have no dangerous animals here. In other countries it can be a safety issue. In particular where there are bears it's wise to keep your eyes open for signs that show they may be around. Even so there can be unexpected meetings when neither you nor the bear are aware of the other's presence until they come suddenly into view. I have three times rounded a corner on a trail to meet a black bear coming the other way. In each case, after a few interminably long seeming frozen seconds, the bear ran off, once to climb the nearest tree and gaze back down at me.

My closest encounter with a grizzly bear was due to my own carelessness. I was on a trail high in the Canadian Rockies on a grey, drizzly day. My hood was up and I was staring down at the muddy earth in front of me as I trudged along. The wind was in my face – so a bear ahead wouldn't smell me – and there was a noisy creek not far from the trail, so a bear probably wouldn't hear me. I should have been looking round and occasionally making a noise. A movement at the corner of my vision caused me to glance round. There, coming towards me, was a huge grizzly, its head down as it snuffled amongst the vegetation. In quick succession I felt elated, excited and terrified. A grizzly bear! Heading towards me! The bear seemed unware of my presence. I knew I needed to let it know I was there before it was too near and thought I was a threat, I clapped my hands, shouted and jumped up and down, feeling very silly. The bear responded, lifting its muzzle and sniffing the air before ambling off beside the creek and away. Feeling relieved I watched it turning over rocks and rooting amongst bushes until it disappeared. I'd never seen a grizzly bear before. It was magnificent.

Other potentially dangerous animals are moose and bison. I've encountered several of the former and mostly they have run off, but on one occasion I came upon one in the rutting season that was thrashing a small tree with its huge antlers and stamping on the ground. Fearing it might decide I was more interesting to fight than a tree I made a long detour round it. Bison I have only encountered once, on a ski tour in Yellowstone National Park. On the edge of a thermal area a herd was scraping away the shallow snow to feed on the grasses beneath. Survival in harsh winter conditions is difficult for bison so it's important they are not disturbed. In this case we were some distance away and were able to watch them through binoculars and take photographs with telephoto lenses.

Whether bears or grouse, snakes or bison, any wildlife encounter is a wonderful experience, a connection with nature that, whilst usually momentary, is also deep and satisfying. As with the adder and the grizzly, meeting an animal can transform an otherwise uninspiring day. The time I felt this most was after a long, and difficult ascent on a cross country section of the Arizona Trail. I had reached a ridgeline in a foul mood, fed up of the heat, the thorny vegetation and the lack of water. Suddenly, a great bald eagle flew right in front of me and settled in a tree. My mood was transformed by the sight of this magnificent bird. All was right with the world. Wildlife can do that. It's worth seeking out.

Night hiking

Early one autumn I was camping high in Coire Garbhlach above Glen Feshie in the Cairngorms when I was woken by a powerful gusty wind shaking the tent. Reckoning I would get no more sleep and knowing it would be light in an hour or so I packed and set off into the black night. Slowly the darkness resolved itself into shades of grey. The hills were almost black against the slightly lighter overcast sky, the ground mottled with tussocks of pale grass and clumps of dark heather. Once my eyes had adjusted I could see just enough to walk without my headlamp and I began to enjoy being out in the night, out in a mysterious world that held the promise of innumerable possibilities. The coming of dawn, with flat light and a grey sky, was a disappointment. The world was ordinary again.

Having walked in the night many times I wasn't concerned at the idea of hiking down the rough corrie though I knew I would need to take care and progress would be slow. Time passes differently when walking in the dark anyway. The concentration required, even on easy terrain, means that the minutes flash by unnoticed. This is when walking without a light. Once you switch on a torch or headlamp you are locked into its beam and all that exists beyond that cone of light is blackness, broken by faint silhouettes of trees or hills. Inside the light the world is familiar but it is so small and restricted that I find it confining. Only on the darkest nights or in the densest forests do I use a light when walking. I always have one handy though, so I can switch it on if I walk into a black space under a tree or boulder and suddenly can't see. I may need it to check the map too. I find my eyes recover in a few minutes if I only have it on briefly.

When there's a big bright moon a light may not be needed at all, especially on open terrain where the ground is pale and eerie and you can see faint shadows. Walk into a forest however and the bright moon can be a problem. Where it shines in open glades and meadows the walking is easy but, as with the light from a headlamp, outside the moon's light all is black and invisible. I sometimes use a light more under a full moon than on a moonless night.

Walking under a bright moon is wonderful though, with the landscape a shadowy reflection of its daytime self. The yellow-white light shines off pale rocks, birch bark, pools of water and anything light–coloured so they shimmer softly. Shadows are solid black with no detail, anything could be in them. Lit areas are cool, bleached of colour and tone. The world is lovely and mysterious.

When there's no moon and the sky is a brilliant mass of stars, walking is harder, not because you can see less but because that great canopy of the universe is distracting, luring the eyes upwards to gaze out into the infinite. Then I stop frequently to starwatch without risk of falling.

At other times the sky is overcast and holds little of interest unless the wind tears the clouds apart to reveal a solitary star or planet, suddenly bright and sharp in the black sky, or the moon half hidden. Mostly, though, an overcast sky brings the eyes down to the landscape, to the dark columns of trees and the unusual shapes of boulders.

Whilst there is much more to see at night than is imagined by those only used to lit streets, or who always use a headlamp, one of the joys of night hiking lies in the amplification of the other senses. Hearing becomes much more acute. Tread on a stick and the crack as it snaps sounds like a gunshot. The rustle of a mouse in the grass sounds like a deer is crashing through the undergrowth. This loudness makes night hiking in bear country, which I have done quite often on walks in North America, interesting. Concentration and stillness is required to adjust any sounds closer to daytime reality and accept that a bear would actually be making much more noise and it's a small mouse you're hearing. The sense of smell is stronger too. I've often smelt the rankness of a deer or the sharp stink of a fox without ever seeing the animal. The aromas of trees and vegetation are distinctive and sometimes I can identify what plants are around me by the smell.

Sometimes night hiking is unintended, as it was that time above Glen Feshie. Often though, I set out to walk in the night, especially in the winter months when darkness is long. Rather than cram as much as I can into the seven or eight hours of daylight I set off before dawn and walk

241

long after sunset. Because finding a camp site in the dark can be difficult I usually select an area in advance where I know there will be suitable ground and cast around for the best spot when I arrive. This doesn't always work in unknown country where I have to guess from the map where good camp sites might be found.

One day on the Pacific Northwest Trail I lingered on a summit to watch a dark red sunset. From the map I thought there should be flattish ground and water not far from the top, but the trail led down a broad ridge with nowhere to camp and no water. An almost half-full waxing moon appeared in the sky followed by a single bright star. I followed the stony trail as it zigzagged down, just able to see it against the darker undisturbed ground either side. A ragged edge of dark forest rose to meet me. In the trees I was in and out of the moonlight and the walk became hypnotic as I descended thousands of feet for several hours before finally reaching a meadow and a creek. It was a glorious descent and, tired though I felt, I was glad I hadn't found a camp site any earlier.

The colours of autumn

Summer fades, nights grow crisp, nature changes. In autumn the natural world speeds up and there is a strong feeling of flux and impermanence. The slow, almost somnolent, feeling of high summer has gone.

Life changes for backpackers and hikers too. As the nights close in suddenly there's no longer seemingly endless daylight. Nightfall has to be taken into account again. Dinner is cooked and eaten in the dark. If there's far to go so is breakfast so you can set off with the dawn. Every year I'm surprised at how quickly the long days of summer disappear. Surely it can't be dark already? Better check those headlamp batteries.

Visually, autumn is a time of wonders and beauty. The colours of the trees are best known, the gold and yellow of birches, aspens and larches, the red of cherries and rowans, but other vegetation changes too. Hill grasses turn orange and red, giving a bright sheen to the slopes. Bracken, a fly-ridden jungle of dense green in summer, turns orange, then brown as it gradually collapses, opening up areas for walking. Red hips and haws colour hedgerows. The last flowers have gone but fungi appear in subtle shades of fawn and yellow with the occasional burst of a bright red white-spotted fly agaric.

Nature is quieter now with bird song dwindling and summer visitors gone south, but there are other sounds that conjure up the thrill of the wild. Far above long skeins of geese announce themselves with loud rhythmic calls. In the woods and on the hills red deer stags roar and grunt, challenging rivals and laying claim to hinds. Hearing this sound on a dark night when alone in a tiny tent far from other people really tells you that this place is wild.

Autumn weather brings the first snows on the summits, though it often goes fast. Storms are more often wet and windy, tearing the dying leaves from the trees and filling the streams. Then there are the calm days with mists drifting over the landscape and the clear nights when the first frosts decorate the grasses and ice forms on puddles and pools. Spiders' webs sparkle with frost and dew and hang mysterious in early morning mist.

Autumn is subtle and magical. Gone is the harsh brashness of summer with its sharp vivid colours and hard sunlight. When the sun shines now it's softer, casting long shadows and sliding through the trees.

243

For walking and backpacking autumn is a wonderful season. It's my favourite for forest walking and camping. The colours are glorious and the ground crunches after a frost. I love swishing through fallen leaves too, watching them flutter into the air and settle into intricate patterns of shapes and shades. Sitting on a log watching the trees and the wildlife is now enjoyable again. The midges that keep me moving in summer are gone whilst the penetrating cold of winter has not yet begun. In sunny spots protected by trees it's possible to feel quite warm. I have dozed off in autumn sunshine on occasion.

Camping is more pleasurable too, again because of the absence of midges. I now only close the tent to keep out rain. Otherwise the doors stay wide open and I sit in the entrance watching the light fade and the sky darken and the first stars appear. Waking before dawn, I see the process in reverse as the stars fade and the light strengthens and grows. In summer I would be trapped in the tent, hiding from the biting hordes.

There are many places I like to visit in autumn that are especially impressive. In the Cairngorms upper Glen Feshie echoes with the roaring of stags while bright golden flashes of scattered birches light up the crags. For forest glory Glen Affric stands out with tremendous swathes of colour set against the dark green of impassive pines. If the hills above are touched with snow the scene is perfect. Loch Lomond is also beautiful in autumn. Here there is the yellow of oak leaves to add to the mix of colour. When I lived further south I always tried to visit the Lake District in autumn, especially Borrowdale, whose woods I would look down on from a high camp.

Above the glens the hills have lost their brief summer green and are returning to brown and grey and fawn;

faded quiet colours that nevertheless are pleasing to the eye. On clear days the light can be sharper than in summer with no heat haze to blur distant views. Rocks are no longer warm to the touch and scrambling can quickly chill the hands. Autumn rains fill the streams and send them crashing down the hillsides. Mountain storms feel more serious than in summer, colder and with the threat (or is it the promise) of snow.

Whilst autumn can feel quiet and still, at the same time there's a sense of urgency, an awareness that this won't last, can't last. Winter is coming. Nights grow longer, temperatures fall, the leaves drift down and the colours fade. All too soon the world will be bleached and pale, waiting for the first blanket of snow to bring it back to life. Until then the autumn is here and to be enjoyed.

Backpacking and the weather

The weather is a pervasive factor in any backpacking trip, especially in Britain where, changeable and fickle, it can affect a walk at a moment's notice. Even when the forecast is good that doesn't mean the actual weather will be, at least not all the time. In some places good weather is predictable and reliable. I once spent six weeks hiking in the High Sierra in California. It drizzled once and looked like it might rain twice. Otherwise it was warm and sunny every day. I took a tarp but only pitched it a few times. Mostly I slept under the stars, confident that the weather would stay dry. I rarely do that for even one night in Britain.

This rapidly changing weather had been even more prominent one spring with a series of storms sweeping over the hills in quick succession. I watched for a weather window that meant my first real backpacking trip of the year (by which I mean one on which I move on every day rather than set up a wild camp and stay there a few nights) wouldn't be too much of a struggle with the elements. A few days of fine weather were at last forecast. This was predicted to change the afternoon of the third day so I planned a two-night trip that would see me out of the hills by noon on that day. My intention was to do a circular trip through the two great passes of the Cairngorms - the Lairig Ghru and the Lairig an Laoigh.

All was fine the first day as I crossed below the northern Cairngorm hills - Cairn Gorm itself, Stob Coire an t-Sneachda and Cairn Lochain - then cut through the rocky chasm of the Chalamain Gap and dropped down into the Lairig Ghru. The sun shone and the air was warm. For the first time since the autumn I rolled my sleeves up. The heart of the Lairig Ghru was packed with snow but this was crisp and firm, making for easy walking, easier in fact than when snow free as this area is then a mass of rocks. On the slopes above I could see the debris from many avalanches and at one point the snow was spattered with small stones released by the sliding snow.

Not wanting to camp on snow or melt snow for cooking I dropped down the south side of the pass and found a dry pitch near the infant River Dee. As soon as the sun dropped below the edge of the mountains the temperature fell rapidly and soon a frost coated my tent. Stars began to appear along with an almost full-moon. The mountains darkened, edged black against the sky, snow fields gleaming eerily in the moonlight. I fell asleep with the tent wide open, my last view the shining mountains and bright stars.

A shift in the weather came rapidly in the middle of

the night. At 1.00am a cool breeze woke me and I closed the tent. The temperature was -2°C. An hour later I woke again, feeling stuffy in the sleeping bag. The temperature was now +6°C. An eight degree rise in one hour at a time you'd expect the temperature to fall. The frost had gone and the sky was thick with grey clouds. The following day I continued to the fine pinewoods of Glen Luibeg and Glen Derry and then up the latter to the Lairig an Laoigh. The mountains stayed mostly hidden with just the occasional partial clearance. Interest lay in the trees and the wildlife - a black grouse on one of the last pines before I was above the trees again, a golden eagle spiralling upwards above a steep snowfield which I watched until it was a tiny dot far, far above. The warmer weather had speeded up the snowmelt and streams were full and deep, making for some cautious knee-deep fords. The River Avon, which had concerned me, still had big snow bridges, one of which I gingerly crossed.

Not far beyond the river I found a dry camp site that was sheltered from the wind, at least at that time. Tired after a long day and broken sleep the night before I was asleep early, which proved fortuitous as it was to be another disturbed night. The weather originally forecast for the next afternoon arrived in the early hours of the morning, starting with rain, soon joined by a ferocious wind that shook the tent. Unable to sleep I was up in the dark at 4.00am and walking before dawn in a wind that almost knocked me over several times. Without trekking poles I would have fallen.

These last few hours were the bad weather struggle I'd hoped to avoid and it was with relief that I finally dropped down into the shelter of Glenmore Forest, though even here the wind was roaring in the treetops. By 9.00am I was

247

back at the car, which itself was shaking in the gusts. Half an hour later I was in a cafe watching the rain outside. The trip had been more adventurous but also more memorable than I expected. That's the beauty of our weather. You never know what to expect.

Amongst the clouds

The air was damp and chill and thick with mist. With visibility down to a few metres I wondered whether to go on climbing. Was there any point when I could see nothing? But high above there were hints of brightness and a blue sheen to the greyness, so maybe up there the sun was shining. I climbed on and the mists did indeed begin to dissipate as a cool breeze blew and a watery sun appeared. Soon the mists were gone, the last tattered shreds speeding away on the strengthening wind and dissolving in the now dazzling sunlight. The world exploded outwards from a few hazy boulders and the patch of damp grass at my feet to a startling vista of ranks of mountains fading into the far horizons, mountains that floated in space for below them was the rippling blanket of white cloud that I'd climbed through. I sat on the summit and stared across the land. Everything above 700 metres was sharp and clear, everything below that height hidden. Visibility was superb; the clarity unreal.

Cloud inversions like this are one of the joys of Britain's humid climate and a particular pleasure of camping high in the hills. Once when I camped on the snow-covered summit of Ben Nevis there was a lovely sunset with just a little cloud to the west and the night looked like being clear and frosty. However I woke to find the first grey light filtering through thin mist. Out to the east a pale insipid sun was just visible on the horizon. Slowly it rose through the clouds, putting out more heat and power, and the mist faded and sank down the mountain's flanks, leaving a bright world with tremendous views of the hills all around. Below, the glens were thick with cloud. Above, ranks of cumulus clouds drifted across the sky, covering and then revealing the sun. The world felt fantastically alive, almost unreal in its mobility and sharpness.

Dawn is often the best time to see such atmospheric delights, before the sun's heat dispels the clouds; an advantage of high level camps. Sometimes, as on Ben Nevis, the cloud-filled glens are unexpected. Sometimes the mist can be seen forming at sunset. Once I camped just below the summit of Glas Maol above Glen Shee in the Southern Cairngorms on a dull cloudy evening. As I lay in the tent I watched fingers of mist slowly creeping up from the glen below and crawling across the slopes, reaching me just as I was falling asleep. I felt the first touch of dampness on my face and saw the first drops of condensation forming on the tent. I closed my eyes thinking that the next day could be one of compass navigation in the clouds, but was woken by brightness and heat. A newly risen sun was shining straight into the tent door and the mist was shrinking back into the glens, which were still thick with cloud. For a few hours I walked over dew soaked grass watching the clouds gradually thin and fade until the glens too were shining in the sun.

Against the days of magic and wonder must be set those when the mist doesn't clear. Particularly frustrating are those times when it feels as though the thin cloud could disappear at any minute and there are tantalising hints of blue and glimpses of sunshine. Often it seems that if only the hill was just a few metres higher you would be in clear air. On other occasions the mist thickens and rain falls and it's quickly apparent that there will be no clearance. I experienced this on a camp on Beinn Eighe (which has surprisingly large areas of smooth, flat turf for a Torridon hill). The forecast was good and there had been a lovely sunset with a deep red sky. Waking in the dark I found the open tent full of damp mist and drips falling from the roof. By dawn it was raining heavily and the cloud was thick and I abandoned my intended traverse of the mountain and set off down to the glen. By the time I was off the mountain the burns were foaming with water and the rain was lashing down.

Then there are those days of playing cat and mouse with the cloud, dipping in and out as it hangs on the side of the hills, occasionally sneaking across a col or drifting over a summit. I traversed Beinn a'Bheithir above Ballachulish and Loch Leven in conditions like this, sometimes in bright sunshine with views stretching many miles, sometimes in dense cloud with visibility just a few metres. To the south the cloud wall never wavered, thick and white and implacable. Rising up the side of the mountain it broke on the ridge, spiralling into the sky and breaking into ragged tendrils. Each time I was enveloped I wondered if the mist would stay but then I would suddenly walk out of it and the world would be revealed.

Perhaps the most unusual and magical night above the clouds was on Stob a'Ghrianain above Glen Loy. In the evening I'd watched a huge orange moon rising over the Great Glen and the darkening bulk of Ben Nevis towering above the sparkling lights of Fort William. Dawn arrived with a fiery red sky as the sun lit up thickening clouds. Below this dramatic sky the long lochs to the south and west were totally covered by thick mist, tinted pink by the sunrise, but the dark land was clear with the silhouetted peaks purple in the early light.

This powerful lighting lasted an hour or so before beginning to weaken along with the clearing mist over the lochs. Only those who spent their night high in the hills would have seen the red sky and the mist-covered lochs. Perhaps I was the only one.

Rain and storms

Rain falling gently in soft misty swathes, delicate and ethereal, quietening and blurring the land. Rain driving across the hills, enlivening and invigorating, making the very air alive and full of power. However it comes, rain is an integral part of backpacking and the outdoors. Often it's so dominant that it is cursed and excoriated. Day after day of rain sodden hills and grey skies, night after night of slowly dampening gear inside a rain-lashed tent can become dispiriting. Every flicker of definition in the blanket of grey, every hint of a hazy sun breaking through the clouds is seized upon with hope and anticipation. Maybe now the rain will ease and dryness and warmth return to the land? Maybe.

Sometimes rain seems to be the major factor in backpacking trips. This was much in my thoughts after a month of almost constant wet weather on the Pacific Northwest Trail and again after four days of rain followed by ten more of drizzle, clouds and sodden ground on the Southern Upland Way.

Thinking about the nature of rain and storms I considered the positive experiences they can bring to backpacking. One is that they can be unforgettable. Looking back on trips it's often the wettest and stormiest days that stand out. Indeed, the least memorable days are those

251

with 'nice' weather – hazy sunshine, gentle breezes, light clouds – with nothing spectacular to see and nothing challenging about walking or camping.

When walking in mist and rain it can be hard to maintain an optimistic outlook. I have had plenty of practice, but after years of feeling fed-up I now try to concentrate on the landscape as it is with rain and clouds, not as I might like it to be in bright sunshine. Misty hills and rainy skies are not less real. They are what the landscape is at that moment and views of them are just as valid as ones bathed in sunshine. Indeed, in areas of high rainfall, like the Scottish hills or the mountains of the Pacific Northwest, they may be more realistic.

In the Cascade Mountains on the Pacific Northwest Trail I walked past the classic roadside viewpoint of Mount Shuksan, a much-photographed mountain whose image, shining in the sun above flowery meadows and a beautiful blue lake, decorates magazines, postcards, and biscuit tins. My almost monochrome pictures, taken in the rain, show a dramatic grey rock mountain clad in forbidding glaciers appearing out of swirling clouds. I suspect that Shuksan looks like that far more often than the chocolate box image but it wouldn't sell many products.

Watching the landscape in the rain reveals a different world from the same place in sunshine. Water is a major factor and not just in the form of the rain itself. Waterfalls and rivers grow in size and power and become visually exciting. If streams have to be forded they can be physically challenging too. Just the day after I walked past Mount Shuksan I had the most terrifying few minutes of the whole walk during the ford of a creek that was thigh deep and flowing very strongly with slippery, rolling stones underfoot.

In really heavy rain new streams can spring up, covering hillsides with ribbons of white water. On my summer long round of the Munros and Tops I crossed Bidean nam Bian above Glen Coe in heavy rain and low cloud before descending into the Lairig Eilde looking for a camp site. The slopes were laced with white streaks of rushing burns; the Allt Lairig Eilde was a surging torrent. The summits were hidden in the clouds but the landscape was still tremendous and dynamic. The ground was sodden, water bubbling up at every step, and finding a site that wasn't too wet was difficult. Eventually I camped on a half-dry boggy knoll just big enough for the tent. Once inside in dry clothes and with a hot drink I could look out on the storm and relish its power and energy.

Camping in rain and storms is, in fact, one of the joys of backpacking. Being warm and dry inside a tiny tent while the rain batters on the flysheet is a simple pleasure that never palls. Snuggle into the sleeping bag, light the stove, wait for the water to boil and take the first few sips of a hot drink, which always taste marvellous as the liquid sends warmth surging through your body. The struggle with the storm – keeping dry, navigating in the mist, finding a camp site, pitching the tent, getting inside without bringing wetness in, is over and I relax and settle into my home for the night.

In the British hills rainy camps are often windy ones too, exposed sites on open hillsides swept by the weather. A strong, storm resistant tent gives confidence and security. On sheltered sites, especially in forests, it's calmer and the rain comes downwards rather than horizontally. Sometimes it's even possible to have a warming camp fire.

My thousand-mile walk through the remote Yukon Territory in Canada is one of the toughest I have done and took me through some spectacular wilderness landscapes with dramatic camp sites. Yet one of the most unforgettable nights of the trip was spent deep in the forest. The day had been spent meandering up a wooded valley with few views and difficult boggy terrain. Drizzle started to fall and as dusk arrived had become a steady rain. I camped in dense spruce forest near a deep creek.

Because I was in grizzly bear country I didn't cook or eat in or near my tent in case the smell of food attracted them. Instead I carried a tarp for use as a cooking shelter in stormy weather. On this occasion I pitched it as a lean-to between two big trees. Huddled under the tarp I felt cold and damp so I lit a small fire just in front of it. As the flames flickered and the warmth reached me my sombre mood changed and I felt contented and relaxed. Just feet away the rain hammered down and, although the dark, dripping forest looked threatening and unfriendly, under my tarp it was cosy and comfortable. I cooked over the fire and stared into the flames. Where else could I possibly want to be?

That night and many others has given me a delight in camping in the rain. Knowing I can be warm, dry and comfortable is very reassuring when hiking in damp clothes on a stormy day. Backpacking in rain may not be ideal but it is part of the outdoor experience and one that can still give rewards. The sun will come out eventually.